The World of "Mr. Sheraton"

The World of "Mr. Sheraton"

by

ERNEST HENDERSON

DAVID McKAY COMPANY, INC.

New York

My gracious wife Molly has relinquished this space, her rightful due, to permit a tribute to the American system of free enterprise—Communism's deadliest foe.

E. H.

Contents

[vii]

The World of "Mr. Sheraton"

I.

A Bird's-Eye View of the World of a New England Yankee

I

DURING the Great European inflation that followed the first World War my two partners and I mobilized our accumulated resources—almost a thousand dollars, which were the proceeds of our government war bonuses. German marks, in the years following the war, had fallen to an almost infinitesimal fraction of their former value. We three—my brother, my former college roommate, and I, still in our early and middle twenties—were anxious to capitalize on the opportunities which prevailing rates of exchange offered to those willing to import goods from Europe.

All went well in the first stages of this exciting operation, and our capital began to grow. We were importing cutlery, safety razors, aluminum ware, and other manufactured articles in ever larger quantities, mostly from Germany. Finally, our big opportunity arrived when forty thousand "ersatz" men's suits were offered at twenty million marks apiece—twenty cents a suit. Presently the shipment reached Boston. Surely the following day we would be putting Hart, Schaffner and Marx out of business.

With an old duplicating machine we launched an initial broadside, quoting the latest in men's fashions at sixty-eight cents a suit. Fortunately it was only a trial run and not too many letters were actually mailed, for customers, somehow, were not fully satisfied with the suits, which were made of a paper fiber and, though faultless when worn indoors, did seem to shrink when the moisture outside exceeded a certain critical point. There were few reorders, and for a while we feared our limited resources might shrink as drastically as did our splendid suits when exposed to a sudden rainstorm. Prospective customers seemed to suspect, perhaps by intuition, that, at sixty-eight cents each, there might be a catch.

Then a ray of hope emerged. A Chicago customer had daringly invested in two of our imported creations and had since reordered twice, the latest time in dozen lots. Could our luck be holding? At the time Chicago had a flu epidemic, but that did not discourage our benefactor. The next order called for fifty suits. They were promptly shipped, and we stood by breathlessly. Suddenly from Chicago came an urgent phone call. How many suits were left? Timidly we admitted to 39,900. "I'll take the lot," came from the other end of the line. It was our friend from the Windy City. "Ship them at once," he directed, spelling out his customer's name—one of Chicago's largest undertakers. The flu epidemic, it seems, was spreading, and the moisture content of Chicago's "next world" apparently was not too high.

Perhaps a bird's-eye view of our early business activities, leading up to our interest in hotels, can best be presented by following the example of a distinguished New England man of letters. Prize-winning author John Marquand once started off a best-selling novel with an outline of his fictional hero's "life" as supposedly recorded in his Harvard twenty-fifth class reunion volume. If Marquand, a most distinguished writer, could use this gambit, why not I, though obviously a beginner? True, I can hardly qualify as a fictional character, but despite this, I offer herewith a condensed account of my activities during the quarter-century following graduation from college, the years 1918 to 1943.

"Henderson tells how Harvard boys ran a shoestring into thirty million dollars," was the specific heading in our class reunion compendium.

"When the war was over I returned from France and accepted a job with General Electric in Schenectady. I was helping to build some mammoth electric generators. The company considered my job extremely important; I attached the G. E. nameplates. While I was in Schenectady word came from my former Harvard roommate, Bob Moore, mentioning that courses at the Massachusetts Institute of Technology were less hazardous than suspected. I spent the next year at M.I.T.

"After Tech my brother George, Bob Moore, and I formed a partnership called Henderson Brothers. It was financed by our war bonuses, or what was left after paying the first month's rent. This was in Boston. Our firm name appeared in large gold letters on the plate-glass window with the designation 'Bankers' added. Fortunately in those days there were no laws against exaggeration. For several years we conducted a thriving business in foreign exchange.

"When foreign currencies approached the vanishing point due to the inflation then engulfing Europe, we turned to importing. With a few American dollars we could be millionaires in France and billionaires in Germany. Soon we were flooding this country with foreign binoculars, safety razors, flashlights by the millions, and even a boatload of German dogs that arrived due to an error in the cable.

"In the middle twenties we bought some radio tubes at a great surplus sale in Boston. Thousands were buying eight-dollar radio tubes marked down to a dollar. Carelessly the supplier's name was left on one of the cartons. We phoned him, and soon we too were in the radio business, selling surplus radio tubes by mail order. This led to manufacturing radio sets. Our principal

[5]

customers—World Radio Corporation—bought so many of these that the owners found it cheaper to give us the company than pay us for all the sets. This was in 1926. Later, fortunately, the company prospered, becoming the largest radio business in New England.

"In 1931, my former Harvard roommate and I organized a small investment company called World Investment Trust. [It now bears the more modest title "Investment Trust of Boston," and is no longer very small.] It acquired defaulted securities and nearly worthless common stocks of other investment trusts, companies that suffered heavily in the Great Depression, but still retained some powers of recuperation. As this venture became more interesting than selling radios, the radio company started buying investment trusts instead. In 1937, by buying thousands of shares of stock of other investment companies, shares retaining little virtue except their voting power, World Radio Corporation came into control of several investment trusts having assets of many millions of dollars. The Boston newspapers delighted in the story. 'Harvard boys run shoestring into thirty million dollars' were the headlines, no mention being made of twenty-nine million nine hundred and ninety-nine thousand in liabilities. Six months later security prices were down again, a trend that somehow liabilities seemed to resist.

"Today (1943) many of these trusts have been merged into a single investment company called Standard Equities Corporation. [Subsequently, by a change in name, Sheraton Corporation.] Liabilities have been sharply reduced and assets once more are modest. However, they include an interest in several hotels and other promising real estate. Last among these assets, and doubtless the least profitable, is an iron foundry in Newburyport, Massachusetts. Once known as a 'war baby' [the Second World War was in progress], it was actually perhaps a miscarriage. We discovered that hotel men are not the best iron foundrymen.

However there is satisfaction in making heavy castings badly needed for the war effort."

This was a summary of our first twenty-five years out of college, a quarter of a century rolled up into a small and concentrated capsule.

2

During the twenty-five years following graduation we made considerable progress toward a specific objective. We wanted to build a successful business that would someday be listed among the country's great corporations, and this ambition guided us through the years. We wanted to prove false the theory so widely held in the nineteen-twenties that business was essentially predatory, that businessmen must "cut corners" to succeed. And we wished to contradict the cynics of those "muckraking" days who were sure that "pull," or at least wealthy connections, were needed to get ahead. Eventually we were to discover that a strict code of ethics was actually an essential ingredient for building a successful business.

When our first twenty-five years in the world of commerce and finance were completed, we had gained experience in many fields, including some knowledge of foreign exchange, importing, manufacturing, and investments, and we were beginning to learn about the operation of hotels. This activity, we concluded, offered the greatest promise and a chance to engage in an exciting business venture.

We realized there would be pitfalls in creating a hotel chain, difficulties that had plagued others during early attempts to erect large hotel empires. For instance, the hazards present in the purchase of supplies are a rock upon which perhaps one attempt to assemble a group of hotels foundered. The temptation for profits "on the side" can be an insurmountable barrier to success. To meet this problem we organized a wholesale company owned exclusively by the hotels themselves which comprised our Sheraton system. Profits of the wholesale supplier were to go only to the hotels being served.

Purchasing was only one of the problems to be mastered. We relied on an interesting theory: if real efficiency could be achieved in all phases of a business, growth in a free-enterprise economy should follow almost automatically.

National advertising was one of the forces to be harnessed if we were to reach a big-league status.

Back in 1943, fearful of the expense of large newspaper advertisements, we decided to start our publicity campaign on a rather modest scale. Scatter ads—four or five small two-inch-square insertions scattered in the "run of the paper"—would present our message at moderate cost. The program was launched with great anticipation.

We selected the New York *Times* for this important campaign. Unfortunately a zealous *Times* reporter had dispatched on that very day a story from Detroit which appeared on an inside page, headed: "Prominent New Yorker Jumps from 14th Floor of Detroit's Sheraton Hotel." The article described the victim's distinguished career, listed his many achievements, and told of the widow left behind. His clubs were duly enumerated, but still some space remained at the bottom of the column —just enough for one of our ads. It carried the slogan current at the time: "Always Try Sheraton First."

3

The period following 1943 was one of expansion. Today Sheraton hotels cover the country coast to coast, and there are several in Canada. Among the landmarks of their respective communities are the Sheraton-Palace in San Francisco, the

Sheraton-Blackstone in Chicago, and the Town House in Los Angeles. The latter, following company tradition, recently became the Sheraton-West. Thus it can counterbalance the glamorous Ambassador on New York's Park Avenue, which caused a stir not long ago when it became the even more luxurious Sheraton-East.

A total of four Sheraton hotels in New York City; the stately Penn-Sheraton of Pittsburgh, once famous as the William Penn; the great Sheraton-Cadillac of Detroit; and leading hotels in St. Louis, Boston, and Washington proudly display the new Sheraton banner. The largest hotel in Cincinnati, the recently acquired Sheraton-Cleveland—these and several dozen more among America's great hotels are a part of the Sheraton Hotel System.

Also included in the Sheraton family is the ultra-modern Philadelphia Sheraton with nearly a thousand rooms, completed in 1957. Three more new hotels were opened in 1959. These were designed to provide Binghamton, New York; Dallas, Texas; and Portland, Oregon, with Sheraton's concept of what should be the hotel of tomorrow.

Looking back over the years and recalling the extensive assets once assembled when we were acquiring investment trusts, I realize that these earlier holdings, which despite offsetting liabilities intrigued the headline-writers of the time, represented but a fraction of the assets the company was soon to control. Sheraton over the years has prospered. It is now owned by fourteen thousand shareholders, more than four thousand of them Sheraton employees. If shareholders of large investment trusts holding Sheraton shares of debentures are counted, indirect owners probably now exceed a million.

Besides more than fifty hotels, Sheraton has some large office buildings and a subsidiary making stainless steel trim for the large automobile manufacturers. Unlike those in the days of the early investment trusts, liabilities are now fairly modest, amounting to only about half the market value of all corporate assets.

Although we have made progress toward the goals sought during the depression days of the nineteen-thirties, we are still more interested in looking into the future, than in looking backward. Long-range plans for the coming decade are ambitious, giving rise to hopes that hotels which now comprise the Sheraton chain will someday be but a beginning to what the company may eventually wish to offer as its contribution to the American free-enterprise system.

II.

Early Subjugation

I

M Y parents must have believed firmly in the virtues of a strict upbringing for the half-dozen children they brought into this world. Perhaps a long line of Quaker ancestors gave rise to this conviction.

An early recollection of childhood, a very painful one, dates back to a time when, at the age of six, I was sitting with my mother on the porch of our New Hampshire summer cottage in the small town known as Dublin. Workmen at a dollar a day were digging a cellar for us, for we were to have a larger cottage to care for a growing family. Doubtless one of the genes responsible for my unpardonable behavior at that time drew its inspiration direct from Satan, for when I saw in Mother's sewing basket a new and shiny twenty-five-cent piece, I took it, supposedly unobserved, and hid it under a stone in the dirt being shoveled from the excavation.

I ran off for a moment, and, returning, succeeded with my bare feet—Dublin was barefoot territory for us in those days— in discovering the shiny quarter hidden under the stone. "Look, Mother," I called out as my toes "stumbled" on the silver piece, "see what I found."

Mother's pained expression was the best possible medicine

for an erring six-year-old. Looking very hurt, she quietly suggested I return the coin to her workbasket. Her handling of this delicate crisis was superb, and the crushing sense of guilt I suffered at the age of six was, I believe, an effective guarantee that integrity would govern my future business dealings. The lesson of that twenty-five-cent coin and my mother's skill in obliterating the offending "gene" were important contributions toward laying the foundation for a subsequent hotel empire.

Not many years after the missing-coin episode, my father also took a hand in the process of raising his youngest son. I no longer recall the transgression that ignited this parental wrath, but it was doubtless some form of falsehood, for Father, a strict disciplinarian, permitted no deviations from his rigid code of veracity. I still recall the half-inch welts that rose all over my back as Father's cane expressed his displeasure. Strong medicine, it was a punishment which today, in an age when many of us are growing soft, might seem brutal, but, looking back on that rugged experience, I realize I would not have had it otherwise. The welts eventually disappeared, but the lesson on truthfulness was ingrained in my consciousness. The words "juvenile delinquency" might now be nearly unknown had Father's approach to such problems been more generally emulated.

Additional parental medicine was administered a few years later, a treatment which saves me many dollars a year. At the age of fourteen I was given by my father, himself an avid smoker, a long, cheap, and very black cigar. Although Father liked his daily smoke, he had decided his sons should avoid this particular form of delight, and his strategy was quite successful. Having removed the tip from the ill-smelling stogie, he put this large object in my mouth and proceeded to light it, suggesting I puff as hard as I could.

I was finally advised, when halfway through this rugged ordeal, doubtless after I had turned a grayish hue, that the

[12]

treatment was over. I never smoked again, and if curiosity ever suggested reaching for a cigarette, the memory of that unhappy event discouraged the idea. I sometimes wonder if today there might not be one or two fewer hotels in our collection had the dollars saved on smoking, multiplied through the miracle of advantageous reinvestment, not contributed somehow to the company's growth.

2

I was born in Chestnut Hill, a suburb of Boston. The family, comprising at the time five children, moved shortly thereafter to Washington, D. C., where we remained only a few years. Watching horse-drawn fire engines rushing past our house is among the few vivid memories I have of that time. "N" Street, North West, must have been near a fire station; we children could hardly wait for the next alarm to be sounded.

I can recall, at the age of three, seeing the new century come in, a big event. However, in retrospect, I suspect it was a "preview" that I witnessed, staged some hours prematurely on the eve of the actual event, for my especial benefit. My parents believed in sending children to bed early, and doubtless a mild deception was held less sinful than breaking a strict rule—even though centuries may not recur at better than hundred-year intervals.

Another recollection of Washington dates back to the time the century was already a year old. My sister, Hildegard, a mature young lady of ten, had returned from a children's party at the White House, where Teddy Roosevelt presided. Actually, it must have been his children who ruled the White House, at least on this occasion. The party was a huge success. A pillow fight had developed, and my sister and Ethel Roosevelt, both armed with White House pillows, were holding off the other children, but the battle was going against them when the President of the United States, an adoring and fun-loving father, came to the rescue. Teddy Roosevelt, mounting superior armament—two pillows in this instance, dipped in a tub of water—arrived in time to assist in routing the opposing forces. I remember how impressed Father was on hearing the blow-by-blow account of this White House skirmish. I understand he voted Republican all the rest of his life.

Father, though perhaps an inch taller, was otherwise a near replica of Teddy Roosevelt. At times it must have been embarrassing for him to ride in the Washington street cars, for the resemblance often caused a stir among the passengers.

At another time in Washington, when I was four, Mother had some guests for tea, that former equivalent of today's cocktail party. Since more were on hand than had been expected, the cakes were running low. As the visitors sat near the tea table, Mother, noting the hopeful eyes cast by her youngest at the diminishing supply, offered me half a piece of cake. Such an indignity called for reprisal. Angrily I announced that if I could not have a whole piece I would not take any. Decades have gone by, but a brother and two living sisters rarely let me forget that unhappy occasion.

When summers came around, we would leave for the cooler New Hampshire hills. Families from Baltimore, St. Louis, Boston, and other cities took refuge in the little town of Dublin during hot summer months. On one of these trips, while we were heading north on the sleeper, there arose one of those "one in a million" coincidences which seem to recur with unbelievable regularity. In the middle of the night our train suddenly came to a halt—whistles blowing, red lights flashing in the dark, and uniformed trainmen with lanterns rushing back and forth. Hours passed, and with no explanation, but after much puffing and jolting, the train finally backed away, and then resumed at last its interrupted journey. No clues were forth-coming from the crew other than a routine report: "an unavoid-able delay."

Twenty years had passed when a magazine article, enumer-ating some near-fatal railroad accidents of which passengers were unaware, included a story, time and date recorded, of a Washington–New York express that had been diverted by an open switch. The track ended at the edge of a sharp preci-pice with a vast gorge extending hundreds of feet below. When the train came to a halt, four of the locomotive wheels over-hung the abyss. My sister's diary confirmed the time and the date.

3

My earliest business enterprise, when I was at the age of twelve, produced a profit, but a family subsidy may have played a part. There was no charge for raw materials, two dozen grocery-store eggs that had previously reposed in the family icebox.

I constructed an object that could house the eggs. A small door with a glass window made it possible to see inside, where a flashlight bulb attached to a dry-cell battery threw light on a thermometer visible through the glass. Four legs, once mallet heads from an abandoned croquet set, supported this contraption. A kerosene lamp from a discarded magic lantern was fitted to the side of my apparatus as the heating plant. The entire chicken factory—for this was to be its function—reposed on the dresser in my bedroom in Cambridge, Massachusetts. Research in the family encyclopedia had confirmed that, with the temperature held at a hundred and three degrees for twenty-one days, eggs might possibly hatch.

For nineteen days all went well, and excitement was running high. But trouble came when I put too much kerosene in the lamp and produced a conflagration. The fire, though finally extinguished, did considerable damage. The thermometer was a total loss, for its "ceiling" of a hundred and twenty degrees had been violated. The eggs outwardly had remained intact, but we could not tell whether they had been hard-boiled inside. Hasty repairs to the apparatus made possible proceeding for another two days, but, with a broken thermometer, guesswork had to substitute for more scientific temperature-control. On the twenty-first day, six former grocery-store eggs began a mysterious prenatal ritual, and, after much commotion, a half-dozen genuine though rather surprised chickens of doubtful pedigree made their respective appearances.

The six members of my new family started growing up, to my mother's dismay, in one of my bureau drawers. A month later, invited to visit the family of George H. Browne, head master of the Browne and Nichols School, for a week end in Plymouth, New Hampshire, I was faced with the problem of baby-sitters to watch over my growing ménage. But Amy Browne, my host's daughter, said, "Bring them along," and so I arrived for a pleasant sojourn, accompanied by my six dependents.

Eventually three "home-made" chickens reached a robust roasting age. They were sold to an appreciative neighbor for two dollars and eighty cents—nearly all profit. My first business venture was a resounding financial success.

In later years, as we became interested in hotels, when things occasionally went wrong it was always a comfort to me to recall this initial undertaking and realize that, if accidents did at times occur, all might still turn out well.

III.

Searching for Ancestors

I

SOONER or later in an autobiography the formality of dusting off one's helpless ancestors must be observed. Naturally any genealogical lines leading inconveniently to some colorful horse thief in Virginia may readily be bypassed, even though they could reveal some of the more adventuresome molecules coursing through our anatomy. A Staten Island cousin of mine, stumbling upon such a trail while in search of ancestors, hastily turned to more productive channels on discovering the unfortunate direction in which this one was leading.

Although I don't know how many ancestors I had, I suspect their number was large. Whatever else may have been their attributes, one characteristic they shared in common: on the seventh day of March in 1897, all simultaneously became my ancestors.

My mother, born in England, was three-quarters British and one-quarter German. The Teutonic strain was often emphasized, for I was born on a Sunday, and in Germany, at least, I was a *Sonntagskind*—a Sunday child. This was supposed to bring good fortune.

The German relatives and ancestors we were told about were mostly Von Bunsens. The De Bunsens, a British branch of the family, included nearly half of Mother's eleven brothers and sisters. A cousin of hers was Sir Maurice de Bunsen, a British Ambassador to Spain and Turkey.

Years later, when I was about to graduate from Boston's Noble and Greenough School, a classmate, Aaron Davis Weld, later a casualty of World War I, invited me to his Marlboro Street home, where his family was playing a game of "Knowledge." They—I add in partial extenuation—were among the more brilliant representatives of this New England center of learning. Sensing my embarrassment at the complexity of the questions asked, they selected one clearly earmarked for me.

"What renowned scientist," they inquired, "invented a famous gas burner?"

Expressions on their faces showed they knew the answer, but even this gambit failed with me, and the game was graciously called off. On reaching home I learned we have a German ancestor—or at least a collateral one—for whom the Bunsen burner had been named. Later, on discovering that for several consecutive weeks Davis Weld's report cards showed nothing but tens, a completely perfect score, my feelings were partially assuaged.

As children, we used to hear much of Great-Grandfather Charles Christian von Bunsen, who married a Frances Waddington in England. His wife, later an author, must have been high on the list of best-sellers, even perhaps in this country, if such lists existed here in her day. I reached this conclusion from the many copies of her book, *Life and Letters of the Baroness Bunsen*, that I have been able to purchase at book auctions, sometimes for as much as fifty cents a copy, but more often, I regret to acknowledge, for only a nickel or a dime.

Despite the many copies now adorning our bookshelves, I must confess I never read the entire volume. Its pages, mostly devoted to European figures of art, literature, and music of a hundred years ago, included such names as Mendelssohn, Sir

[18]

Walter Scott, the Duke of Wellington, Wordsworth, Lord Macaulay, and others the Von Bunsens entertained in London, Berlin, or Rome.

Charles von Bunsen, appointed Prussian Minister to the Vatican despite a difference in religion, became a friend and great admirer of Pope Gregory XVI while in Rome, and stories of his intimate walks in the countryside with the head of the Roman Catholic Church have come down through the generations. It appears His Holiness, fond of watching birds in the trees, once tripped on an unseen root. Rising from a painful fall, the Pontiff turned to Great-Grandfather von Bunsen and remarked, "You see, Charles, even a pope is not always infallible."

After his years in Rome, Bunsen became Prussian Ambassador to the Court of St. James's and spent many years in London. It was, however, his wife's sister, Augusta Waddington, and her husband, a tall mining prospector from Wales, who especially interested us.

The mining engineer, Benjamin Hall, perhaps more than any other, was responsible for the action of a mid-twentieth-century Labour government, a hundred and thirty years later, in nationalizing the British coal mines. Benjamin Hall's prospecting apparently had met with considerable success. Starting with little or nothing, he was able to pass down through several generations to a lone surviving descendant, a sixteen-year-old Eton boy, a large proportion of the Welsh coal industry comprising mines which he, Benjamin Hall, had discovered. It is perhaps understandable that in the nineteen-forties a British government should question the wisdom of leaving in the hands of a sixteen-year-old the ownership of such an important segment of the present British economy.

Toward the middle of the nineteenth century, the tall and prosperous Benjamin Hall apparently concluded that the British Parliament buildings, then under construction, needed a clock with chimes. Duly purchased and installed, it became known as

[19]

"Big Ben." At about that time Benjamin Hall became known as Lord Llanover. We have not examined too closely a possible link between these supposedly unrelated occurrences.

Our middle daughter, Penny, was christened Augusta after her great-great grandaunt Augusta Waddington, wife of Benjamin Hall. Our youngest son, Barclay, also owes his name to a British progenitor, and perhaps to the possibility that he might someday wish to cash a check in a distant corner of the British Empire, at one of the Barclay Banks. Our son's name came from Robert Barclay, a seventeenth-century promoter whose wealth apparently resulted in part from a profitable sojourn in prison.

Robert Barclay, during the late sixteen hundreds, was, according to stories we often heard, a small-scale British speculator. He was apparently destined for relative obscurity, for if his investments ever rose by a point or two, the great urge for profits seemed to force him to cash in, thus precluding any prospects of his ever becoming very wealthy. This handicap could have plagued him all his days had not his family, as was true of generations of his descendants, been ardent Quakers. His religious convictions seem to explain his years in prison, as well as the fortune which is evidenced today by a notable banking empire.

Robert Barclay, we were told, had secured, presumably on a narrow margin, a controlling interest in some British textile mills. As the price of the shares went up, Barclay would doubtless have sold, but fortunately British involvement in a Continental war prevented this indiscretion. When engaged in military adventures, the British had a recurring fondness for putting their Quakers in jail, since religious convictions of adherents to this faith precluded the oaths of allegiance British sovereigns cherished.

For the duration of the war Barclay remained behind prison bars, unaware perhaps that a need for uniforms would enrich the textile industry. When hostilities ended, Robert Barclay, finally released, found England greatly impoverished, but with one notable exception: his textile monopoly, entitled to receive large sums from London banks, was doing very well. As the story goes, in the ensuing depression many banks could not meet their obligations, and the wealthy textile firms took them over. Thus, many became Barclay Banks. Whether the story is wholly accurate is perhaps open to question, but at all events, Robert Barclay was an ancestor, a grandfather with many "greats" attached. The Barclays, Waddingtons, and Gurneys, families that often intermarried, recurred at frequent intervals on various branches of Mother's family tree.

The Gurneys were sometimes referred to in England, specifically in *Alice's Adventures in Wonderland*, in the tones with which we upon occasion allude to Morgans and Rockefellers. Sad to relate, this was of little help to the Hendersons in the U.S.A. Fifty years after my appearance in the world I received a legacy from a Gurney ancestor who had bequeathed what was perhaps a lordly sum at the time, to be divided equally among all descendants alive a century later. Partly, I suppose, because of British taxes, more, perhaps, due to depreciation of the pound, but most, presumably, on account of the fertility of her descendants, we Hendersons, some years ago, each deposited in our bank accounts the princely sum of $158.

An overzealous German aunt, eager to press for such mileage as existed in the British branch of the family tree, succeeded in tracing our lineage, I trust through reasonably legitimate channels, through four or five generations of Richard Grenvilles (each spelling his name with a quaint variation), through William the Conqueror, all the way back to Charlemagne. The pleasure Aunt Marie von Bunsen derived from this subtle accomplishment must have been somewhat diluted on learning that she had reached Charlemagne by way of an offshoot of the family tree which led to King Charles X of France, unfortunately better known as Charles the Simple.

[21]

My father, whose name I inherited—embellished with a "Jr." which I later discarded—came from Staten Island, New York. He graduated from Harvard in 1883 and acquired in Berlin both a Ph.D. and a lovely wife, a daughter of the youngest son of the Chevalier Charles Christian von Bunsen. Mother in her early years commuted between Germany and the western borders of England. Summers were spent at Llanover, one of the great Welsh estates near Abergavenny that were handed down by Big Ben Hall; for the winter she would return to the von Bunsen house in Berlin.

It was from Mother's Berlin home that one of her early recollections came. Some twelve years before her marriage, at the age of eight, she saw the triumphant homecoming of Bismarck, following the birth of Germany as a unified nation. Bismarck had reached the crest of his eminence in 1871, after the peace conference of Versailles that brought to an end the Franco-Prussian War.

Bismarck was an interesting paradox, who has risen and fallen in American esteem according to the state of U.S.–German relations. During recent world wars, he was considered a demon, a war-monger, and a reactionary, sharing with the Kaiser and Hitler responsibility for unleashing Germany's supposed lust for conquest. That, however, was not the American point of view when the "Iron Chancellor" was alive, a time when sentiment mostly favored the Germans.

It is interesting that, in the decades following the Franco-Prussian War, Bismarck was to inaugurate the first social-security laws of any land—laws which in later years would be models for much of Franklin D. Roosevelt's New Deal legislation. It would seem, however, that Bismarck's pioneering in social progress did not arise solely from humanitarian impulses. As a brilliant statesman, he perceived that the quickest way to deflate the power of socialist opponents was to take the lead in old-age, unemployment, and other forms of welfare legislation. This pioneering in the evolution of social responsibility was under way in Germany when Mother was a very young girl.

Mother's youth, divided equally between England and Germany, must have been especially interesting. She was doubtless one of the very few presented as a debutante both to Queen Victoria in London and also at the German Imperial Court.

2

If I was born with a silver spoon in my mouth it must have been silver plate, for my parents were able only with great difficulty to put their six children through school, and later through various colleges.

Father, a historian, pursued a far from lucrative career. His best-known work, ironically called *A Short History of Germany*, comprised two enormous volumes. Since his studies required research in France, England, and other European countries, we children were taken abroad nearly every second or third year. Usually one or two would be deposited in different parts of Europe to learn languages. Otherwise our education was divided between Boston and Cambridge schools, private or public— depending, no doubt, on the circulation of the latest history book.

The royalties that Father received on his books, though small, were fortunately fairly persistent. Although he died in 1928, a check for some $2.50 still periodically arrives from Macmillan, indicating that at least a few copies of *A Short History of Germany* were sold since the previous accounting.

Father's burdens were partially eased by the fact that his own father died during an interim between two of the major depressions which so often plagued the previous century, and this made possible something of a nest egg for the surviving children. The value of each legacy unfortunately was in inverse ratio to the number of those alive—close to a dozen, if I counted

[23]

them correctly. The death of John Cleves Symmes Henderson, the source of these welcome legacies, marked the end of an interesting career, one always an inspiration to his many grand-children. Three times he had made a sizable fortune only to see it lost in an ensuing depression—or financial panic, as these phenomena were called in his day.

I remember some impressive prints on the walls of Hender-son & Company, a New York Stock Exchange firm near Wall Street headed by one of my father's six brothers. The prints showed some large mid-nineteenth-century American Rubber works outside of Paris, the scene of one of John Henderson's ventures which subsequently succumbed as a disastrous business cycle took its toll.

The interesting point about my grandfather's financial affairs, one often emphasized as we grew up, was that on each occasion when his financial world collapsed, leaving behind mountainous debts, he refused the more painless path of bankruptcy as a means of wiping the old slate clean. Instead, setting forth again, with less than nothing to start with, he proceeded to make a new and larger fortune in a different field of endeavor, eventu-ally reimbursing the creditors of the previous misadventure.

After his third failure and subsequent recovery, perhaps sens-ing the need for an investment that could survive future crises, he decided to consider real estate. Among several opportunities, the choice finally narrowed to two alternatives: some land on Staten Island, and several undeveloped acres on the southern tip of Manhattan. But the elderly man, now cautious after many failures, insisted that an analysis of the soil be made. Lower Manhattan near Wall Street must have lacked the de-sired fertility; and so a hundred living descendants now share in some miscellaneous acres on Staten Island which, with some difficulty, earn each year just about enough to pay the accruing real-estate taxes.

John's father, Judge Thomas Henderson, also an interesting

figure, came to America as a youngster from England late in the eighteenth century. An early Cincinnati settler, he, with two friends, laid out much of that Ohio city. His antecedents remain a baffling mystery.

Apparently the judge and his friend John Cleves Symmes, after whom the judge's son was named, planned Fountain Square as the focal point of what was to be the city of Cincinnati. Little could he have guessed, as the seventeen-hundreds were drawing to a close, that a century and a half later the dominant building overlooking Fountain Square would be the city's largest hotel, destined to become an important link in a hotel system his own great-grandson would head.

Before leaving London for the United States, the judge, a contemporary of Thomas Sheraton, may perhaps have known that illustrious gentleman. If perhaps their paths did cross, Thomas Henderson could hardly have guessed that the future hotel on Fountain Square, in common with fifty others throughout the continent, would bear the name of that famous creator of eighteenth-century furniture design.

IV.

Early Education

I

It was during one of Father's many trips to France, in Versailles, that I had the combined experience of attending my first school and becoming involved in my first love affair.

As the youngest of five children—the sixth was to arrive later (much later, my sister Frances emphasizes)—I had remained with the family. Father had settled abroad for the winter in the shadow of the Palais de Versailles, engaged in getting some new angles on Marie Antoinette's past. Near our apartment was a school called "Le Petit Lycée des Jeunes Filles," attended by two hundred girls and three boys. I was one of the three boys.

With all those girls to choose from, I could hardly have done better in drawing a deskmate: Colette D'Aron, exquisite, exotic, chic, and a little coy. I fell desperately in love with her, despite her advanced years; in those days, I must have liked older women. Colette was nearly eight. I never saw her afterward—though perhaps a French lady now presumably in her sixties, doubtless grandmother of a dozen or more, is blissfully unaware of the havoc she once played in the emotional life of an American six-year-old.

I spoke both French and German in those days, better perhaps than English. Today, however, these languages are a major struggle for me, perhaps because the vocabulary of a six-year-old, especially the sweet nothings useful when whispering to Colette, is of little help when conversing in French on economic theories, or when dwelling on international politics. Besides, both Germans and Frenchmen handily beat you in the duel of foreign tongues. Europeans, learning languages so they can actually speak them, have an unfair advantage over Americans, whose schooling rarely produces that desired result.

No wonder that, when attending compulsory French classes at Noble and Greenough in Boston, I was surprised to find myself near the bottom of the class. French, after all, I could only speak, read, and write—better, perhaps, than could my teacher. Unfortunately, my classmates could conjugate irregular verbs, and, whatever might be the virtue therein, they at least could pass exams that I was sure to fail.

Another recollection of days at Noble and Greenough still remains. Old Mr. Noble—doubtless approaching ninety—one of the country's great authorities on the classics, was still teaching Latin despite seriously faulty hearing. Unwilling to admit to his infirmity, and as co-owner of the school hardly subject to involuntary retirement, he doggedly retained the prerogative of sole purveyor of Latin, until finally his career came to an abrupt end. My classmate John Davis was the immediate cause. Johnny had diagnosed correctly the impairment in the headmaster's hearing. When asked by the elderly teacher to translate a certain paragraph of Cicero, he began to recount with simulated hesitancy, his eyes appearing to follow the text, the details of a recent fishing trip. Old Mr. Noble, observing Johnny's lips to appraise the fluency of the translation, commented on the unaccustomed proficiency.

"Well done, John," he said cheerfully.

The uproar that greeted this "exposure" sounded the death

knell of a great teaching career. However, my success in surmounting the rigors of Latin entrance requirements at Harvard provided strong evidence that old man Noble, though nearly stone deaf, could still accomplish miracles. Hardly could I have entered Harvard when I did, had it not been for the wizardry of George Washington Copp Noble.

2

Father, perhaps like many American parents, had determined in advance upon the careers his three sons should follow. Brother George would be a banker, my oldest brother, Gerard, a scientist. I was to be an electrical engineer, doubtless because of Father's discovery that at the age of sixteen I could disconnect the run-down batteries operating our front doorbell and substitute new ones, miraculously restoring thereby the interrupted service. Father's literary career had insulated him from the worlds of electricity and mechanics, so prowess in such nebulous regions, no matter how rudimentary, evoked visions of a great scientific future for at least two of his three sons.

One of the instances when parental wrath descended upon us with unusual fervor was when Father discovered that Gerard, instead of pursuing a scientific career, had applied and been admitted to the Harvard Law School. His displeasure was only mildly assuaged when Gerard graduated at the head of his class, with the second highest honors ever awarded a graduate of that institution. I believe Louis Brandeis may have enjoyed the top honor.

At the age of thirty-five Gerry entered the law firm of New York's ex-Governor Nathan Miller, the name becoming Miller, Otis, Farr and Henderson. This partnership lasted less than a year, for an eye infection brought a sudden end to what might have been a notable career. It proved fatal within a week.

Gerry's widow raised three children and put them through college with comparative ease on the interest received each year from Gerry's share in the firm's fees earned in connection with a railroad reorganization.

In 1928 neither sulpha drugs nor penicillin were known. Had they been discovered a few years earlier, an exciting future might have been Gerry's.

3

Since Father's plans for making a scientist of Gerry had failed, he took extra pains to see that the education of his youngest son should follow the desired pattern. Once more in Europe in search of historical nuggets, he deposited me at the age of sixteen in Hanover, Germany, a city boasting both the purest German and one of the best European technical colleges.

During my year in Hanover I found I could augment a somewhat meager allowance by reading aloud to an American expatriate, a former Harvard chemistry instructor named Rothman who had suffered an almost worse than fatal accident in Cambridge. He had moved to Germany, where, relatively unknown, he could avoid the burden of sympathy from his former acquaintances. Rothman had examined too closely a container of acid with a flame underneath—a Bunsen Burner, presumably. As he peered at the mixture it began to boil and three drops flew upward. One hit his necktie, burning a hole through the fabric. The other two struck his two eyes.

Rothman arrived in Hanover and became associated with Walter Bergius, one of Germany's top physical chemists who had already achieved fame by devising a formula for diminishing the pangs of starvation, an ordeal soon to face his nation. He had discovered a chemical process for converting seemingly worthless sawdust into glucose from which some partially palatable nutrition could be extracted. I met Bergius again in 1936 when, as a leading European scientist, he was honored at Harvard's Tercentennial Exercises.

While I was in Hanover, Bergius and Rothman were developing an interesting invention—a mercury arc rectifier that could convert alternating into direct current. I was permitted to serve as a substitute for Rothman's eyes during those exciting experiments. I can still recall the flash of electrical sparks jumping under the pressure of high voltages, the ghostly glow of greenish incandescence inside large glass tubes as rarefied mercury vapors were subjected to powerful electrical charges, and the sharp odor of ozone that permeated the laboratories as monster switches were thrown in and out.

Rothman did not survive the First World War. The combination of a physical affliction and finding his native America at war with the country he had adopted was evidently too painful. When the war was over we were shocked to hear he had found an open window high up in a tall building—and that was the tragic end.

That the work of Bergius and Rothman eventually bore fruit came to light forty years later when I chanced to be in Toronto. Fred Kummer, Sheraton vice president and brilliant chief engineer, was taking me through the King Edward Sheraton, our popular Toronto hotel, and explaining the electric installation, which operated with exceptional efficiency. In a room marked "Danger—High Voltage" was a device changing alternating current into the direct current needed for hotel elevators. A mysterious green glow in a large glass tube alive with a spluttering mercury arc revived memories of those Hanover experiments. "So you have a mercury arc rectifier," I remarked casually. Fred, I presume, still wonders how a mere hotelman could fathom these technical intricacies.

When the conversion of one of our Midwest hotels to alternating current posed a problem, Fred told us that mercury rectifiers might reduce by a hundred thousand dollars earlier estimates for more conventional equipment. Little did I imagine, when working in the Bergius laboratories, the extent of my subsequent interest in the success of those early experiments.

My stay in Hanover lasted through July, 1914, and the family, reunited on the Hamburg-American liner *Cincinnati*, sailed for Boston just one day before the First World War broke out. But before I describe the journey home, there is another event to record which occurred a few weeks before. If my troubles on that occasion did not actually cause World War I, they should at least have been a strong contributing factor.

Hanover, once ruled by Kings George I and II of England, had a British sector that played a significant role in the social life of the community. Recently the once popular yearly Anglo-German Ball had somehow become an Anglo-American affair. It was the top social event of the year, and the most prominent Englishman and the leading available American were British and American chairmen on this important occasion. The spring of 1914 was to be no exception, but, lacking a prominent American, the committee invited me—by now a seventeen-year-old student and perhaps the only American in Hanover—to serve as the American co-chairman.

Sensing the significance of this international event, I invited Susie, the lovely sixteen-year-old daughter of Dr. Bergius, to be the lady of the evening so that together we might uphold the prestige of the United States.

Arriving by taxi at the ballroom entrance, Susie at my side, and observing that the taxi meter called for seven marks, I reached for a ten-mark gold piece brought along for this purpose. The taxi man, accepting the coin with a deep bow, conceded the generosity of the gratuity. It was worth it, I thought, for Susie, very beautiful indeed, obviously deserved to be impressed; and anyway, was I not to be honored as the most important—if perhaps the only—American then in Hanover?

As Susie and I entered the ballroom, dancing automatically stopped and couples stepped aside so the representative of America and his lady could pass. We began to cross the floor, heading for the flag-bedecked American Box, to the stirring measures of "The Star-Spangled Banner," a musical effort into which the German orchestra, struggling with unfamiliar measures, was none the less blasting all the decibels at its command. As Susie and I, the center of all eyes, reached the middle of the floor, a commotion brought the music to a sudden stop. Our taxi driver had rushed into the room, shouting in the loudest of tones.

"You've cheated me, you've cheated me," he shrieked at me so even the deaf could hear. There he stood, clutching a new and shiny coin resembling a German ten-mark gold piece. In terror I reached for the pocket of my tuxedo, a suit I had not worn since leaving the U.S.A. The ten-mark coin was still there. The taxi driver was holding a new, shiny American one-cent piece.

Three weeks later World War One broke out. I still sometimes wonder—was there perhaps a connection between these two disasters?

The day after we boarded the *Cincinnati* the holocaust was raging. We were on a German liner, a potential British prize, in waters controlled by British men-of-war. Racing toward America, our lights extinguished at night, we were pursued by several British warships. Somehow we escaped, and reached eventually the sanctuary of Boston Harbor.

A fellow passenger who spent many evenings playing bridge with my parents was a teen-age student on his way home from France. Today, representing precisely one-half of our brilliant team of distinguished Massachusetts Senators, and a senior member of the Senate Military Affairs Committee, Leverett

Saltonstall, that fellow passenger on the *Cincinnati*, is now rendering valuable services to the nation.

4

In the autumn of 1914 I became a freshman at Harvard. The following spring, while pursuing the popular collegiate pastime of attending a dance I fell into conversation with a classmate, a fellow member of the stag line. Both of us agreed that the choice of partners was substantially below specifications. All, we concluded, were presumably Radcliffe girls. This implied that they were studious, probably wore heavy glasses except at dances, and were fatally damned in the eyes of the sons of Harvard. Today, I hear, things are very different, and Harvard boys are eager for dates with Radcliffe girls, provided the girls will overlook the woeful judgment once displayed by a former misguided generation.

The student I met on that memorable occasion agreed with me on many subjects as the evening wore on. In fact, we got along so well that he asked me to spend the weekend at his family home in Wayland, a dozen or so miles away. I gladly accepted—and ever since, with surprisingly little difficulty, we have agreed on almost every subject. This is how I met Robert Lowell Moore, my roommate for the next two years, a partner in all business ventures since those early days at college, and, at present, Sheraton's board chairman.

Bob Moore was the owner of a contraption he sometimes called, with some lack of conviction, an automobile. It was a Metz, which had, instead of a conventional transmission, a big flat wheel and a large steel plate at right angles to it. One of these was attached to the engine and the other to the rear wheels, and, when the two were pressed together with sufficient determination, the car would move forward. This was called a friction drive. The car had no floorboards, and I was soon to discover that a passenger had distinct merit, if he could be induced to push with both feet on one of the shafts; under such prodding the otherwise reluctant Metz would become inspired and could travel twice as fast.

I sometimes wonder nowadays whether Bob Moore's interest in his future college roommate on the occasion of our first meeting was not somehow related to the advantages of having a passenger along.

We must have been a familiar sight on Brattle Street or Massachusetts Avenue, Bob at the steering wheel and I with my feet protruding beneath the chassis, coaxing a few extra miles per hour out of our dashing conveyance. As recognition for my contribution, I had the prerogative of manipulating the large klaxon horn, a device which never failed to keep clear the traffic lanes ahead. A mere fire engine chancing to follow behind could scarcely have expected much attention from any of the awed bystanders.

The partnership Bob and I formed was an immediate success, providing a pleasant association and a welcome source of financial dividends. We both liked to buy broken-down automobiles, take them apart in our college-dormitory yard, and reassemble them in the hope of making a profitable sale. A further financial merit of these carefully rejuvenated cars was that they could be rented to our classmates, who, allergic to nearby Radcliffe, needed transportation for their periodic fifteen-mile trips to Wellesley. Even our wealthier classmates preferred ours to the cars of more conventional rental agencies, for rejuvenated jalopies were more subject to breakdowns at strategic intervals. Ralph Damon, a classmate, was an occasional customer. We once offered him a rebate when an old Stoddard Dayton had broken down, but he firmly refused. Perhaps, he explained, we should have a bonus.

Ralph Damon later headed the American Air Lines and eventually became president of T.W.A. Even more important in our eyes, he was an effective Sheraton director until his recent death—a loss most keenly felt by the entire business community.

From buying up and renting old cars in our spare time, we eventually graduated to a more lucrative phase of the automobile business, one Bob Moore and I indirectly helped pioneer. We had discovered in those early days—some years before Ford put trucks on the market—that ambitious firms were buying up new Fords, removing the unused bodies, and welding in place heavier rear axles. By mounting a truck body on the reinforced chassis, they could deliver a serviceable truck—and we could buy the new but surplus bodies cheap.

Realizing that Ford parts were interchangeable, we found we could buy old second-hand Fords, substitute the new bodies, replace the ancient brass radiators with ones of a newer vintage, and thus create nearly new 1915 cars. We sold these for half the cost of new cars, and business was rushing. Even classmates liked our modernized product, for they could now take their girls for drives in seemingly new cars without sacrificing the prospect of occasional breakdowns on lonely country roads.

5

At times, while at college, we attended what were known as the Salem Assemblies. These dances were exciting affairs that usually lasted quite late, and transportation back to Boston was difficult, especially if our rebuilt Fords were all spoken for. Sylvia Benson, one of the more popular Salem belles, lived in one of the large brick eighteenth-century sea-captain homes that still bear testimony to Salem's former maritime grandeur. Even the widow's walk on the roof was intact, that elevated railed passageway where a wife would spend hours awaiting a glimpse of a distant sail to herald, or perhaps warn, of the return of a long-absent husband bringing his clipper ship to port.

Sylvia often brought home, after the dance, several of the out-of-town students invited to Salem, no doubt, to reinforce the indispensable stag line. She would give us a midnight breakfast of milk and scrambled eggs, and a bed for the night. There always seemed to be plenty of rooms where we could get some needed sleep.

On one of these pleasant occasions, when more of us were on hand than usual, a young Boston lawyer and I were assigned two large beds under the attic rafters. Although a stranger, this young lawyer was a useful companion, for he too would be leaving by the morning "Narrow Gauge" for Boston, and, as we both had early engagements, we could help each other wake up.

My appointment was in connection with our first real-estate venture. Bob Moore and I, now sophomores at Harvard, had purchased, with profits from our rebuilt Fords, some land on which we planned to build some multiple stalls—a so-called community garage. To establish title to the land, we needed a signature from a person we were to meet on the fifth floor of a Franklin Street building. The next morning, my document in hand and my attic companion following, I struggled to catch the Narrow Gauge train.

Having reached Boston by ferry—a necessary adjunct in those days to the Narrow Gauge railway—we proceeded from Rowe's Wharf to our respective destinations. We both headed for Franklin Street, entered the same building, and, on the fifth floor, suddenly discovered that his was the signature and mine the document for which we had rushed to Boston together at that uncouth hour. How much pleasanter, we reflected regretfully, it would have been to pass the document from one attic bed to the other. This was one more instance of the million-to-one coincidences that seem to recur with such regularity.

Perhaps another million-to-one event took place during my

early days at Harvard, although at the time it seemed unimportant. A classmate, Johnny Davis, dared me to walk the seventy-three miles from Cambridge to Dublin, New Hampshire, one pleasant spring evening. Had we realized what odds might have been quoted against completing such an unconventional journey, perhaps even from Lloyds of London, we might have been more prosperous during our later college days.

We started early in the evening and reached Concord, Massachusetts, fifteen miles on our way, where a soft field offered some needed rest. Too cold to sleep, however, each of us soon discovered the other was wide awake, so we walked all through the night to keep warm. We took a short midday nap under a warm May sun, continued our unrecorded marathon, and reached Dublin early that evening. Our speed, we calculated, had been nearly three miles an hour, including "stops."

Observing in a recent issue of the Boston *Herald* a front-page story, headlines and picture thrown in, suggesting that the hiking record had fallen to a present-day Harvard student who took a fifty-six-mile jaunt in less than a day, I wondered if we had not missed a chance to claim in our time a world's record. We had failed to draw even an honorable mention from the Boston *Herald*, leave alone a front-page picture.

During that long walk I enjoyed a small advantage over my classmate, for, accustomed to barefoot summers in New Hampshire, my feet were fairly tough. Johnny developed some minor complaints: a postcard mailed to his family en route mentioned "blisters the size of New York" on both feet.

V.

The Coming of War

AFTER completing two and a half years of college, we became convinced that entry of the United States into World War I was a virtual certainty. I suspect many of us by that time were also sure that, however real was the danger of German armaments, impending examinations presented an even greater terror. Most of us were soon in uniform.

Once in the Navy, I discovered I was destined for the career of an electrician third class. The wavy lines on my sailor-suit sleeves, emblems presumably passed out almost at random, indicated that I was to be a radio operator, and soon I was attending a Navy radio school. A month later I was in Rockland, Maine, where Uncle Sam, to maintain communications with a twenty-mile-distant island, had requisitioned the private radio station of a young Rockland boy. Three of us newly created operators arrived, manned the equipment the local radio ham had ingeniously devised, and every hour on the hour sent out a call consisting of three mysterious letters. Crackling back through the ether would come the comforting response, the same three letters repeated. They confirmed that in the interval the island had not been captured.

Nothing was more enjoyable than those pleasant months as

a radioman in Uncle Sam's delightful Navy. As sailor boys we almost owned the world. To the beauties of Rockland, we were heroes defending our country, and their former beaux no longer had a chance. Months later, when we were transferred to the Naval Air Service, having discovered this more direct approach to a coveted ensign's commission, we learned that, once you were in an officer's uniform, the fun was largely over. Ensigns were a dime a dozen, while sailors with their white hats and bell-bottom trousers literally reigned supreme.

After aviation ground school in Boston and flight training in Pensacola, I earned my Navy wings, on the eve of my twenty-first birthday. The wings meant some days' leave before I sailed for France, duly fitted out with the gold bar of an ensign on my shoulder boards. A detour by way of Wheeling, West Virginia, used up the first few days.

Shortly before joining the Navy I had met Mary, the daughter of James G. Stephens of Wheeling. She had come to a dance in Cambridge while visiting some cousins, and never before, I was sure, had so beautiful a girl been in New England. Accordingly, it was essential that three at least of the precious days of leave be allotted this West Virginia city. After all, what was more important than having Mary see the new uniform, the golden wings that now adorned the coat, and the large gold stripes, seemingly as broad as those of an admiral.

Apparently the strategy worked, for some years later, after the war was over and the business could afford a raise, I had the pleasure of changing both names of Mary Stephens to Molly Henderson, an expedient dictated by prior claims of several other Mary Hendersons in the fairly immediate family.

The three days in Wheeling were naturally over too soon. There was still time for short farewells to my own family, and before long an Army transport was steaming through submarine-infested waters, bringing me safely to a French port. After a few days in Paris, punctuated by occasional bursts from German

Big Berthas now finding the range of the French capital, we were off to a seaplane base near Bordeaux to receive additional training on French flying boats. We were then sent to Italy as ferry pilots to bring Italian-built Caproni trimotored planes to the Navy bombing squadrons based in northern France.

While we were in Italy, word reached us from Washington that Navy pilots must henceforth be able to fly at night, since daylight bombers were suffering from the growing skill of German ack-ack gunners. This produced a critical dilemma. No one in our small group of Navy pilots was trained to fly at night. Swallowing our pride, we turned to the U. S. Army, which sent us from nearby Foggia an Army major originally from New York. He was Fiorello La Guardia, more affectionately known as the Little Flower when he later became Mayor of New York. Fiorello had been up three times at night and accordingly was now rated an expert. I was to be his first pupil.

That night we took off in the dark. Nothing was visible beyond the dull red glow of our three belching Fiat engines. Over the roar of the motors I heard Fiorello's voice, shouting that things were somehow different this time; on his previous night flights there had always been a full moon.

Eventually the Little Flower, pointing from our open cockpit in a generally downward direction, drew attention to a speck of light, evidently a distant farmhouse. We were delighted until we realized it came no nearer. Fiorello again shouted above the roar of the motors: "That's no farmhouse, it must be a star; we must be upside down."

Struggling with the dual controls, we somehow righted the universe, putting the star where we thought it belonged; but by now it was clearly time to return, provided we could agree on a suitable direction. Finally, despite the darkness, by some gracious miracle our wheels touched the ground. La Guardia reached for the ignition and turned it off.

"How in the world," he asked in amazement, "did you make such a perfect landing?"

"Heavens," I replied, looking at the dual controls, "I thought you made the landing."

I never saw Fiorello again, though I sometimes shudder to think how close New York City once came to doing without its Fusion mayor.

My next flight did involve tragedy. I had landed in Turin before heading across the Alps for France; the rear motor had been giving trouble, but I was assured that one of Italy's top mechanics would soon restore its faltering vigor. Obviously there would be no delay, since the Italian's first furlough in years was to start when the work was completed. Unfortunately his mind was on other things. An ominous thud, followed by sharp screams from bystanders, was the first indication of trouble, and expressions of horror on their faces confirmed the tragedy. The mechanic had failed to observe the turning propellor blades. It was a frightful spectacle, and I was greatly shaken by the fatal horror of it.

When work on the offending motor had been completed, we continued on our interrupted journey, gaining altitude in a cloudless sky in order to cross the snowcapped mountains separating France from Italy. An assistant pilot was at my side in the open cockpit and a Navy mechanic sat in the rear, separated from us by a huge gasoline tank serving both as backrest for the pilots and as a container for a ton of high-volatility aviation gasoline.

As we reached the needed altitude our attention was suddenly attracted by the excited mechanic's frantic signaling from behind. The rear motor was ablaze in a sheet of flames.

Pushing forward the controls, I almost dived the giant Caproni in the direction of the Turin airfield, but an observant citizen below somehow noted our plight and sounded a general fire alarm. We landed, all right, though it was not my best exhibition of aerodynamic skill; even so we received perhaps the most unusual reception ever accorded a visiting American pilot. At the far end of the field where the burning Caproni was coming to a stop, the flames now creeping forward as our speed began to slacken, a reception committee of three vehicles awaited us: a fire engine, an ambulance, and a hearse.

The fire was eventually extinguished, and when the customary autopsy on the delinquent motor was completed, the trouble was revealed. In the crankcase were the remains of a machinist's hammer evidently forgotten by the late lamented and obviously distracted Italian mechanic.

For a while we enjoyed better luck, at least until reaching Dijon in France, where a week's delay kept us firmly grounded for repairs on a leak in the water jacket of one of the motors. That week, spent mostly biting our fingernails at the pleasant Hotel de la Cloche, was eventful in one respect: a six-month accumulation of mail, after pursuing us through most of Europe, finally caught up with us. Some twenty letters from Wheeling received top priority.

The enforced stopover in Dijon might have been even more eventful had I discovered that my brother George, now an infantry captain, was spending several of those same seven days in Dijon, also at the Hotel de la Cloche. Our paths simply never crossed. In this instance a one-in-a-million chance was apparently destined to misfire.

After Dijon, our repairs completed, it was only a matter of a few hours to reach Orly Field near Paris, which we did on November 11, 1918. The war suddenly had come to an end.

Never could the excitement of the Paris crowds on that memorable occasion, that spontaneous outpouring of emotion that greeted the end of the war, be duplicated elsewhere in the world. Lights were once again ablaze, flooding the whole of Paris after long years of blackouts. Joy and tears were choking everyone. Millions of people—all were in a frenzy of excitement. Soldiers, sailors, girls in uniform from many allied nations joined in the great jubilation. Bands of happy people formed great circles by clasping hands and danced on the streets in rings around any soldier in uniform, imprisoning him within the circle until each beautiful mademoiselle in the ring had been kissed. And then at the height of this tremendous fervor all was suddenly quiet. We stood in front of the great opera house. An immense shaft of illumination coming from a powerful searchlight, normally perpendicular in search of enemy sky raiders, but now lowered, was casting its brilliant beam on the roof of the Madeleine. From this aerial perch, one of France's leading prima donnas was singing the "Marseillaise," while awestruck thousands below listened breathlessly.

Not far from the Opéra, in the small hours of the morning, a collection of captured German machine guns, cannon, and other great engines of war, was still on display to delight the delirious crowds. By coincidence, they were on a sidewalk near the Paris office of the American Express Company. An exuberant United States sailor, noting the fortunate juxtaposition, produced a pair of tags and addressed them, via American Express, to his Newark, New Jersey, home. He attached them firmly to two of the more costly exhibits. A month later, I subsequently learned, two priceless German war trophies were duly delivered to the sailor in New Jersey, a testimonial to the infallibility of the American Express Company.

VI.

Early Business Experiences

I

AFTER our education was completed and World War I was over, yet long before our interest in hotels had begun, we ventured into various fields of endeavor. Our first undertaking was to deal in foreign exchange. My brother George, my former roommate, Bob Moore, and I, after the end of the war, had discovered we were wealthy. We could muster total resources, the proceeds of our war bonuses, of a thousand dollars. This we considered an enormous sum, though it was somewhat depleted by the month's rent we were asked to pay in advance. With this initial munificence we started in business in a ground-floor office on Court Square in Boston. Since there were no banking laws in those days to interfere, we proclaimed our mission to passers-by, in gold letters on our plate-glass window, as:

HENDERSON BROTHERS
Bankers
Foreign Exchange

We could sell our own drafts drawn on European banks, and bravely we opened bank accounts in five European capitals: Paris, London, Rome, Berlin, and Vienna. In each instance we deposited in the leading bank the magnificent sum of one hundred dollars. We arranged to have printed some impressive international checks, and if our customers sometimes hesitated, failing perhaps to recall among names famous in international banking that of Henderson Brothers, this deficiency was soon overcome when they saw our beautifully engraved "cheques" drawn on such impregnable institutions as the Deutsche Bank in Berlin and other financial giants.

Fortunately checks purchased by customers could go forward only by mail—not even by air mail in those early days. We received cash in advance, including our modest commission, and could thus send money to foreign banks by cable. With inevitable delays in the mails, funds in foreign banks accumulated, and our balances gradually assumed more respectable proportions. Eventually the banks began to forget their shock at the effrontery of American "bankers" who opened accounts with those microscopic deposits.

Our most memorable achievement in foreign banking occurred in the days when gyrations in exchange rates were often quite spectacular and sometimes so unpredictable that even the larger banks could not always keep all their departments posted on temporary changes in rates. The trust department of a large Boston bank, with forty thousand dollars' worth of French francs to sell, was seeking a better price than their own foreign department had offered. Noting this opportunity, and taking advantage of a momentary flurry in the rate of exchange, we bought the block from the bank's trust department and resold it, at an agreeable profit, to the foreign department of the same institution. This fortunate transaction doubled our initial capital. But this was not all. We received warm thanks from both departments of this obliging bank, and each department head, unknown to the other, complimented us for our skill in executing the respective buy and sell orders.

A few months ago, after thirty-seven years had elapsed, I

gathered the courage, while addressing a Boston audience, to recount this adventure in arbitrage. To my consternation, I then saw the head of the foreign department of that Boston bank in the audience; he had been with the institution all those years. Not in the least annoyed, this veteran of foreign exchange came up afterward to express delight at having helped in the launching of our early business careers.

2

In spite of occasional windfalls, the lure of foreign exchange began to dim, for we were discovering that the potentialities of foreign imports with wider margins of profit could be even more intriguing. Through the German banks, which now displayed greater deference as the American dollar gained in prestige compared with the falling German mark, we began to receive leads for importing German products. Resolved to participate in this more enticing field, we again summoned the window-lettering artist who had once established us as "bankers," and suggested adding "and importers" in equally conspicuous gold leaf to our plate-glass window.

Orders were quickly placed, and foreign shipments began to arrive. With our duplicating machine we were soon barraging prospective customers, proclaiming the virtues of imported German jackknives, binoculars, or practically anything a few hundred dollars of capital, magnified by the magic of inflation, could buy in France or Germany.

The climax of our importing adventures came when inflation was shrinking the German mark to microscopic proportions and German adding-machine makers were reaping a golden harvest, for every few weeks their former equipment became obsolete as newer models with extra banks of zeros were ordered.

Almost everyone engaged in business in or near Boston began

to dream of cashing in on the depreciated German currency. In one instance a dog-dealer wondered if German police dogs did not perhaps come from Germany and could be imported. We added this query to a cable requesting quotations, but there was no response and we supposed our agent must have thought it facetious. Six months later, we heard an irate voice over the phone from the piers where freighters usually docked, insisting that we forthwith unload our new consignment. We were expecting nothing, but, impelled by the urgency in the voice, we hurried to the pier.

There, at the Mystic Wharf, was a small German freighter from the decks of which rose an incredible bedlam from fifty yelping dogs. The bill of lading was in our name. We soon began to appreciate the urgency in the troubled agent's voice.

Examining the cargo more closely, we discovered that half the shipment consisted of handsome German police dogs, the rest, of mongrels of assorted sizes, varying perhaps from an admixture of dachshund and cocker spaniel to something that might trace its lineage with equal propriety to a collie or an Irish setter. A further disquieting circumstance was that the nondescript twenty-five had collars bearing no relationship whatsoever to the size of the mongrel necks assigned to them. By a strange coincidence, there were just twenty-five members of the crew, counting the captain. Expressing surprise on seeing an exquisite dog in the private quarters of each member of the crew, we were told that German sailors always travel with their own pet dogs. However, since the freighter's itinerary had included a stopover in Halifax, we felt that a little canine hijacking in the back streets of Halifax might offer a more plausible explanation. We firmly refused the shipment unless the status of the heterogeneous mongrels was adjusted. This produced a complete deadlock.

Days went by. Somehow a Boston newspaper picked up the story of the fifty unclaimed dogs, creatures unfamiliar with our language, abandoned at the entrance to their promised land. The accounts, spreading to other papers, were at first inconspicuous, but gradually were elevated to the front pages, and finally, rising to screaming headlines, were reinforced by more detailed stories, embellished with a "dog interest" angle, appearing in the Sunday supplements. Here were fifty foreign visitors to an inhospitable shore, dogs without a country, dogs no one wanted. Doubtless the hearts of the readers bled profusely.

A week later, breaking all maritime precedent, but doubtless responsive to the strain on members of the crew from days of continuous bedlam, the freighter, hauling up anchor at dead of night, set sail for Hamburg. The departure was without benefit even of clearance papers. The mixed cargo of fifty dogs had been abandoned on the unfriendly pier.

Major repercussions followed. Who would feed the unwanted dogs? Feeling a contingent obligation, we arranged for food and water. Water was ruled to be permissible, but the Treasury Department, which had jurisdiction since customs formalities had been neglected, was pondering the question of how anything —food, in this instance—could be added to an undeclared shipment without doing violence to sacred Treasury regulations. In the midst of this awkward dilemma, with newspaper headlines still screaming, the Animal Rescue League, that lone agency that transcends human laws, seized the dogs, good and bad alike, and provided food and shelter.

And so a month went by, and the international incident could be forgotten—but not entirely. A small newspaper notice in the classified columns announced that fifty dogs, description conspicuously omitted, would be sold by the Animal Rescue League at ten o'clock on the following Monday.

Although this particular morsel escaped the vigilance of the headline writers, it at least caught our attention. When ten o'clock drew near on the following Monday, with two hundred dollars in our pockets—enough, we hoped, for the fifty dogs—we approached the scene of the sale. Our path unfortunately was blocked. An accident, perhaps, had caused some crowds to gather. With important business in hand, we pushed past the multitudes.

"Hey there," shouted one man upon whose toes we may have trod. "What's the hurry? Don't you think others might like those dogs?"

And so we learned to appreciate the potency of classified advertisements. Not only were crowds visible far up and down the sidewalks, but hundreds of automobiles, many with out-of-state number plates, brought prospective buyers to the Treasury-sponsored sale.

The first of the dogs was held up by the auctioneer, and the opening bid, we noted to our dismay, exceeded our resources of two hundred dollars. That first dog, sold for three hundred and fifty dollars, was actually the only bargain of the day. The crowd, sensing that the supply would not equal the demand, began to bid in earnest. Four, five, and six hundred dollars became the prevailing rate. When the last of the real police dogs was sold, the mongrels started to appear, and bidding within the hall began to falter. This was the signal, however, for those in the street, a block or more away, to make themselve heard, though none at that distance could possibly see the dogs. A ferocious pseudo-airedale that had wantonly attacked the auctioneer brought five hundred dollars from a pedestrian who was obviously unaware of the assault.

Each successful bidder was given a receipt for his cash and a number that represented his dog. He could claim his purchase the following day. Sales by Uncle Sam were of course final—no exchanges or refunds. We returned to our office, our two hundred dollars still intact.

A year passed and the dog episode was nearly forgotten when one day we heard a peremptory knock at our Federal Street office door. A severe-looking official, with "U.S. Treasury" written menacingly above his visor, asked for someone in authority. Cautiously we bade him enter. Such were the intricacies of import regulations that we could never be altogether sure we had not made some mistake.

On hearing that the police dogs had prompted the visit, we hastily proclaimed our innocence, pointing out that we had no connection with the now famous shipment; we had not even ordered the dogs. At most, we conceded, we had asked for a quotation. This seemed to be of little help. The official, clearly disturbed, said that a problem had arisen, one never before encountered in the century and a half of Uncle Sam's sojourn in this pleasant land. Without a solution, the Treasury could never close its books on the dog episode.

He began to explain. The Treasury Department had sold the dogs in accordance with accepted procedure. The auctioneer's ten per cent, which had top priority, had been paid. Then came the cost of food and lodgings at the Animal Rescue League. Rates, though doubtless close to those our Sheraton-Plaza would gladly charge for luxury suites, were apparently no hindrance. That bill was also paid. Next came the Treasury's right to collect the unpaid duty—twenty per cent, I believe, of the invoice price. Looking back on this strange event, I think our government worked rather hard for a somewhat meager return. With German marks on the toboggan, the invoice price of eight hundred million marks on which duty was assessed had shrunk so drastically in terms of our money that the twenty-per-cent levy amounted to only two dollars and forty cents, now that funds were on hand for meeting this formality. The government meticulously withdrew its two dollars and forty cents, thus collecting in full for the unpaid duty.

The transportation company came next, provided the funds held out. The freighter which had abandoned the shipment had asked for eight hundred American dollars, which were also paid —and still large sums remained, a circumstance perhaps unique in Treasury experience. The potential beneficiaries, however, were not yet exhausted. The German shipper, whose drafts were unpaid, could now present a claim for eight hundred million marks, but with vast inflation under way in Germany these millions were worth only twelve dollars and forty cents. This too was paid, and still a balance remained.

This was the predicament the Treasury Department faced when it sought to balance its books. An abandoned shipment sold for unpaid duty had produced more than enough for all existing claims. Perhaps our position could be re-examined. Had not the dogs after all been intended for us?—that is, if the Treasury wished to add to the list of potential beneficiaries. We began to see the light. Yes, we volunteered cautiously, if it would help, we were, after all, the intended consignee.

Greatly relieved, the official thanked us warmly and handed us a United States Treasury check.

"Now," he said, "we can close our ledgers."

The check was for twenty-eight hundred dollars.

In subsequent years additional police dogs arrived, but we were never again plagued by substitutions. We will gladly acknowledge, however, that troubles encountered on that memorable occasion were small if measured in terms of the help received from Uncle Sam and from the publicity provided by obliging Boston newspapers.

Soon the Treasury sale was forgotten, for we were turning our efforts to new items coming from across the Atlantic.

3

An elderly German gentleman walked into our Court Square office one day with a pair of gray German Army binoculars given him as a sample with the understanding that a ten-dollar commission would be his if he could induce some American firm to order a reasonable supply. We sent for the glasses, as he suggested, and a hundred binoculars arrived. Then our troubles began. There were only a few optical dealers in Boston, and interest in each instance was negligible beyond the purchase of a single pair. We were always given the same story. The lenses were beyond reproach, doubtless a bargain. Could the buyer purchase a single pair for himself? The store of course was not interested; "customers never buy binoculars with a gray military finish."

For months we made no headway. Even the conscientious German with his ten-dollar commission presumably had pangs of conscience, for, though probably nearly penniless, he had offered to give us the money he felt he had never earned. Luckily, we refused; after all, if things go wrong, should one not be a good loser? Soon the situation worsened, for our Hamburg agent, assuming the glasses were selling fast, had shipped—fortunately at his own risk—an extra lot of two hundred.

It was at about this time that J. Angus Connors, Esquire, appeared upon the scene. He owned what was known as an Army and Navy store, which could sell almost anything, no matter how hard it was to move. He looked at the gray war glasses and pondered for a moment. Could he have, say, a case of a hundred with the right to return the unsold glasses? Our first impulse was to enlighten him, to suggest two or three pairs might last for many weeks; but we reconsidered. After all, had we not taken psychology at Harvard? At such a crucial moment, should we discourage a promising prospect?

Angus took the glasses and headed for his small Back Bay shop. A half-hour elapsed; then our phone began to ring. Angus was on the line. Would we mind sending the remaining two hundred pairs? Customers were getting impatient.

Convinced that Angus was completely mad, we nonetheless summoned a taxi and on the remote chance that some binoculars had been sold, took the extra glasses along. As we approached, we were startled to see a sizable crowd milling about his establishment, gazing from the sidewalk toward the roof of a nearby building, binoculars pressed to their eyes.

Angus had ignited a chain reaction by handing out "free trial" glasses to passing pedestrians. Each, looking through the German lenses, attracted additional viewers and in less than two hours the last of three hundred sales, each at nine dollars and eighty-five cents was recorded on the happily jingling cash register. Angus had made a cool thousand-dollar profit in two hours of selling, oblivious to the plight of traffic officers rushed to disentangle the growing traffic jams.

Additional shipments of binoculars in ever larger quantities continued to arrive from Hamburg. Eventually Angus sold over four thousand pairs, using his sidewalk selling technique, all before the more conventional optical outlets discovered that they too could participate in this great bonanza.

At this time we made the useful discovery that we too could sell glasses at retail, using mail order advertisements. We placed a one-column insertion in the *Literary Digest* to proclaim the virtues of Germany's military lenses, all for $9.85. We were soon decidedly in business; quantities of checks began to roll in. We received nearly a hundred the first day after the initial advertisement appeared, thousands more before the pleasant stream of orders from this first insertion finally ran its course.

We tried a number of different magazines, using a simple device to "key" the potency of various publications and their resistance to the inevitable attrition which the law of diminishing returns imposes on advertisements repeated too often. "Keying" consisted of using different addresses for each publication, rather than the more conventional department number—L2, for instance—to designate, perhaps, insertion number two in the *Literary Digest*. Our system was more subtle, though it must at times have confounded astonished postal authorities. Since our real address, 93 Federal Street, lacked suitable variety, we expanded it. We brazenly added numbers 91 and 95 to the entrance of our office building, with the hope that the landlord would not object. But this was not enough, as business increased. We needed more variations, and so we added in our advertisements all four points of the compass, providing thereby a dozen extra alternatives. If an envelope with a coveted check inside was marked 91 South Federal Street, *Liberty* magazine received the credit; one with 95 East Federal Street might owe its inception to an advertisement in the *National Geographic*; and so on with other combinations.

In this connection, I have a gratuitous tip for prospective advertisers. Although thirty years have passed since our binocular advertisements appeared in the *National Geographic*, we still occasionally receive an envelope marked "95 East Federal Street" enclosing a check for nine eighty-five—a tribute perhaps to the frugality of doctors, who rarely discard publications that seem to retain eternal power to soothe the ills of waiting patients.

After selling Germany's surplus military binoculars for a year or more—nearly two hundred thousand of them—we finally exhausted the supply. This created a crisis, for the demand not only continued, it was actually accelerating. Obviously we could not start a new war for the sole purpose of replenishing the supply of these military glasses; there must be an alternative. Hastily Bob Moore and I journeyed to Göttingen, a small German university town where a factory had once turned out the original glasses. Now the plant was shut down. Göttingen, besides its famed educational institution, had no important industry other than its optical works, and the normal output of this factory, designed for the luxury trade, had been unable to cope with an era of postwar austerity. The number of unemployed had risen sharply. With difficulty we located the Herr Direktor who had headed this now defunct enterprise and proceeded to negotiate. Before leaving, we persuaded him to reopen the factory so that exact duplicates of former Army glasses could issue again from the original assembly lines.

A year later, after thousands of the new glasses had been sold, Bob and I, once more in the vicinity of Göttingen, decided to visit unannounced the Herr Direktor whose establishment was meeting so well the insatiable American appetite for German "military" binoculars. Our train reached the town at noon, but we had evidently chosen a holiday, for streets were filled with crowds and banners were flying everywhere.

Hoping that, despite these festivities, we might still locate the managing director, we discreetly left the train by way of a rear platform to avoid delegations poised to welcome some visiting dignitary apparently expected on the same train. After successfully detouring the crowds, we approached the factory, where the director greeted us with evident astonishment. His surprise was not at our unexpected arrival; news of a visit by men with orders from America had apparently leaked out. The amazement was at our escaping the vigilance of the assembled members of the reception committee.

The Herr Direktor, realizing the predicament, rushed us back to the waiting train so we might once more alight from our railroad coach, this time on the main platform, to receive the greetings of the Burgomeister and hear the speeches of those awaiting our arrival. Then, ceremoniously escorted between two brass bands, a pair of bewildered Americans still in their early twenties proceeded to the optical factory to be formally presented to the Herr Direktor.

4

Soon after our return to the United States, I began to consider other vital matters not directly connected with the commercial aspects of the importing business. In this instance, at least, foreign imports were not involved, for it was to be a domestic affair. I contemplated a crucial trip to Wheeling, West Virginia, and the "import" of a young and beautiful bride. The date for wedding bells had been set.

Not until shortly before had it occurred to Mary Stephens, soon to become Molly Henderson, that marriage would involve anything beyond settling down in her own home town. Fortunately, in order to dispel any lingering doubts, I brought along an impressive second-hand Cadillac, one of not too ancient a vintage, considering our still limited resources. It was tuned up and polished for this gala event. Presently the knot was happily tied.

The journey back was to be our honeymoon. And so we started off, in gradual stages, to cover the eight hundred miles to Boston. Why we were not arrested on that agreeable occasion for discovering the merits of one-armed driving will always remain a pleasant mystery.

A memorable stop on that delightful homeward journey was an overnight visit to the summer home in Elberon, New Jersey, of Solomon Guggenheim, one of the seven interesting brothers who so ably guided the destinies of the copper world for an entire generation. Sol Guggenheim's daughter had been my sister's roommate during a winter in Germany and, as a result, we came to know the family well. Sol's wife told Molly how, not so many years before, she and her husband had started married life in a third-story Flatbush apartment. The fabulous millions that emerged from the creation of a vast mining empire had all been achieved in a single lifetime.

Eventually we arrived in Boston to begin the excitement of setting out on a new and adventurous career—that of family life, which would mean greater responsibilities and therefore a quest for new opportunities. These abounded at the time, for we were progressing along the path later to be known as the "roaring twenties," now already well under way.

VII.

Other Business Ventures

I

ONCE settled in a two-room apartment in Cambridge with my lovely young bride, I faced the question of how to support a wife, and perhaps eventually a family.

Up to this time we had gained experience in foreign exchange, in importing, and in the distribution of merchandise from Europe. In the early nineteen-twenties the greatly expanding radio business was capturing everyone's imagination, and we felt that surely radio offered a chance to make the proverbial fortune.

Those were the days of battery sets with their three large dials for tuning in various radio stations. We could see an appreciable discrepancy between the prices of finished sets, then in great demand, and the cost of component parts—particularly if we took advantage of mass-production prices suppliers of tube sockets, transformers, and other necessary ingredients were quoting to chain-store operators. S. S. Kresge was striving valiantly to meet the demand from the "do it yourself" technicians who were eager to hear KDKA or WJZ on their home-built radio apparatus. We too had concluded we could build a radio.

We went to the makers of mass-produced parts to establish sources of supply, a furniture manufacturer in Grand Rapids provided walnut cabinets designed to put other set-makers to shame, and we assembled a beautiful and workable receiver. Coils we wound ourselves, and the necessary soldering we accomplished on a production-line basis that even Henry Ford could hardly have scorned. We sold the finished receivers for half the cost of Freed-Eisemann or other well-known makes then sweeping the country. Our sets worked well, and orders began to come in. Those were exciting days.

Soon we needed larger quarters, for we shipped sets to Australia and many parts of the United States, and in London large advertisements over Selfridge's name proclaimed the excellence of our American five-valve wireless.

In Boston things were different. This was a hard market to crack. We didn't pretend to be prophets, but we evidently had much in common with practitioners of this art, for we were clearly not recognized in our "own country." After all, here in Boston, didn't everyone know we were just young fellows assembling ten-cent-store parts in an upstairs loft, calling what emerged a radio? Actually, the mass-produced parts often outperformed those the more expensive set-makers were using. Marshall Field's in Chicago was selling our receivers in quantities and frequently reordered. Its customers were getting excellent results, but that was nearly a thousand miles away. In Boston defenses erected by buyers of our great department stores against a purely local product remained virtually impregnable.

One Boston merchant, however, finally began to show some interest after he had tried a set in his home, perhaps on a favorable night, when Omaha had come in on the loudspeaker. Previously with a Freed-Eisemann, possibly under less favorable atmospheric conditions, he had scarcely heard New York, and then only with earphones.

The merchant was Eli Siegel, who operated a time-payment jewelry store on Washington Street. A pioneer of the dollar-down and a dollar-a-week technique, he had built up a large and profitable installment business when such devices were in their infancy. Eli maintained that economies from volume operations could offset the higher costs of selling on time. After all, if houses were bought on monthly mortgage payments, why not diamond rings and watches on installments?

Cognizant of his success in many lines, Eli was ready to tackle anything the public wished to buy. Everyone wanted radios, and the fact that they had not previously been offered on an installment plan meant nothing to him. He knew the public was interested, and the magic of a newspaper advertisement quoting radios at a dollar down was instantaneous. The jewelry store was swamped. Diamonds and watches were almost forgotten. Loudspeakers, storage batteries, and the sets we were supplying began crowding aside wrist watches, fountain pens, engagement rings, or whatever else had been warming the hearts of the dollar-a-week adherents.

But the momentary glint in Eli Siegel's eyes was not to last. Delivery problems, difficulties with installations, and subsequent calls for service were strange to an organization accustomed to regulating watches, polishing silver, or setting diamonds in rings destined for some lovely feminine finger. A new store, financial backing, and an organization to cope with the trials of a new industry were needed. A single advertisement had proved that the business was there, and Eli Siegel would learn to harness it.

He told us of a friend, a furniture man named Carl Canner, who had just sold his business for a half-million dollars and was seeking new fields to conquer. Thus we learned of Carl Canner's fantastic career.

A dozen years before, with his single suit of clothes on his back and ten dollars in his pocket, he had arrived, an emigrant from Russia. After finding a job in a furniture store, he kept his eyes open and learned the tricks of a trade as he acquired command of the English language. Fortified with a knowledge of furniture, he answered an advertisement of a furniture store for sale. The widow and sisters of the late owner had inherited the business and were desperately seeking a buyer. A hundred and fifty thousand dollars was the asking price, and Carl knew the value was there. The only drawback was that his original capital, ten dollars, had not been appreciably augmented during his years of apprenticeship at a very low wage. However, Carl was never deterred by minor obstacles.

"I'll buy the entire business," he announced, "but only on one condition." His own financial resources, he conceded with a modicum of understatement, were at the moment somewhat strained. If the sellers wanted all cash, well, it was doubtful that the deal would merit his attention. But if they would turn over the business at once—lock, stock, and barrel, including cash, inventories, and other assets on hand—he would issue his personal note for the entire amount. Ten thousand dollars he would pay in a couple of days, the balance in monthly installments. The sisters were jubilant. They would have their asking price and would not be obliged to learn the business.

Carl took over at once. With money enough in the till, now available under the terms of the agreement, the first payment was duly met. World War I was raging, and prices were beginning to rise. Every month, by means of special sales, enough cash was raised to meet the next payment. In two years the last installment was paid and Carl owned the entire business. Five years later, a larger nearby store, unhappy with the growing competition, paid a half-million dollars to buy him out. That was the source Eli Siegel would tap to finance his radio venture.

Eli and Carl got together, and a hundred thousand dollars of Carl's new wealth provided the resources for an enterprise named "World Radio Corporation."

The company grew like Topsy. Hundreds of sets were sold each day, but the more the company sold at a dollar down, the faster its affairs became tangled, and the more difficult the problem of meeting growing obligations. Our firm of Henderson Brothers—the designation "bankers and importers" now deleted

—was the sufferer from the principal headaches arising from the company's desire to sell too many radios with insufficient funds. One day we were summoned by Canner and Siegel, who told us the company could not pay for the thousands of sets that were purchased. They did not, however, wish to see us lose, for they had appreciated the credit extended. They had brought with them the stock certificates representing ownership in the company, with the shares endorsed over to us. By accepting the stock, we would own everything in the company and, if we ran the enterprise well, we could eventually pay ourselves, from the assets of the business, all that the company owed us.

We were amazed, for, had they wished, they could have left us little more than an empty shell.

As the new owners of World Radio Corporation, we immediately went to work. We strengthened the credit department so losses could be reduced. We found that an efficient service department, by bringing inoperative sets back to life, would mean delinquent payments could be revived. Soon cash began to come in and "frozen" debts began to thaw. The company grew, and within a couple of years we had thirty-five branch stores in all corners of the New England states.

One of the largest items of overhead for this growing enterprise was newspaper advertising. But publicizing thirty-six stores throughout New England was no more costly than running ads for a single store in Boston, for all New England read the Boston papers. This was a lesson that was to help twenty-five years later, when we realized that budgets for promoting hotels through magazine advertisements could be far more effective when the cost was divided among fifty different units.

As a result of the expansion and growing success of World Radio Corporation, a company once riddled with debts, Bob and I had become something of a curiosity among Canner and Siegel and their friends. Our good fortune in reviving the company where others had previously failed was considered, in those knowing circles, a distinctly unaccountable phenomenon.

2

When the depression of the nineteen-thirties was under way and security prices were tumbling dramatically, Bob Moore and I became intrigued by the opportunities that stocks and bonds, selling in some instances for only a few cents on the dollar, could offer if the depression, like preceding upheavals of this nature, should eventually come to an end.

Boston, even in those early days, was recognized as the capital of the investment-trust industry. Why shouldn't we participate? All we needed in 1931 was a friendly lawyer with enough spare time to draft a declaration of trust. Such a document, ten or twelve pages long, could set forth in legal language, interspersed with the requisite quota of "whereases," that an entity had been created to purchase and hold securities, one that could attract needed funds by selling its own shares to the public. The modest legal cost, plus a twenty-five-dollar filing fee, was all that was required. Our ambitious title, World Finance Investment Trust, later shortened to World Investment Trust, was finally converted, in deference to a rising New England conservatism, to Investment Trust of Boston.

Partly because of fortunate timing deep in the days of the depression, and partly owing to a somewhat unique system of arbitrage, the fund began to prosper. We were largely buying and selling undervalued shares of other investment trusts listed on the Stock Exchange. By using a slide-rule formula Bob Moore and I had devised, our trust, small with respect to shares sold, was growing rapidly as far as its own assets were concerned. The system, though viewed with skepticism by the financial community, worked well. A few years later an issue of the *U.S. Investor*, listing the records of appreciation of several trusts during a number of up-and-down swings of the market, placed our fund in top position for performance. Quite recently, a similar tabulation, covering the past fifteen years, was published by a leading financial service; again this fund, Investment Trust of Boston, is credited with the highest appreciation of any such fund during this more recent period.

In the early days, when assets rarely exceeded a million dollars, newspapers did not hesitate to quote our shares daily under the heading of investment trusts. Perhaps the name World Investment Trust conjured up in their minds a quite impressive operation, rather than one involving but a few hundred shareholders. Today with assets of over sixty millions, the trust must sometimes argue to convince editors it is sufficiently large to justify inclusion in the daily financial pages.

Although by no means the sole reason for an outstanding performance by Investment Trust of Boston, the record of one of its more modest holdings, purchased years ago, has been at least reasonably acceptable. This investment consisted of a few hundred shares of Sheraton stock costing originally some eight thousand dollars. Following several stock splits, some impetus from the repercussions of inflation, and perhaps some advantage from certain hidden potentialities of hotel chains, the present value of these Sheraton shares is over a million dollars, more than a hundred times the original cost.

The board of trustees of Investment Trust of Boston, expanded over the years, now includes some of Boston's top financial leaders, and accordingly Bob Moore and I no longer dominate the fund's affairs. However, it has been a great satisfaction to observe the progress of this venture. Investment Trust of Boston today is among the more conservative and better-known investment companies, organizations that are playing a growing role in reshaping investing habits of the nation's small and medium-sized investors.

Our experience with Investment Trust of Boston, since it so often held shares of other investment companies, gave us an intimate knowledge of what is known as "leverage." This characteristic, sometimes useful and occasionally disastrous, results from the presence of senior obligations, which produce an effect similar to that of buying securities "on margin," magnifying the benefits of rising values, but operating in reverse when market values shrink. Ours, not primarily a "leverage trust," was a so-called "open end" fund, which meant its shares could be sold in any quantities, provided the public would purchase them. Owners could cash in at will at the "asset value."

The investment companies whose shares we were purchasing were different. These had non-redeemable shares and were usually subject to large amounts of senior securities providing this so-called leverage, fortunately without involving all the risks of holding stocks on margin.

Being familiar with leverage, we became interested in an investment company that had fared especially badly during the depression. By 1934 signs of recovery were appearing, and the leverage of the company might now be helpful in a period of rising values.

It had originally been organized by a group associated with a Boston bank that succumbed during the 1933 banking holiday and, despite all efforts at resuscitation, was never revived. Its security affiliate, Beacon Participations, Inc., now an orphan, and once the possessor of millions in assets, had figuratively lost its shirt in the early nineteen-thirties. The remaining assets amounted to less than a quarter-million dollars in 1934. Senior obligations consisting of preferred shares, were still outstanding, and these, including unpaid dividends, represented a liability of nearly two million dollars. Obviously the Beacon common stock, with only a quarter-million of assets in the fund, was far "under water," and would remain so unless the value of these assets could be lured back to a level exceeding the two millions due preferred shareholders, who were entitled to a first call on all assets.

It was the common stock of Beacon that was offered to us, and for ten thousand dollars World Radio Corporation, now out of the radio business, purchased them. But even at this point, restrictions were imposed. Borrowings by Beacon Participations were to be limited; there was to be no undue "pyramiding" of assets. Furthermore, no salaries could be paid; and finally, and this was the harshest blow of all, shareholders wishing to surrender their shares for redemption could do so during the ensuing year, receiving their full proportion of assets in return. Obviously, if all the shareholders cashed in, nothing would be left, and our ten-thousand-dollar investment would be worthless.

There was one additional circumstance which might somehow help. A preferred stockholder had brought a suit, which had been pending for several years, against the former directors, charging liability for some unwise investments. In the event of a recovery, stockholders who had liquidated would still receive their proportion, and the balance, if any, might help the company.

We paid the ten thousand, accepted the restrictions, and now controlled Beacon Participations. The following year, as I recall so vividly, was, I am sure, the longest 365 days ever recorded. One by one, preferred stockholders were turning in their shares for redemption. Would they all cash in during that nearly endless year?

When the redemption period was finally over, almost one-third of the preferred shares had been liquidated. But, with rising markets, the remaining assets were still worth two hundred and fifty thousand dollars. Accordingly, our common stock was now less "under water," and happily no longer subject to attrition from continued liquidation. The lawsuit, furthermore, was going badly for the old directors. None, as far as we knew, had profited personally from the transactions complained of, yet they were all at a disadvantage. Hindsight made it easy to pinpoint errors of judgment. At times, unfortunately, they had acted on advice not wholly reliable. Even though our sympathies were largely with the directors under attack, our company eventually became the beneficiary of one hundred and forty thousand dollars of recoveries from these rather harsh lawsuits. What seemed especially injust, though doubtless legally correct, was that the only director with sufficient resources to satisfy an adverse judgment—upon whom, therefore, would fall the major burden of possible liability—had not even attended the directors' meeting at which the matters complained of had allegedly occurred. An operator of supermarkets —or whatever their prototype was in the early nineteen-thirties —he was about to discover that a legal web could trip him up under the theory that absentee directors must still know what has transpired at a properly convened directors' meeting.

In looking back, we still recall at times the suspense during the period of liquidation in 1934 and remember the gloom we experienced on seeing so many shares surrendered. Perhaps that former feeling of gloom is now reciprocated by some who did turn in their shares. After various subsequent mergers, each Beacon shareholder with the courage to hold on, eventually received Sheraton shares in exchange. These today are worth some two hundred dollars for each dollar available to those back in 1934 who "ran to cover."

With the year of grace concluded and the threat of further liquidation past, our interest turned to investments which offered the best promise of appreciation. Leverage investment company common shares made perhaps the poorest showing during the declines of the early nineteen-thirties, but they might now have good prospects of recovery. Some of these shares, however, when measured by our "slide rule" calculations, were selling for far less than, and others for nearly twice, their theoretical value, if one took into account the leverage they possessed. By purchasing only "undervalued" shares, we found we could do relatively well even during falling markets when leverage worked against us.

While following this slide-rule approach we acquired large quantities of Standard Investing Company shares at "undervalued" prices—so many that ultimately we had control of the company. Standard Investing had millions in assets, but unfortunately most of these would soon vanish, for a bond issue with but a year or two to run, was approaching maturity. Most of the assets would then have to be sold to meet claims of bondholders. This was 1937, and a new market collapse faced us. The single circumstance that saved our financial world, as Standard Investing bonds came due, was that our real-estate holdings and the leverage securities in our portfolio, despite widespread skepticism, actually outperformed many "blue chip" securities that were taking a heavy pounding.

When the Standard Investing Bonds were finally paid off, less than a quarter-million of assets remained, but among these was control of our first hotel, located in Springfield, Massachusetts, some other scattered real estate, and the germ of a good idea. We believed that, if we could build an efficient management company, we could accelerate recovery in our real-estate holdings and thus reverse the losses the depression had caused. This was the goal we set out to reach.

3

Our entrance into the financial world was not to be without its difficulties. As outsiders to the New England financial community, we were sometimes resented, and our problems were magnified when we acquired a majority of the shares of a certain investment company bearing a harmless-sounding name. Careful audits had confirmed that the assets held were all as represented, and since the common shares of this company seemed undervalued, we eagerly made the purchase. Soon we found we had a bear by the tail.

We examined the extensive records as they reached our Boston office. They revealed that companies, too, can have a rather questionable past. The former name had been changed, perhaps in the hope of burying the company's colorful history, but it had at one time been, not an investment trust, but a large utility holding company organized to control several impressive public-utility empires. Although it once had enormous sums in its treasury, amounts which in 1929 probably exceeded a hundred million dollars, it subsequently shrank until its assets were only a few millions. This in itself was not extraordinary, for of course other companies had suffered in the depression. In this instance, however, things were different. Perhaps F.D.R. was right in casting skeptical glances at the pre-S.E.C. gyrations some financing had involved. We were about to receive a dramatic postgraduate course in the high finances of a previous generation. All that was needed was for us to study this one-time holding company's affairs.

The startling phenomenon of this financial epic was that the former holding company had survived the market crash of 1929 without loss to any investor. All the millions originally subscribed remained intact during the early disastrous plunge of crumbling security prices. It was when these many millions had been raised, but before an investment program was adopted, that financial clouds gathered and the panic of 1929 broke loose.

With such an auspicious start, with millions of plentiful 1929 dollars in the treasury during a depression when dollars were becoming scarce and valuable, extraordinary results might have been achieved, but somehow they failed to materialize. A company that seemed destined for a notable record was apparently to give a deplorable showing. It had fallen under the spell of what was not necessarily the best of the holding-company managements, and things began to happen. Little by little the cash dwindled and unfortunate investments appeared in the portfolio, securities the selection of which could scarcely have been attributable to an infallible financial genius. Losses were unbelievable. Within a few years, only one-twentieth of the original millions remained. Even the once somewhat doubtful holdings that still retained a semblance of their former value began in turn to disappear as even more questionable issues took their place. Finally, when signs of better times appeared and rising prices gave hopes of recovery, these prospects for salvage were often denied the hapless holding company. For a small consideration, options had been granted certain fortunate individuals for securities that retained some likelihood of recovery. Yes, the S.E.C. was clearly created none too soon.

But the past could not be as easily buried as some people perhaps hoped. Lawyers for minority shareholders were beginning to appear, and they usually had a good nose for promising situations. Following the affairs of this investment company under its new name, they sought out its new quarters in Boston and demanded access to the books, hoping, with some justification, that pay dirt might linger in the company's colorful past. That was how we found we had a bear by the tail. We were loath to produce records for strange and prying lawyers, knowing that innocent directors who had served at times on the board might perhaps get hurt. We also suspected the real offenders were far beyond reach.

Our dilemma was soon solved by the attorney we retained, Irvine Shubert, later to become our Sheraton general counsel. He told us we must call in the S.E.C.; otherwise we too could be charged with impeding the course of justice. A couple of S.E.C. accountants casually appeared at our office and began glancing at the books. Their reactions on seeing the records were instantaneous, resembling those of a fire chief reaching the scene of a conflagration. A general alarm, or at least the S.E.C. equivalent, was promptly sounded, and a dozen or more S.E.C. accountants arrived under full steam. They dived into the records as though this—which perhaps it was—might be the greatest of all their "discoveries."

Up to this time our interest was academic, as we thought we were mere observers on the sidelines. The early history of the company could hardly have been our responsibility, or even, we erroneously supposed, of any direct interest to us. Our only possible concern related to existing conventional hold-ings—General Electric, DuPont, or whatever other investments the renamed company held. But soon we were taking a most lively interest in proceedings. Rumors reached us from obscure sources, indicating that if we continued revealing records to the S.E.C., or permitted lawyers to see the books, we would have good reason to regret it. We soon discovered just what was meant. The books, however, remained open; our attorney told us there was no other choice.

Presently minority-stockholder suits against former directors were under way, charging that losses in the tens of millions had been suffered, and demanding restitution. Some of the defend-ants, assuming incorrectly that we, the present company officers, had caused these unpleasant developments, started igniting back-fires aimed at discouraging us. Lawsuits charged us with mon-strous irregularities. We were soon to learn that any persons with funds to hire a lawyer could bring whatever fictitious charges they wished against whomever they wanted to annoy. Newspaper stories were simultaneously planted, suggesting we had misap-propriated funds and converted assets, and in fact hinting that we had committed virtually every known depredation related to financial manipulation, a subject with which our tormentors seemed quite familiar.

Word occasionally reached us, suggesting that these "trivial annoyances" could easily be ended, should we agree to call off the wolves. Some people apparently assumed that if we were subjected to sufficient provocation, troublesome minority-stockholder suits would end. They were very wrong. Alluring prospects of large legal fees were quite sufficient to whet the appetites of hopeful lawyers who perhaps only in theory represented the interests of minority stockholders.

Our position was a strange one. Although dedicated to the principle that success could come without sacrifice of integrity, we were nevertheless being publicly charged with stealing from our shareholders, an awkward experience for one who recalled the anguish caused by a twenty-five-cent piece that "vanished" when I was six. Even friends wondered, with so such smoke around, if flames might not be lurking somewhere.

This being subjected to pressure through countersuits was a curious experience. A hundred thousand dollars, we calculated, were spent with leading law firms in an effort to scare us off. Our attackers, clearly not "pikers," at least had a motive; it was more surprising that quite prominent law firms should take part in this delicate form of coercion.

A somewhat embarrassing problem would occasionally confront our persecutors, who realized that legal expenditures incurred to apply pressure on us might be wasted if the cases ever came to trial and evidence was needed to substantiate the reckless charges. A simple, quite ingenious device served to meet this recurring hazard. When no further grounds could be conjured up for delay, and the cases were about to come up for trial, the opposing lawyers would be summarily dismissed and other law firms would be substituted. Under such circumstances, the courts always seemed willing to grant further extensions so the new lawyers would have time to study the "facts." When postponement was secured, the screws could again be applied. At the time, our acquaintances, on passing, would often turn the other way. After all, they read the newspapers; something obviously must be wrong.

Eventually the original suits against former directors came to a head. Although by then out of our hands, they were finally settled through payment in partial restitution to the injured company of nearly two million dollars—a modest amount, we thought, considering the losses actually suffered. The statute of limitations had outlawed most of the claims. Immediately following this settlement, all suits against us were dropped, because of "insufficient evidence," according to the official records—an understatement, we concluded, for as far as we knew there was no evidence at all.

Although some unpleasant scars remain from this questionable use of our courts of law, a minor satisfaction can be recorded. One of the many defendants, who perhaps participated in the multi-million-dollar settlement, though I am sure he took no part in the plundering of the former holding company, subsequently became a good friend of ours. For years, until his recent death, he invited Molly and me to attend the annual horse shows held on his beautiful country estate and insisted we join his more intimate circle of friends in his private garden on those colorful occasions.

Those nerve-racking days of our exposure to fantastic lawsuits are fortunately nearly forgotten; however, through these strange experiences we learned to appreciate the advantages of financial regulatory bodies.

VIII.

Early Hotel Experiences

I

OUR first introduction to the hotel business was shortly after the 1933 banking holiday, when Franklin Roosevelt had just become president. A real-estate man told us of a building in Cambridge that had been completed only four years before and had opened its doors on the day of the 1929 stock-market crash. Known as the Continental, it seemed to be a glorified apartment house.

Six months later a Boston bank foreclosed the mortgage. As though in retribution, the bank itself soon became submerged in the intensifying economic whirlpool then engulfing the nation. Eager to end the mounting deficits, its receiver decided to sell the Continental at almost any price. Bad luck, however, still plagued this ill-starred enterprise. At the hour of the sale a veritable cloudburst discouraged the few potential bidders not previously dissuaded by the assorted collection of claims, liens, and other imperfections in the title encumbering this relatively new property. We were virtually the only bidders.

We often hear how "fools rush in where angels fear to tread." Whatever our role, it was clearly not, in the eyes of our friends, that of the angels. However, as sole bidders, we felt no compulsion to reach very high. If ours was a foolish offer, which of course it was—well, the closed bank could always turn us down. We offered less than one-third of what the property had cost to build only a few years before, and only twenty-five thousand dollars was to be in cash. If the bank accepted our proposal we would be the new owners, subject of course to diverse liens, mortgages, and operating deficits. This brick building had cost close to a million dollars in 1929.

Few in those depression days wished to assume new obligations, least of all ones involving real estate enmeshed in title deficiencies. This may explain why our offer was accepted. Although little cash was needed, we looked for a partner willing to share the risk. It was a good idea, for we began to realize our new and exciting project was more like a hotel than an apartment house. There were a large ballroom, an adjoining garage, and one hundred and fifty furnished rooms, most of them dismally vacant.

An interesting discovery, one that gave promise of a profitable future in this new activity, and therefore perhaps a factor some years later in the establishment of Sheraton Corporation, was the magic of a rugged padlock. Presently we learned what miracles it could perform.

Finding that operating losses of the Continental were really staggering, we began to understand the urge that prompted the closed bank to consider an expeditious sale and realized something must be done at once. Supplies were running low. Storeroom shelves were nearly bare—with one notable exception. Hundreds of tins of a particular brand of canned goods were on hand, nearly enough for a whole army. A strange circumstance about these attracted our attention. From each label, a piece the size of a postage stamp had been removed. "Why?" we inquired with some curiosity. We soon learned that numbers had originally appeared on the labels, and when these numbers were forwarded to a certain address, the lucky number won a prize. Employees of the Continental were continually winning prizes.

These amounted, obviously by coincidence, to just ten per cent of the orders placed with the supplier during the preceding thirty days.

A strategic door led from a food-storage room to a section of the adjoining garage where employees, or at least those who could afford such luxuries during depression days, were expected to leave their cars. A shiny new Oldsmobile was usually visible directly beside the storeroom door. On this door we snapped our padlock and threw away the keys.

Not many days after this unpardonable action, resignations began to come in at a rising crescendo that soon reached overwhelming proportions. Fortunately the employees who quit by the dozen, saying they had better opportunities elsewhere, eased a fairly crucial problem of overstaffing. Of course there was no connection with our padlock, but it was interesting that, despite the depression, the hotel gradually began to convert red into black ink on its financial statements. Not many years later, the Continental was singled out as perhaps the most profitable hotel of its size in the country. This was our introduction to the potentials of hotels—and, incidentally, to the merits of a reliable padlock.

Our success with this Cambridge hotel suggested the idea of larger operations in this lucrative field. The investment companies previously "assembled" had assets of only a few hundred thousand dollars, for the Standard Investing Company bonds had been paid off. We now used these remaining funds for the purchase of those quite unpopular real-estate securities still available at bargain prices. In passing, I might add that, at least in our experience, securities of an intrinsically sound character, perhaps momentarily low in public esteem, often presented the most interesting investment opportunities.

Among the defaulted securities we acquired was a block of bonds of the Stonehaven Hotel in Springfield, enough to give us control of the property. As our experience with the Continental had demonstrated, with recovery in sight, we could anticipate notable results if real estate should make an expected comeback, particularly if we accelerated the process by lifting a hotel out of receivership and providing an energetic management.

Elmer Boswell, the Stonehaven's resident manager, greeted us cordially when we arrived to take over the property. We brought along evidence of ownership of more than half the outstanding "defaulted" bonds, and, owing to this technicality, we could now issue orders. With perhaps unnecessary tactlessness, we asked Elmer if he would take charge of the operations on our behalf while we looked for a new manager. Our plan was based largely on the false assumption that, with so much red ink in evidence, a change in managers was inevitable. We were very wrong.

Elmer was like a minister without portfolio. His salary was less than that of the chef, and he had very little authority. He was not even allowed access to the kitchen, an indication of some of the problems hotel managers encountered in those somber days of receiverships.

However, he was willing to overlook the matter of a temporary assignment, and seemed on the whole pleased with the new turn of events. Did we really mean he should have, at least until further notice, full charge of operations? We readily agreed. At this point Elmer, offering some feeble excuse, suddenly withdrew. When he returned we inquired where he had been.

"In the kitchen," replied.

"What happened?" we asked.

"I fired the chef," was the calm reply. Elmer apparently had little enthusiasm for divided responsibility.

Elmer has been with us ever since, one of the company's most highly valued assets. Under his able direction, the two-hundred-room Stonehaven began to prosper, and earnings in a year or two helped us acquire two more hotels, each the size of the Stonehaven.

It was at this time, early in 1939, as possessors of three small hotels, that we began to develop some ambitious ideas. Perhaps we might someday have a large chain of hotels. Cherishing this somewhat nebulous dream, we began to consider the advantages of a single name for the prospective empire. In addition to the Springfield property we had the Lee House in Washington and a hotel known as the Sheraton on Boston's Bay State Road. The latter, with an expensive electric roof sign, left us little choice in the selection of the new name for our future domain, for it would have cost a small fortune to change the letters of sign. Our hotels in Springfield and Washington thus became Sheraton hotels.

We had some interesting experiences with our original Boston hotel, which had a rapid succession of managers during the early days. One of these, whose sojourn on Bay State Road was of limited duration, did not seem to like employees. He kept a sign on his office door emphasizing this point by saying that no employees might enter. A local newspaperman, the arbiter of his paper's gossip column, discreetly referred to this episode. He mentioned the manager of a hotel "less than a thousand miles from Boston"—a designation evidently calculated not to exclude this local enterprise—who had a message on his door devised apparently to discourage employees from seeing the boss. "As a matter of fact," the column suggested, "they can't. The manager doesn't work there any more."

In that same Boston hotel, I remember visiting Spencer Sawyer, one of the able managers who once headed the enterprise. It was a holiday. Spencer was easier to see on such occasions and glad to talk about the progress he was making. Ordinarily he was busy, and I, only an owner, could add little toward making the property pay.

Next to the manager's office was a small banquet room from

whence issued perceptible signs of gaiety. On inquiring, I learned a glamour girl from a nearby suburb was having a wedding reception. Spencer was obviously chagrined to find that his boss had never even heard of the prominent young lady honoring his establishment.

The conference over, I left Spencer's office and, entering the corridor, observed a charming spectacle. There, in full regalia, was the bride, surrounded by a half-dozen handsome ushers, to each of whom she was giving a ceremonial bridal hug. As the last received his due, I thought I could pass unobserved—but this was a miscalculation. The bride, not even looking at me, mistaking me for number seven, gave me a bewitching bridal kiss. Just then, my predecessors having all vanished, Spencer emerged from his office, somewhat startled. He evidently wondered whether he could ever again believe a single word I said; so I "had not even heard of" that famous glamour girl.

Later, at this same hotel, I discovered with pleasure that my son Ernest III had accepted a lowly position in one of the hotel kitchens so he could learn the culinary mysteries of hotel procedure. He had decided that, should he advance in his father's business, he would do well to have personal knowledge of what went on behind the scenes.

Many celebrities had permanent accommodations at this original Sheraton Hotel. One of these was Ted Williams of Boston Red Sox fame. One time, I remember, a pretty young seventeen-year-old from nearby Concord had reached the conviction that nothing really mattered more in this difficult world than getting a genuine autograph of her famed baseball hero. Realizing how important such things can be, I inquired of our general manager if her desire could be gratified. Soon a regulation baseball appeared, bearing the authentic inscription, "With greetings to Sally," followed by the coveted signature. It was to no avail. Someone previously had played on Sally's gullibility by presenting her with a spurious note from Ted, and she was sure the baseball likewise could only be a hoax. Calmly she tossed the offending "fraud" into the Concord River, aggrieved that any one should trifle with her deep emotions. I never heard what happened later when Sally learned that the treasure so lightly cast aside was really quite authentic.

It was many years later, after we had control of Boston's more magnificent Copley Plaza, that the Boston Sheraton, a landmark that gave its name to some fifty units in our hotel system, was finally offered for sale. In 1938, when the country was still deep in the depression, it had cost all of one hundred and sixty thousand dollars. Ten years later, when it was sold, it brought a mere million dollars.

2

We purchased the Copley Plaza in 1941. This was an exciting milestone. As one of the country's important hotels, it enjoyed a world-wide reputation, though the luster, after many years of deficits, was becoming rather dim.

Shares of stock originally worth one hundred dollars each represented the actual ownership, but because of the long period of persistent losses, they were now selling at a dollar a share. Even brokers buying them for our account were baffled by our recklessness. Did we not know the certificates were practically worthless paper?

By 1941 we had more than half the voting shares, and so we attended the annual meeting. The directors were literally astounded. That anyone would want these nearly valueless shares had never even entered their minds.

This was our introduction to our first "major league" operation. Although it was a great opportunity, some Bostonians were understandably resentful. It was all well enough for some young Boston fellows to take over a few outlying hotels, but this was different. The Copley Plaza was an institution, a landmark, an actual part of the city of Boston.

We went to work with prodigious zeal, for success was now imperative. Our future would depend on how well we could meet our new responsibilities. Carefully we studied all phases of the business, determined to show that prolonged years of deficits could now be brought to an end. We started off, however, with a major indiscretion. We had wantonly canceled some "untouchable" insurance policies. Having several hotels, we could save by taking advantage of what might be considered wholesale rates available on so-called blanket policies. This, in the eyes of some proper Bostonians with an interest in the insurance business, was an unpardonable sin, one that could involve repercussions, since Boston's better clubs allow members blackball privileges when new names come up for consideration. Though aware of the magnitude of our crime, we still at times persist in placing insurance with the "wrong" firms when such indiscretions are advantageous.

One Sunday, shortly after we secured control of the Copley Plaza, I was called unexpectedly to New York. The problem of cashing a check arose and, checkbook in hand, I stopped at the cashier's window. The young lady politely asked for my credit card. Taken somewhat aback, I admitted I lacked that means of identification, but hastened to explain I was the president of the hotel.

"Sorry, sir," she apologized, "but the last person with a bad check told me that story."

A passing newspaperman rose to the occasion. I was duly identified.

We retained on the Copley Plaza board several "outside" directors, feeling that, with Boston's welfare at heart, they would have no conflicting interests. One of these directors, eager that nepotism be rigorously excluded, when the question of a decorator for a new cocktail lounge was discussed, insisted the job be awarded on merit, rather than to someone's brother-in-law, or perhaps to some friendly first cousin. We all readily assented. The lounge was to be in an area unused since the hotel was built, which could now start to produce revenue. Turning to John Buttrick, who had raised the specter of nepotism, we asked, "Why don't *you*, John, select the architect-decorator?" John had excellent taste and would make a wise selection. When the new room was nearly ready, and the chosen architect was applying some finishing touches, John and I looked in to admire his work. High on a stepladder was the expert John had selected. I don't know who was more surprised when from up on the ladder Hampden Robb, a distinguished Boston architect, greeted me most cordially, saying, "Why, hello, Cousin Ernie."

Our new manager was making progress and the hotel was gradually emerging from an extended siege of continuous red ink. Many things were beginning to happen. There were even prospects of dividends on what was once almost worthless stock. An indication of the changes occurring was given by the florist who had a lobby concession. The hotel gave him a monthly honorarium of three hundred dollars to help support this needed adjunct to a luxury hotel operation. One day he paid us a visit and indicated a willingness to forgo his usual subsidy, should we wish him to do so.

"On the contrary," our manager explained, "we want *you* to pay *us* three hundred a month."

"As you wish," said the friendly florist. "How long a lease may I have?"

When the hotel was built, in 1912, labor was cheap and uncomplaining. Waiters were forced to cover unconscionable distances and to climb long flights of stairs to serve exacting guests, but in those days this was of little concern. Now things were different; union wages were rising sharply. It would be hard to

[81]

move the kitchen to the lobby floor, but if we couldn't bring the mountain to Mohammed, perhaps Mohammed would be willing to move. For sixty thousand dollars the principal dining room could be transplanted to a lower level. Waiters could halve the distance covered in their accustomed shuttle between temperamental chefs and ever-demanding diners, and avoid the endless stairs. Payroll savings and faster service would earn, we estimated, some forty thousand dollars a year, a better return at least than the more familiar three or four per cent paid on government bonds.

Other improvements soon followed. How well they would pay off depended on a simple mathematical test. The normal return on hotel investments, enhanced by the "leverage" of mortgage financing, is close to fourteen per cent per annum before, and perhaps ten per cent after, allowance for corporate income taxes. The extent by which we could exceed normal expectations was the measure of the desirability of contemplated projects.

Using a ten-per-cent return after taxes and amortization of costs as the amount necessary to justify improvements, we were constantly searching for projects that would produce at least twice this yield, in order to provide a doubly worthwhile investment. In this way, we could add two dollars in value as indicated by "capitalizing" these earnings—for every dollar expended. This, in brief, is the principle we used in order to lift ourselves up by our "bootstraps" from a company with one or two hundred thousands in assets twenty years ago into one with several hundred millions today.

Favorable depreciation allowances on new projects, particularly since enactment of the 1954 revenue laws, have been an additional incentive to make improvements. These allowances have reduced the burden of taxation, making us less envious of oil prospectors with their twenty-seven-per-cent depletion benefits. The new revenue laws were thus a great boon to the hotel industry.

Modern accounting, unfortunately, does not always reflect the added values created by improvements until a property is actually sold. The increase in net worth resulting from improvements, especially those that add more than their cost to the value of a hotel, has been an important factor in the progress of our business. We estimate these "unrealized gains" periodically by measuring the indicated market value of all Sheraton properties over and above their respective mortgage debts. This we accomplish by multiplying by ten the annual net earnings after deducting a realistic amount for depreciation, not the accelerated depreciation we are permitted when reporting company earnings. Our yardstick indicates over a hundred million dollars of value is not recorded on our official audited balance sheet.

In case a meticulous security analyst observes these unorthodox comments and possibly elevates an eyebrow, I hasten to add that the amount of depreciation deducted for this purpose is usually between two and three per cent of the indicated total value of the property, land and furniture included; the actual amount of this composite average depending on such matters as age, location, and certain other factors.

Using our valuation formula, we proceeded with our face-lifting operations at the Copley Plaza, seeking twice the added income needed merely to justify these expenditures. We ordered new carpets, designed new kitchen layouts, and installed new bathroom fixtures or items such as colored plate glass, known as carrara glass, to replace aging bathroom tiles.

Soon we discovered that a decorating department should have a high priority. Selecting a capable specialist able to produce "rooms of tomorrow" became a particularly pressing project. How could we find that person, someone to create not just what we might like? We, after all, would not be paying for hotel

[83]

rooms; our guests were the ones we must please. Finally we had an idea. We invited eight highly recommended experts to take part in a decorating contest. Each was given a suite that needed attention, together with a budget of three thousand dollars. The instructions were to transform the suites into "rooms of tomorrow" that would fire the imagination of the traveling public. The work should be daring, and yet reflect the utmost in good taste. All contestants went to work, and on the target date a thousand guests arrived, invited to inspect the new creations. We provided cocktails, for guests should be in an appreciative mood. We showed them the eight completed masterpieces and asked each to cast a ballot for the suite of his or her preference. When the returns were in, it was Mary Kennedy by a landslide; and ever since that fortunate day, she has been the arbiter of the decor of the well-appointed Sheraton bedroom, lobby, or banquet hall. Without Mary Kennedy, life for traveling America, at least in our prejudiced opinion, would be distinctly less agreeable.

We proceeded with the new decorating program in Boston with ever-increased vigor under her direction. The new look we were achieving was to contribute amazingly toward restoring and eventually exceeding the former prestige of what was once the noble Copley Plaza.

But today the Copley Plaza is no more. By unanimous corporate resolution, some five years ago, the name was daringly changed to the Sheraton-Plaza. We had deliberated ten years before summoning the courage to take this momentous step.

However, there was still a minority interest in the hotel, which could technically veto participation by the Copley Plaza in Sheraton's national advertising program. A change in name would resolve this problem.

Boston was in an uproar. Predictions of impending ruin echoed everywhere. Even Boston's most famous dowager honored us with four pages in longhand, describing in colorful language the enormity of our transgression. Such attention from so lofty a source gave us cause for concern, until Page Browne, an observant company vice president, finally noted that our influential detractor had not been inside the hotel in perhaps a dozen years. A potential loss of patronage from even so distinguished a personage could hardly wreck the establishment.

Two days had passed. The famous Hildegarde was singing in the hotel's Oval Room, and Molly and I, both ardent Hildegarde fans, had asked for a small table to entertain a few guests. Nearby was a large table bearing a conspicuous "Reserved" sign. Soon we saw approaching with a group of notables, all eyes turned toward her, our recent critical correspondent. Easily the most prominent of all proper Bostonians, she is affectionately known by her many admirers as the one and only Miss Boston.

An interesting result of the Copley Plaza's transformation into the Sheraton-Plaza was the number of friends who complimented us on the addition of one more unit to our ever-growing chain. Book matches, monograms on towels, insignia on china, glasses and silverware had for years proclaimed the Sheraton affiliation, yet many guests were unaware of the association until the name was changed.

Repercussions from dropping the Copley Plaza name were, as I have said, immediate, prolonged, and violent. Even today, fortunately on a diminished scale, some rumblings still persist. However, in Boston we never quite suffered the excoriation achieved on a similar occasion in Worcester when the Bancroft Hotel became the Sheraton. We were never quite sure if newspaper outbursts that followed this overt act were solely due to removal of the Bancroft name or whether failure to re-elect to the hotel's board of directors a distinguished former incumbent possibly played a part.

The morning the Bancroft became the Sheraton there appeared on the Worcester newsstands an impressive issue of that city's morning paper. Headlines across the entire front page could hardly have been blacker had a real war been declared, rather than what we considered a purely local skirmish. Noting Worcester's location somewhat to the west of Boston, they proclaimed: "Barbarians From the East Desecrate Memory of Worcester's Greatest Citizen." George Bancroft, once an American Ambassador to Germany, was a founder of the Naval Academy at Annapolis.

We soon learned that when a hotel name was changed, denunciations would rise to a ringing chorus, but so too would the earnings of the hotel. Perhaps we were substantiating the creed of a well-known though now departed Boston politician. His Honor was reputedly fond of publicity—favorable, of course, if possible, but "bad publicity was much better than no publicity at all."

3

Changing a hotel's name unfortunately is not the only cause for irritation in connection with hotel operations. Lapses in service sometimes arise, and we are always grateful for criticism. Compliments, of course, are a waste of time; little can be done about them except an occasional raise for a manager, and that is always expensive. Fortunately travelers can run hotels better than the management, and we capitalize on this useful circumstance, for it is costly to hire inspectors to report on deficiencies when customers do it for nothing. A little prompting helps at times, so occasionally we lead with our corporate chin. When the flow of complaints runs low, we often leave questionnaires in hotel bedrooms.

Replies to questionnaires always arrive in quantities, and all are duly scrutinized. Brooks Fenno handles this delicate operation with consummate skill. He has a talent for "turning the other cheek" with most disarming charm, even in the face of unreasonable communications. For the benefit of a large number of letter-writers, who may wonder if we pay attention to their assorted gripes, let me add that the meticulous Brooks always informs the manager as well as the offending or praiseworthy employee, enclosing photostats of the communications.

Brooks is methodical. He tabulates complaints and compliments according to categories, keeping track of such breaches of propriety as failure to honor confirmed reservations, delay in the appearance of a breakfast tray, or even that greatest of mortal sins, ringing the wrong room when a call was left for 6:15 A.M. For purposes of scrutiny the statistics are invaluable. As a more immediate index of performance, Brooks uses a simpler device. When the proportion of complaints to compliments is more than fifty per cent, he knows at a glance some management is slipping. Should the proportion rise to sixty per cent, drastic action looms. And if the proportion of compliments is excessive, this too can cause concern. Has the manager been giving away all the profits?

Complaints are always taken seriously. Many are constructive, and numerous Sheraton policies have emerged from the solicitude, or perhaps letter-writing talents, of some of our worthy guests. But although we have received a number of complaints, we have the pleasure of knowing other businesses also have troubles. Transcontinental railroads are apparently no exception.

Once the president of a large railroad received a strong denunciation threatening not only cancellation of future travel on his line, but, far worse, a hint that valuable freight might go to a hated rival. The difficulty had occurred on a westbound sleeper. The trouble: bedbugs. Almost immediately the railroad sent a most abject apology, signed by the president himself. With deepest remorse he explained that never during his twenty-five years with the road had such an unfortunate catastrophe occurred. Investigation had followed at once, and not only the conductor and porter, but presumably even the engineer had been fired. The customer's feelings softened. Had he perhaps been overhasty? Could not the incident at least this once be overlooked? Unfortunately a penciled note, obviously included by mistake, fell from the open envelope, a memo from the president to his secretary. "Send this S.O.B.," it read, "the usual No. 4 bedbug letter."

When, at a recent dinner in Boston, I met the distinguished head of a great transcontinental railroad, I was unable to suppress this charming story. He at least, I felt, should be amused. I was hardly ever more wrong.

"Unfortunately," said the rail magnate—a little icily, I thought, certainly with no trace of amusement in his voice—"part of the story happens to be true. You see," he explained, "I ought to know." My face turned its accustomed shade of red.

4

Among our particularly good friends in Boston are the Paul Ceresoles. Linda, one of the city's leading glamour girls, and her husband, Paul, are often seen dining out at Boston's exclusive restaurants, but they don't, we feel, patronize the Sheraton-Plaza as much as they should. The trouble, we are forced to conclude, dates back to a time, many years ago, when the Oval Room was the scene of particular merriment on the night before the Harvard–Yale football game. Linda and Paul had reserved a table, and the service apparently was less than perfect. The next day at the Harvard stadium our paths somehow crossed and Linda caught me by the sleeve.

"Since we are such good friends," she started to explain, "I think you really ought to know. The service in the Oval Room last night was really beyond words. An aged waiter," she confided, "looking as though he were ready to die any minute of a heart attack, finally succeeded in taking our order and then never reappeared." They had eaten no dinner. Even worse, they had missed the first act of *South Pacific*.

The following morning at the hotel the manager, looking quite disturbed, called me to his desk to report a major misfortune. His oldest employee, a veteran Oval Room waiter had been stricken with a fatal heart attack.

The Ceresoles were advised of this tragic development, but to this day, I am sure, they believe that in our zeal for the glory of Sheraton we contrived the disaster as an alibi. They are sometimes seen at the Ritz, but, despite these occasional lapses, we continue to count them among our better friends.

There was a costly incident at our famous Boston hotel during World War II, when rent controls raised many acute problems. The highest room rate paid for any specific accommodations during March 1942 fixed the rate for the rest of the war, and we felt that the enforcement of this rent-control law was perhaps tinged by the anti-business bias generated during the Roosevelt era.

The hotel had a luxury bridal suite, for which the established price was twenty dollars for single and twenty-four dollars for double occupancy. A visiting business executive had occupied it during most of the crucial month, thereby establishing the twenty-dollar single rate. But on the final day of March a somewhat impoverished sailor, interested in only a minimum rate, arrived with his bride at the hotel for their wedding night. He was soon to rejoin his ship and head for hostile shores. The manager had a big heart, and also a son in the service. The bridal suite was available, and the newly married couple was checked in at the hotel's seven-dollar minimum rate as a patriotic gesture to a potential future hero.

Since the suite had brought only twenty dollars during the base period, the price was fixed at that figure and single and double use were treated alike. Years later came an official audit seeking deviations from the prescribed formula; heavy penalties awaited infractions of wartime edicts. When the bridal suite came up for scrutiny, single occupancies at twenty dollars were readily approved, but for each instance of double occupancy, a more normal status for a bridal suite, an overcharge of thirteen dollars was recorded. Treble damages were assessed for each transgression, so we paid several thousand dollars in fines, but that was not all. Henceforth the prescribed card quoting compulsory frozen rates must appear in this nuptial suite, showing:

Single occupancy $20

Double occupancy $7

We often pondered the prospective injury to a traveling executive's morals should he, upon observing this illuminating interpretation of the law, contemplate the possible financial advantage of seeking a lovely companion willing to share, for a stipend of less than the posted differential, this commodious suite.

Some years later at the same hotel, when I was attending a Sheraton dinner-dance—now an established Boston tradition—my status as a hotel man was seriously questioned. In the ballroom I was introduced to a charming young lady, and as we danced to the strains of pleasant music, I realized I must make a special effort to remember this glamorous partner. Since names during introductions register poorly, I asked her to repeat hers. She seemed somewhat surprised.

"Do you know, Mr. Henderson," she said, her big eyes rolling, "this is the third time you have been introduced to me?"

I must have turned unusually red, that accomplishment at

which I always excel. Noting my embarrassment, she tried to make amends.

"Oh, it doesn't matter," she said. "Of course, Mr. Henderson, it doesn't matter—that is, unless you expect someday to be a politician, or have secret hopes of becoming a hotel man."

I was so overcome by her innocent remark that her name again escaped me. However, I look forward to a fourth introduction. Next time I promise to remember.

My injured feelings on contemplating the doubt cast upon my ability in my chosen career were somewhat assuaged when recently I met a distinguished celebrity, also for a third time. I had met him once in the elevator of our Boston hotel and a second time elsewhere. The third occasion was at the Metropolitan Club in New York, where Bill Chadbourne, one of our Park Sheraton Hotel directors, introduced me to him. Each time this prominent personage graciously expressed pleasure at meeting me. I was delighted; I began to feel better. He was James Aloysius Farley.

5

Soon after we acquired the Copley Plaza, the Beaconsfield in nearby Brookline became a part of our growing chain.

It was an old hostelry of about two hundred rooms. Business had been quiet during the depression, and the management had found it cheaper to seal off surplus facilities than to pay for redecoration. As a result, much of the house was out of commission. The hotel had formerly belonged to the Harry Paine Whitney estate, and perhaps this circumstance accounted in part for the lack of profits, for sometimes tax losses are almost as useful as earnings, if tax brackets are sufficiently high.

One day we received a visit from a distinguished New York lawyer, a charming Manhattan blueblood, who wanted to talk about the Beaconsfield. He told us one hundred and fifty thousand dollars was the best offer he could obtain for this venerable property, and he wanted a better price. Very simple, we suggested. With fifty thousand down and the rest on extended mortgages, we could offer two hundred thousand. The New Yorker began to shown interest; he was getting nearer his goal, which was three hundred and thirty thousand dollars—the extra thirty, we assumed, to make up the preceding year's losses. The prospect began to interest us also. Obviously he was not expecting much cash, a scarce commodity for companies interested in expansion. Twenty-five hundred in cash, we volunteered, without questioning the asking price. The balance would be in mortgages secured by the property he was offering us.

"Agreed," said the distinguished New Yorker without any hesitation.

That was in 1941. Three years later, as the earnings increased and refinancing became feasible, we paid off the last of that purchase-money mortgage. The estate had realized more than twice what others had been willing to pay, and yet we too had few grounds for complaint. As the years went by, earnings increased. Not long ago we sold the hotel. Our initial investment of twenty-five hundred dollars had grown to a million and a quarter, and at that, I think, we sold too cheap. Besides, the price was exclusive of the proceeds of a nearly new garage "thrown in" by the kindly New Yorker to secure more adequately the mortgage he was taking back. The garage had brought an additional hundred and fifty thousand once it was put on a paying basis.

Other hotel transactions could scarcely be expected to equal, percentagewise at least, our success with the Beaconsfield. However, the techniques which made the Beaconsfield and Sheraton-Plaza hotels successful were repeated in many parts of the country. Now that three hotels recently constructed are completed, there are more than fifty units in the spreading Sheraton chain.

6

One of our first New York hotels was purchased from the Bowery Savings Bank, which had acquired it by foreclosure during the difficult days of the depression. This hotel on Park Avenue, known as the Russell, was being managed, together with several other foreclosed properties of the Bowery Savings Bank, by the illustrious Emil Ronay. This distinguished hotelier was to be glowingly written up in the *Saturday Evening Post* as a great hotel "doctor" capable of resuscitating financially ailing hotels. We were in great awe of him and accordingly, when the bank sold us the Russell with the stipulation Ronay should remain at least two years as manager, we readily agreed.

Shortly thereafter Ronay, his stature enhanced by the accolade from the *Saturday Evening Post*, arrived at our Lincoln, Massachusetts, home for an unexpected visit. It was wartime, and servants were unavailable. Our twenty-room home was maintained principally by the efforts of Molly—an undertaking which involved, during my frequent absences from Boston, even the shoveling of soft coal into the locomotive-sized boilers which kept the house from freezing.

Molly greeted our surprise visitor with mixed emotions. She had prepared a skimpy dinner—probably stew and cabbage, or whatever else chanced to be on hand—and to serve it to so illustrious a gourmet, accustomed no doubt to delicacies of world-famous chefs, was almost unthinkable. However, when dinner was finally over, the great Ronay commented on the "most delicious food." Molly, frozen by the apparent sarcasm, all but burst into tears. Later, looking back on this visit, we concluded that after a lifetime of food from hotel kitchens he had probably really enjoyed this unaccustomed fare, and presumably actually meant the nice things he had said.

The two years of Ronay's stewardship of the Russell hotel

eventually came to an end, and we took over the management ourselves. Whether the subsequent improvement in earnings was due solely to the stimulus of a wartime economy that brought added business to hotels, or whether we too perhaps were learning the art of doctoring ailing enterprises, may never be fully settled, but the fact remains that as the years went by the Russell's growing earnings, reflected in its rising value, eventually quadrupled, largely a tribute to the skill of Dorothy Clary, our only woman hotel manager.

We later acquired other New York hotels and became interested in selling the Russell in order to finance improvements in some of these larger ones. The stumbling block was the capital-gains tax payable unless there were offsetting losses, which are rare during periods of inflation. One opportunity did arise, but the desired tax losses would "run out" unless we sold before April 30, the end of our fiscal year. Since real-estate sales often require months of planning, we negotiated the proposed sale well in advance. It was to a large university, which planned to purchase the hotel and lease it back to Sheraton—an attractive undertaking for an educational institution, involving little if any risk. All was arranged when, only a few days before the zero hour, bad news came from the university treasurer. The deal would have to be called off. He was most apologetic, but unforeseen problems had arisen. Two new trustees had joined the board of his institution. Being bankers, they were skeptical of a transaction to be completed on such short notice and doubtless thought it had all the earmarks of a "high pressure deal." Their signatures were required, and they couldn't even be reached for they had gone out of town.

Greatly disappointed, we simply had to forget the entire transaction. Not only was an opportunity to salvage some substantial tax benefits lost, but we were almost equally grieved that efforts to contribute to the financial program of a distinguished educational institution had failed. After all, with the level of academic overhead a continuing problem, additional earnings for a university could do little harm. However, we knew we should not cry over spilt milk.

That evening, Friday, April 29, our vice president Page Browne and I attended a testimonial banquet at a competing Boston hotel. Arriving late, we were taken to a small table held for latecomers and were joined by two New Yorkers also present to honor the guest of the evening. Their train to Boston had been delayed.

Introducing ourselves, we learned they were officers of a large New York bank. When they heard of our interest in hotels, they began to ask about one on Park Avenue named the Russell, telling us of a somewhat "questionable" transaction in which they had been urged to participate. As trustees of a prominent university, they had almost been pressured into a precipitous purchase.

At last we could tell our side of the story, explain why time had been so important, and say how sorry we were that the university could not benefit by an unusual opportunity. As we outlined the details, the bankers became interested. The next day, Saturday, they told us, their bank would of course be closed. But if we still wished to sell and would catch the midnight train for New York, they would telephone the president of their bank and the treasurer of the educational institution. There was still time to meet the approaching deadline.

The following day in New York, the treasurer of Syracuse University, in the offices of the Guaranty Trust Company, gave us a certified check, and a multi-million-dollar transaction, because of a one-in-a-million coincidence, was successfully completed.

The university has apparently not regretted this miraculously revived transaction, for we have been unable in recent years to repurchase this Park Avenue property even at a substantial advance in price.

IX.

Dublin, New Hampshire

NEARLY every business career has some roots in early childhood environments. Dublin, New Hampshire, where we spent our summers as children, undoubtedly left upon one of its youngsters a fairly vivid imprint. It is a small village of some six hundred inhabitants during the winter months, but expands to many times this number during the summer. It is perched on the side of Monadnock Mountain in the southwest corner of the state. Dublin Lake, fed by cool springs, is more than a mile long. I swam the entire length once and ever since have admired British Channel swimmers.

Climbing Monadnock, 3300 feet high, was a favorite sport for youngsters. I suspect nowadays the coming generation, accustomed to automobiles, would prefer helicopters when contemplating the ascent. In our day two and a half hours were required to reach the top. I claim the record for coming down in twenty-one minutes flat.

Dublin was at its zenith during the days of William Howard Taft and Woodrow Wilson, when several of the principal foreign embassies, seeking escape from Washington's July and August, set up summer headquarters there. Franklin MacVeagh, Secretary of the Treasury under President Taft, built a summer mansion of thirty rooms with some ten bathrooms, and here, on several occasions, he entertained the President. This house, abandoned in 1937 after the great depression had wreaked its damage, was to be acquired "for a song" seventeen years later. It was purchased and rehabilitated by a certain Boston hotel man—but this part of the story follows later.

My earliest recollection of the MacVeagh home is of a reception tendered President Taft in 1910. All Dublin was invited—even I, a thirteen-year-old. After standing for nearly two hours in a slowly moving line, I considered it a matter of great import when the President's huge hand—Taft weighed some three hundred pounds—was finally extended to me. Unfortunately he was looking in the other direction; the occasion was perhaps less momentous in his life, for a passing acquaintance engaged his attention until I was swallowed up in the receding line. He did not even look down to see whose hand he had shaken. At a tender age I thus discovered that to a United States President the experience of meeting a thirteen-year-old was not necessarily of world-shattering importance. Unfortunately I was too young to cast a vote of protest for any political opponent.

Back in the days of Taft, Dublin's summer colony included some well-known artists, authors, and others weighed down with scholarly pursuits. Mark Twain spent several summers there, but his talents were not always fully appreciated. He liked to read from his manuscripts to large audiences assembled at the homes of neighbors in order to test the reaction to his latest chapters. Occasionally annoyed when passages predestined for peals of laughter somehow misfired, he was even more exasperated when audiences were sometimes convulsed over situations supposed to elicit more sober responses.

A constant hazard at these Mark Twain readings was the danger they might persist for many hours, during which rigorous attention was demanded. Dr. Dellinger Barney told us that his wife, while attending one of these extended séances, cautiously reached for her knitting—to no avail. Mark Twain spotted the infraction. Stopping his reading to peer at the hapless offender, he remarked, "I beg your pardon, Mrs. Barney, was I disturbing you?" Although one of our great American authors and lecturers, Mark Twain may have been somewhat less than a genius on occasions when he read aloud.

Another Dublin resident was the artist and naturalist Abbot H. Thayer, considered by many the discoverer of protective coloring. While still in my teens, I saw a demonstration of his skill. He had produced a piece of stone carved to resemble a duck. Painted to match the roadway, the object had a very dark brown back, and much lighter colors on its belly.

In broad daylight Thayer placed the duck, supported by a stiff wire, in the roadway and led me twenty paces away. Turning, I was sure the object had vanished; nothing was visible at all. A few paces nearer, and the wire could be seen—nothing else. Another few paces, and the duck began to take form. Yes, Abbot Thayer had indeed mastered nature's secret for deceiving the human eye.

When World War I was raging, deceptive markings to disguise merchant ships falling prey to German torpedoes became a matter of national necessity. To meet this emergency, Dublin's great naturalist was offered an impressive financial inducement to guide a Navy program for confusing the enemy with camouflage. Despite a threatening specter of poverty, Thayer declined. It would mean military activity, and this his conscience would not then permit.

Subsequently, as the fever of war rose, realizing human lives were involved, Thayer offered the British a new type of uniform designed to render their soldiers partially invisible. This the British flatly rejected, concluding, no doubt, that fitting their men with unbecoming rags could injure morale more than could a mere reduction in the deadliness of approaching German bullets.

When Abbot Thayer sold a painting, usually a semi-annual event, the few hundred dollars received were always deposited in an earthenware jar resting on the family mantelpiece. A grocery bill or the cost of a pair of shoes could be taken care of by reaching for this substitute for the First National Bank.

One Thayer family treasure, the wedding silver, was never to be used. Held inviolate as a nest egg, it was hidden in a corner of the cellar, a poorly kept secret, doubtless known to all of Dublin. However, this was an honest community—with one possible "exception." That was when the silver disappeared.

There were three Gerrys in Dublin, all in their teens: my oldest brother, Gerard; Jerome Brush, the son of George de Forest Brush, who rivaled Thayer as a top old-school artist; and Gerald Thayer. These three knew that Henry Dion, Dublin's intrepid constable, although the owner of a formidable pistol, was nonetheless thoroughly harmless, for his once deadly weapon, now rusty, could no longer shoot. Believing the Thayer silver to be inadequately protected, the three Gerrys formulated a plan to stage a make-believe robbery.

Removing the silver one night from its usual hiding place, they carefully secreted it elsewhere in the cellar—all but one or two pieces. These they dropped with care on the stairs to the kitchen, where Papa Thayer would be sure to find them in the morning when fetching water for the kettles on the kitchen stove. It was now midnight; the three desperadoes would have several hours' start before Henry Dion could be alerted to initiate his deadly pursuit.

Light snow had fallen, for it was late in the fall. But Henry Dion's task was not to be made too easy. He would have recourse to two bloodhounds, now superannuated, to be sure, relics of a scare of earlier years, which would of course be pressed into service when the enormity of the crime was weighed. The progress of the dogs must be impeded.

The three boys, their task accomplished, set out for the woods, heading up a rarely frequented slope of Mount Monadnock, making sure their trail in the snow, at least in the initial stages, could be followed by their prospective pursuers. Halfway up, the three began to double up on their tracks, making a few complete circles to confound, if possible, pursuing canine noses. Finally they headed back, covering their footsteps as best they could, and reached our summer cottage, which was closed for the winter. Exhausted, they fell asleep in an attic bed.

It may have been noon when they were rudely awakened. Barking dogs and heavy footsteps could be heard. Henry Dion was mounting the attic stairs.

"Surrender," he roared, "or I'll shoot to kill."

The three pulled the covers over their heads as the steward of the law advanced, reinforced by farm hands with pitchforks pressed into emergency service. "Surrender." The command was repeated as the minions of justice burst into the attic. Henry Dion, clinging bravely to his rusty gun, spotted the three forms under the blankets and daringly tore off the covers, revealing the trio, all sixteen-year-olds, looking into the once dangerous end of a superannuated revolver. For the rest of his earthly life Henry Dion could never forgive these three desperate troublemakers.

The Thayer story is incomplete without reference to an early Thayer painting once found by the children in an old closet— a landscape portraying Monadnock in midwinter. Early rays of a January sun were casting long shadows from snow-covered evergreens. It was Thayer's first and perhaps only picture not dedicated to glorifying womanhood in some ethereal form. He didn't like it, and few knew it existed.

Young Gerry Thayer, finding the painting, promptly nailed the unframed canvas to a beam in the cowshed, hammering a spike through the picture itself. Perhaps the compulsion of youngsters to plaster rotogravure pages of Sunday papers on walls of a stable had led young Thayer to display this neglected scene where cows at least could enjoy it. For a year it hung there, unattended, until suddenly half of Dublin appeared, in the midst of a raging thunderstorm.

Lightning had struck the hay stored above. More, perhaps, to impress the crowds than to save an object of value, Gerry entered the burning building and ripped the painting from the wall, to the plaudits of cheering onlookers.

Some months later Thayer died, leaving a score of unsold canvases as the children's legacy. The pictures went to New York, a sale was arranged, and the first picture went on the auction block. It brought a higher price than Thayer ever received while alive. Soon the law of supply and demand was asserting itself. As each picture was sold and the supply diminished, the paintings brought more and more. Finally the picture of Monadnock was offered, with the large hole through the canvas. Forty thousand dollars—or twice this figure, in terms of today's more anemic dollars—was the successful bid. Altogether a quarter of a million was realized, and the children were now rich.

The tragedy of Thayer's career was that while he was alive his output had exceeded the demand, and so his paintings never brought a price commensurate with their true worth. As a sad finale to the family epic, only a few years after that momentous auction, nearly all the money was gone; but now the once dependable earthenware jar still resting on the family mantelpiece could no longer be replenished.

Besides famous pictures Dublin also boasted other forms of art. One of these was far more interesting. George Grey Barnard was a sculptor whose fame was widely proclaimed, especially when the Rockefellers purchased his "Cloisters" in New York to transform into a museum. It was not, however, Barnard's notable sculpture we admired, but rather his prowess in producing a beautiful daughter, then seventeen, which seemed an even greater accomplishment. Vivia's beauty exceeded by far that of her father's other works of art.

For me, however, life had become quite difficult. Barnard had spent his childhood in France, and was evidently imbued with the French concept that the daughter of a well-to-do family should not even speak to a boy until marriage had been arranged by the omniscient parents. I suspect George Barnard considered forty years of age quite young enough for any such unhappy contingency.

Fortunately I had an ally in Mrs. Barnard, who evidently concluded my intentions were honorable, and occasionally I prevailed upon her to call me on the phone and tell me when she and her husband would be out for dinner. If I would bring Vivia home safely before their return, all would then be well.

Taking Vivia out meant calling for her on my motorcycle, which was equipped with a tandem seat. This she would bravely mount, and miles of thrilling country roads through New Hampshire and nearby Vermont made me exceedingly grateful on these moonlight occasions for the "conspiracy" between her mother and me. My gratitude was further strengthened by the many sharp curves of the narrow country roads, for then Vivia would be forced to choose between braving strong centrifugal forces or holding on to me more securely.

One of those thrilling evenings we thought would be the last. The crucial deadline of 10:30 P.M. was drawing near. Still some miles from Dublin, the throttle wide open, we were speeding up the Peterboro Hills toward home, when disaster struck. Our rear tire burst, and motorcycles carry no spare.

With only minutes separating us from impending paternal wrath, we calmly considered our plight. Peterboro, like most New Hampshire towns, retired early, but fortunately a light was visible. The milkman who covered the route to Dublin was reassembling his Ford delivery car and was encountering difficulties. Here was my chance, for I was on familiar ground. We struck a bargain. I would assemble the engine in return for transportation to Dublin.

Never was a job more expeditiously completed. The dinner party in Dublin might last longer than expected; there might still be a chance. Moments later, we were on our way. We practically flew. Stutz Bearcat racers of that era could scarcely have kept pace with our now inspired delivery car. Dublin residents the next morning would doubtless be receiving rather more butter than milk.

Breathlessly we approached the rear entrance to the Barnard home just as headlights from the large black family Studebaker were visible entering the driveway. Vivia scrambled through a kitchen window and, as I learned afterward, leaped fully dressed into bed, for her parents always kissed their daughter good night no matter how late the hour of their return. Her father's kiss indicated all was well, though a squeeze on the wrist from her mother suggested one of them, at least, had not been fooled.

Despite its occasional breakdowns, my devotion to my magnificent motorcycle was almost equal to my admiration for the lovely passenger who occasionally graced its tandem seat. It had cost, second hand, only fifty dollars, yet it was almost as thrilling to me as the possession of another hotel might be today. Abbot Thayer could scarcely have found more pleasure in contemplating his priceless canvases than I derived from gazing at the majestic cylinders or the spokes I kept so well polished. Pride of ownership is a powerful force. A miser counting his stacks of gold presumably knows this, just as did I when admiring this roaring gasoline demon.

We made many trips, my motorcycle and I. One of these was when Hamilton Montgomery, now a prominent dermatologist of Rochester, Minnesota, invited me for a week end at his family summer lodge on the side of Hurricane Mountain in the Adirondacks. The motorcycle and I were off, taking to the narrow though often scenic roads. Although there was no room for a suitcase, I managed to solve the problem of extra clothes. When I arrived at "Glenwood" the Montgomerys expressed surprise at the weight I had put on. It was only temporary, I explained. I was wearing two suits of clothes, a bathing suit, a pair of pajamas, and several changes of underwear, one over the other. This was cheaper than shipping a suitcase by express.

A particular friend in Dublin had a home on the far side of the lake. It was he who some years later introduced me to the potentialities of real estate. Robert Sterling of New York had spent his summers in New Hampshire since before the turn of the century. By pouring thousands of dollars into defaulted real-estate securities during the depth of the depression, paying only a few cents on the dollar of their original cost, and holding them through various reorganizations, he had achieved impressive results. The effect on him of these many millions was practically zero. He still drives around Dublin in a beautiful 1938 Dodge, thus putting to shame the town's other millionaires, most of whom are occasionally seen driving even new cars, provided these are no more ostentatious than a Ford. Foreign cars are a possible exception, a Jaguar or two being reasonably acceptable when a degree of eccentricity is to be desired. Cadillacs are rare, being driven mostly by year-round residents, sometimes called "the natives," a designation that could serve in retaliation for whatever epithets the latter doubtless use when referring to the summer invaders. The year-round residents, though usually forced to make a year's living during three short summer months, could nonetheless afford quite expensive cars.

There was in Dublin, years ago, a prominent summer resident named Guy Currier, who lived near us when we were youngsters. At the time he must have reached a high plateau in the motion-picture hierarchy, for he had been given elaborate professional projection equipment with which to transform an old New

England barn into a glamorous private movie palace. As children we occasionally saw in Dublin the latest Hollywood productions weeks before they were seen on Broadway.

Guy Currier was an exemplary husband. Though often away on business, he never failed, however far from home, to call his wife on the long-distance phone. On one such occasion, so at least it was rumored, cross words were momentarily uttered, marring an otherwise unblemished record. In response to her husband's daily inquiry if anything unusual had happened, Mrs. Currier replied, as was her custom, that nothing worthy of mention had occurred; but then, on reflecting, she added, "Well, yes, one thing; that Burnett estate in Peterboro you liked so much—it was sold at auction this afternoon. It actually went for a song."

This was what caused the words that allegedly came between them. "How could you have let them sell when you knew how much I wanted it? Why on earth didn't *you* buy it?" he demanded.

For a moment she hesitated, and then calmly added, "As a matter of fact, I did."

Next, of course, to the motorcycle escapades, my most memorable recollection dates back to the time of President Wilson's administration. Dublin's leading summer resident, artist, raconteur, and impresario, officially Joseph Lindon Smith, was known to all of Dublin as just Uncle Joe. He was asked to stage one of the magnificent outdoor pageants for which he was justly famous, in Cornish, some seventy miles away. Many of Dublin's summer colony, children and grown-ups alike, were given on such occasions frocks or tunics from Uncle Joe's reservoir of medieval costumes so they might be transformed into elves, fairies, sprites, and other characters in his spectacular extravaganzas. The scene of the pageant was an outdoor theater with a stage all of grass. Pines, spruces, balsams, and other evergreens provided the rustic backdrop. The seats, in amphitheater style, could take care of an audience of several hundred, and many came from Dublin for this special occasion. The size of the Dublin contingent was an added mark of devotion to Uncle Joe, partly because at the time motor cars were primitive, but especially because New Hampshire dirt roads were even more so.

The visit to Cornish was one of the rare occasions when Father momentarily relaxed his otherwise tight rein on the delicate family exchequer. For once the Hendersons had rented a car, and Father and Mother and four of us children made the trip. The breakdowns and tire changes so common in the era made us arrive late in the outskirts of Cornish, but we were not the last. A car with District of Columbia number plates was just ahead, and another, similarly equipped, followed close behind. Little did we dream that one held men of the White House Secret Service; the other the President of the United States.

The late arrival of Woodrow Wilson meant the performance was delayed. The Hendersons, unaware of the presence of the famous visitor, were surprised to be virtually lifted from our car, rushed through an arch of roses, and assigned flag-bedecked chairs in the pit just in front of the stage. The curtain, rising at that moment, cut off all possible retreat. Regaining my senses, I beheld the President sitting at my side; Father was next, then the First Lady, and finally the rest of the Hendersons. I suspect the faces of the Secret Service, if recorded on some color chart, would appear somewhere in the region between scarlet and vermilion.

After that amazing experience in full view of Uncle Joe's many admirers, we must have risen perceptibly from the level of a lower rung of the Dublin socio-economic ladder. Our insistence that it was all a mistake had never been taken seriously; had not the President, perhaps assuming we were his hosts, greeted us with warmth and cordiality right under the eyes of the entire audience?

But although the family prestige may have experienced a

measurable rise, since we owned no motor car and could boast but a fraction of the retinue of servants deemed requisite, we were still to remain in a relatively modest position on Dublin's financial ladder. At the other end of the scale of opulence were Mr. and Mrs. Winston, a delightful couple, though perhaps unaware that the feudal system was no longer in existence. They had horses and bridle paths on their large estate, gasoline launches on Dublin Lake, and when they went to a tea party the question would inevitably arise if the Daimler limousine or the Mercedes cabriolet, each with its retinue of chauffeurs and footmen, should be used. The coterie of Winston servants received five dollars apiece a week, outrageously in excess of the customary four ordinary residents paid.

The Winston quota of domestics had been augmented in 1914 by three stewards from the German liner *Crown Princess Cecile*, a ship which, like the S. S. *Cincinnati*, had been interned in Boston Harbor. Unlike most German stewards, these spoke no English, a misfortune that caused one, at least, some momentary discomfort. With war raging in Europe, it had become mandatory for the ladies of Dublin to occupy themselves with useful pursuits. Rolling Red Cross bandages or knitting socks sufficed for most, but not for Mrs. Winston. A course in lifesaving, she thought, could better serve the national emergency, and so she set out to master the latest arts of resuscitation, such as rolling victims over barrels to restore their breathing. One of the German stewards, now a Winston butler, was wading in Dublin Lake one day as Mrs. Winston was returning from her lifesaving lesson—it was the day the barrel technique was demonstrated. Tripping on a submerged rock, he fell almost beyond his depth, gulped much water, and was momentarily speechless. Mrs. Winston, noting some empty barrels on the pier and seeing her butler submerged, remembered the lesson of the morning, dashed fully clad into the water, and bravely hauled the unhappy victim onto the pier. As only gurgles issued from her hapless minion, who under the circumstances was hardly able to protest, Mrs. Winston lifted him across the nearby barrels for the prescribed treatment.

Happily, somehow the waiter survived.

When the war ended, Winston, having put everything he, as well as much that others, possessed into building wooden ships destined to end hostilities by breaking the submarine menace, suddenly found himself penniless with countless half-built wooden ships on his hands and no more hostile submarines to which they could be exposed.

A few years later, I saw the Winstons once more, now no longer in the Mercedes limousine, but on Second Avenue in New York, emerging from a delicatessen store. Each had under one arm a large loaf of bread. Dublin's most colorful family was never to return. Feudalism may at that moment have come to an end; yet the Winstons were sincerely missed by those who once had known them. Dublin would never be quite the same again.

Nearly all of Dublin's summer homes are hidden from view at the far ends of long driveways, for it was essential that each should have a view of Monadnock and, if possible, of Dublin Lake too. In this semi-artistic, semi-literary colony there was an enduring passion for the rustic, and virgin woodlands were highly prized by all, including our nearest neighbor, Grenville Clark, one of New York's most distinguished lawyers, whose wife owned thousands of evergreens stretching far up the mountainside. Dublin people were touchy about their trees; our neighbors the Clarks were no exception.

One summer the town was in an uproar because somewhere on the Grenville Clark family acres, perhaps a mile or so up the mountainside, a branch or two from some of the millions of trees that made up the wilderness had been brutally chopped off. It was a bad summer that year, for all trees were held in reverence, and the offending vandals had not been apprehended. At the turn of the century Dublin had witnessed a famous murder. That could be forgotten, but wanton injury to a tree was different. Grenny Clark was unhappy. After all, branches, once severed, could never grow out again.

This was the summer of 1938, the year of the big New England hurricane. Because of the altitude, the devastation on Monadnock was especially severe. On the Clark acres alone, some fifty thousand trees were uprooted, to say nothing of millions of branches destroyed. Grenny's reaction understandably was awaited with trepidation. As the story goes, Grenny stepped out the next morning on his porch to view the extent of the destruction. Turning to his wife, he allegedly observed, "Fanny, you know, I don't think we ever before had quite so good a view of Monadnock."

Grenny may have achieved fame for leadership in national affairs, for his part in organizing the Plattsburg camps of World War I, for the initiation of the Selective Service Act of 1940, and more recently for making important contributions to the prospect of international disarmament; but to us his greatest role was when he served as one of the seven Fellows of Harvard College. A major function of this group recurred at twenty-year intervals or so, when a new president of Harvard was to be elected. A. Lawrence Lowell was soon to retire, and so the Board of Fellows was convened. According to rumor, six of the seven ballots had been cast for the new president, three for James Bryant Conant and three for Grenville Clark. Grenny was then called upon to cast the seventh and deciding vote, and Conant became president of Harvard.

Although Grenny vehemently denies the accuracy of my version, I still adhere fundamentally—give or take a quibble or two —to this story, believing some minor discrepancy, perhaps excessive modesty, or possibly failure to appreciate the extent of the sentiment favoring him for president, accounts for his disagreeing with it.

Our nearest neighbor on the other side, Mrs. William Amory, had a large and beautiful house surrounded by a wilderness of trees. Her husband on his deathbed had warned her that if she ever built another house, she should call in an architect. When she felt an urge to build a log cabin in a particularly cherished retreat at the end of a wooded lane, a place where she and her daughter could commune with the stars and God, she remembered the dying words of her husband and immediately phoned Boston's leading architectural firm to ask that a member of that distinguished organization be sent forthwith to Dublin.

Yankee shrewdness evidently still flourished. A young architect arrived who was obviously helpful. He pointed out that a one-room log cabin might prove in some respects deficient; after all, modern civilization required certain limited appurtenances. Mrs. Amory readily agreed, and a bathroom was quickly added to the plans. How right her husband had always been. But that wasn't all. The architect wondered if the daughter's nurse would not sometimes accompany them. Here was clearly another oversight. Then there was the question of possible guests. After all, one must be hospitable. Mrs. Amory fully agreed, and two more rooms appeared on the plans. And so it went. The cook would need a dining room and of course a kitchen too. Encouraged, the architect discovered more and more niceties that would surely be required. An extra wing, for instance, would meet a desire for seclusion should too many guests arrive, and of course a cellar could house the heating equipment since temperatures are low during autumn nights. A great ballroom became a "must," for after all, the daughter, growing up, would someday have a coming-out party.

Thus it was that one of Dublin's famous showplaces evolved, a great Italian villa, but an even greater tribute to the business acumen of a charming though ingenious young architect.

Mrs. Amory was of French descent and accordingly, when America entered the First World War, hearing that I, her neighbor's son, would soon sail for France, decided something must be done for the youthful Navy pilot heading overseas. I received word before embarking to stop while in New York and pick up the best silver wrist watch Tiffany could offer. Taking kindly to this generous thought, I soon possessed one of Tiffany's finest, complete with seventeen jewels.

Soon thereafter, we arrived at the French seaplane base near Arcachon. The sand on the beaches there, however, was too much for my Tiffany masterpiece, and so when Saturday brought us our weekly day off in Bordeaux, I entrusted it to a woman watchmaker, a widow carrying on for her departed husband lost in the war. No receipt was needed, she explained. She would have the watch ready the following week, when we would again be in Bordeaux. But that following Saturday never came, for special orders sent us to Italy and after that to northern France. When the war ended, we returned to the U. S. A. without ever approaching Bordeaux. As I had neither the name nor address of the lady watchmaker, the Tiffany timepiece was clearly a casualty of the Great World War.

The following summer in Dublin, on meeting Mrs. Amory, I constantly had to cover my wrist. How could I ever explain? A year later, when I was again in Dublin, the dread of meeting Mrs. Amory was even more acute. Another such summer would be unbearable; something would have to be done, and I determined to send a post card. I remembered that the jewelry shop was two blocks down from the railroad station and one block across, and I drew a sketch on the address side of the postcard. A square marked *Gare du Nord* showed the station, and a diagram showing two streets down and one across ended in a second square marked *bijouterie* for the jewelry store. On the back, I inquired if the Tiffany watch left by the *pilote américain* could still somehow be traced. If Madame would kindly quote the charges I would gladly forward a check. Almost in no time a little box arrived from France, and inside was the missing watch, now as good as new. A small accompanying note explained Madame had always been sure the *jeune américain* was still alive, and would someday send for his watch. There would be no charge.

Now I could once more face Mrs. Amory.

The Dublin Lake Club was the center of most activities, and the principal event of the season was the annual fancy-dress ball there. My sister Edith was nearly my size, making it relatively easy for me to appear dressed as a girl. The slight discrepancy in my figure presented no serious difficulty, for this was a tennis club and tennis balls were plentiful.

My prolonged disgrace in Dublin was due to the misfortune that one of these needed props had not been adequately secured, and repairs became urgent. The dressing room to the left of the corridor was marked "gentlemen," but to one in my feminine attire the door to the right seemed more appropriate. My wig and my sister's dress would be my *cachet* for admittance. But I miscalculated; the uncooperative tennis ball must have caused my downfall. The powdering of feminine noses ceased abruptly when a maidenly scream signaled the exposure of the fraud. My disgrace continued for a considerable number of years.

Before we leave Dublin, one more occurrence should be chronicled.

Next to the fancy-dress party at the club, the most scintillating event, at least in the eyes of many, was the annual chauffeurs' ball held at the town hall. There were probably more servants and chauffeurs than summer residents in Dublin in those days— alas, days that failed to survive the advent of the income tax. Among the servants were always many comely Irish colleens, whose adornment on these gala occasions was usually supplemented from the wardrobes of their employers. To many in Dublin these town-hall festivities perceptibly outshone the affairs at the Dublin Lake Club. In the main event, the grand march, the question of protocol was a matter of great urgency, and precedence rested on the financial eminence—as nearly as could be determined—of each respective employer. The Dan Catlins, the George Markhams, both of St. Louis, were readily evaluated for this vital event. Their chauffeurs would be near the head of the line. The Winston chauffeurs, however, demanded precedence. Their boss, they argued, had liabilities exceeding two million dollars, a financial pinnacle no others could possibly match. The Winston chauffeurs always led the grand march.

X.

Making Hotels Pay

I

MAKING new and successful hotels out of old ones was even more exciting than making "almost" new Fords out of their predecessors while we were still at college. With hotels we could almost see the business grow as attractively decorated suites took the place of "tired" and sometimes threadbare facilities. While we sought new business through modernization, we could make inroads into the hotel's overhead by studying the operations.

Many preliminaries were often necessary to convert old and occasionally insolvent hotels into better and more profitable ones. First we made sure we had an able manager. The existing one, though he may not have been effective under former owners, often had all the needed skills and might simply have lacked an opportunity to exercise the talents he possessed. Sheraton allows its managers almost complete autonomy in the operation of hotels

On one unfortunate occasion this policy somehow backfired. A manager asked for forty thousand dollars to complete some unfinished rooms to take care of expanding business. The funds were appropriated, but the desired extra revenue was nowhere visible. The half-dozen rooms had been beautifully decorated and fully air-conditioned, costly features had been provided, a private revolving bar had been included to impress visiting V.I.P.s, yet no extra income was reported from the new luxury accommodations. Finally we investigated. When the glamour suite was completed, the manager, his wife, and four children had moved in.

Whenever a new hotel came into our ever-expanding fold, food and beverage departments received special attention, for these are the heart of a successful operation. Participation in Sheraton's central food-purchasing organization usually meant getting notably better quality at considerably lower cost. Pre-control system would reduce waste. Uniform portions could save thousands of dollars. And of course some padlocks strategically deployed, devices so effective at the Continental in Cambridge, were considered.

Payrolls of newly acquired hotels always needed study, though a union contract setting out the conditions of work would often limit what could be accomplished immediately. However, one strategem for dealing with excessive payrolls that might threaten the competitive position of a hotel was usually available. This consisted of rescheduling work hours so that the eight-hour day of one man would start perhaps an hour or two before the employee being relieved had finished his work. With such over-lapping timed to coincide with peak loads, two men could often do what formerly required three. Although we were rarely forced to discharge the extra man, we often could, through rescheduling, provide for the expanded business that advertising and added sales promotion was likely to attract, without increasing a once unwieldly payroll.

In almost all instances when a new hotel was added, Elmer Boswell, our general manager, would take over. First he would call a meeting of employees to outline plans for improvements. He would usually astonish the assembled staff by assuring them the new owners had neither cousins nor sons-in-law in profusion anxious to pre-empt their jobs. He would tell them the world was not really coming to an end, that actually a brighter future might lie ahead, one from which they might also benefit. Elmer has a magnetic quality which endears him to those with whom he works. After all, he started as a bellboy at the age of twelve.

Once the ritual of introductory meetings was over, progress was assured, for employees when they wish can greatly influence the success of a business enterprise.

One of Elmer's first activities was to examine the entire building, usually starting with an inspection of the employees' quarters. Kitchens, storage rooms, and employee dining rooms would be examined, with special emphasis on the help's locker rooms, showers, rest rooms, and other remote ramparts that even the more venturesome guest rarely sees. Elmer has long been aware that these shadowy regions are always the most neglected, and preparations for modernization usually start in some of these nether regions. Experience has convinced him that unless employees have good surroundings, we are unlikely to get the desired results. Often at our Boston headquarters we observed that initial requisitions for some newly acquired hotel called for items such as ventilating equipment, new paints in the Mary Kennedy tradition, modern shower heads, or other embellishments for areas guests may never know exist.

After preliminaries are dealt with, other parts of the house receive attention. This is when Mary Kennedy takes over. Her objective is to produce an assortment of lures designed, mostly through the use of pleasing effects, to entice ever larger numbers of guests to Sheraton hotels. Colors and decorative materials, furniture, equipment, and all other ingredients of a hotel's decor come under her jurisdiction. When budgets for improvements are up for consideration we not only calculate the direct benefits to the new hotel, we also consider the effect on all Sheraton guests of observing improvements in a hotel's appearance when "Sheraton," followed by a mandatory hyphen, is added to the former designation. This is part of a subtle campaign to convince customers they should expect more than the ordinary when a prominent eighteenth-century furniture designer's name is appended to a newly purchased hotel.

Although Sheraton's managers have much autonomy, an exception is made in the delicate realm of color selection, for this remains an exclusive Mary Kennedy prerogative.

Mrs. Kennedy has a useful rule for determining the degree of perfection her decorative art has achieved. Her success can be measured with surprising accuracy by the extent of that agreeable and restful feeling one experiences on entering a room after it has had her particular brand of treatment. Whether or not guests are connoisseurs in the controversial sphere of taste, if, on entering a refurbished room, they are pleasantly and consciously at ease, Mary knows her objective has been attained.

Although attractive rooms increase materially the volume of business, other devices also help restore a hotel's earning capacity. Surveys of mechanical and electrical facilities, for instance, are often quite productive. The presiding genius directing this activity is Fred Kummer, whose greatest joy in life is the pursuit of losses he can discover, analyze, and eventually eliminate. Sometimes, with an air of regret, when another hotel comes into our chain, Fred sadly concedes, "This time, we can't save more than a few thousand dollars." Our predecessors, he complains, have done too good a job. On other occasions Fred beams with delight. The possibility of a hundred thousand in savings produces a king-sized sparkle in his gleaming eyes.

Fred can discover amazing discrepancies in operations under his jurisdiction. I recall when coal for a certain hotel was costing far more than his estimate of normal consumption. He soon found the trouble. To each truckload of soft coal delivered, nearly a ton of water had been added just before the weight was recorded. Soft coal can absorb enormous amounts of moisture. It must have been a profitable account for some eager purveyor, though expensive for one of our smaller hotels.

Fred faced a far more difficult problem when he noted the staggering cost of water at one of our resort hotels. Ten thousand dollars a year, enough, perhaps, for a second hotel, were vanishing mysteriously. Sherlock Holmes could hardly have faced a more baffling mystery. How could so much water disappear? "Elementary," must have been Fred's conclusion. It must be going somewhere. Fred was going to find it.

Several workmen one morning started shoveling, under our engineer's direction, and a six-foot trench gradually surrounded the entire building. The quest was not in vain, for they uncovered a large pipe leading in the general direction of a competing hotel. Water could be heard flowing in the pipe. The line was cut, immediately water consumption decreased and ten thousand dollars a year would be saved. We observed no visible repercussions, yet occasionally we wondered if guests at a nearby hotel might not have encountered trouble the next day in drawing their accustomed bath.

We had many devices for improving hotel operations. A favorite among these, when results were less than satisfactory, was to organize what we called "flying squadrons." These were in the nature of task forces recruited from among our Boston executives, designed to improve operations to a level we considered theoretically attainable. "Wrecking crews" was a less complimentary term applied by some of the hotels singled out for such concentrated attention.

The usual roadblock confronting our hard-hitting forces that often converged on the less profitable units was the oft-repeated contention that "here things are different." We were repeatedly told that what could be done in New York or Boston would not necessarily work in Akron or perhaps Detroit. Sooner or later our persistent "wrecking crews" would disprove these recurring alibis. If food costs, for instance, could be held to thirty-two per cent of sales in one Sheraton city without impairment of quality, our flying squadrons would soon demonstrate that a forty-five-per-cent figure was not necessarily indigenous to some other geographical region.

Four or five members usually constituted these trouble-shooting groups. Elmer Boswell, boss of all hotels, and Bob Brush, second in command, were *ex officio* participants. Others might include specialists such as Joe Haddock, head of purchasing, or perhaps Bob Kelsey, our chief accountant. We never knew just what talents were needed; but the important point was that the monthly earnings of hotels marked for such specialized consideration usually responded adequately to these occasional, though sometimes unwelcome intrusions.

Other Boston experts available to hotel managers would also be within reach. One of these, Bud Smith, heads our hard-hitting sales division, a group dedicated to the unwritten law that, if business is in sight, a Sheraton salesman must nail it down. It was Bud who sired the lusty brainchild better known as the Sheraton Sales Blitz.

This unique phenomenon was doubtless influenced by the theory that, though rifles can cause much havoc, shotguns with many more pellets cover a wider range. Bud Smith's powerful Sales Blitzes partake mostly of the nature of saturation bombing, rather than depending on the effectiveness of a few well-aimed missiles.

Each Sheraton hotel has its own sales staff, and so Bud can draft recruits from different units for concentration on a city marked for attack. Like a swarm of hungry grasshoppers closing in on a helpless cornfield, the twenty-odd participants in a standard Sheraton Blitz cover every likely prospect in a radius of many miles. Any conceivable victim, though he may be only remotely interested in some banquet, business meeting, or social gathering, would have little chance to escape. Bud, the commander-in-chief, maps the deadly strategy, personally leading his cohorts into the field, inspiring them with added encouragement when they are about to tangle with such remaining sales resistance as a reluctant prospect can muster.

The results of these blitzes are always dramatic. Whereas Napoleon measured battles in terms of enemy losses or guns captured, Bud counts his successes by the number of conventions booked, or the banquets, weddings, and meetings his task force is able to snare. Thousands of credit-card applications are always a part of the spoils, and business captured from a competitor adds to the joy of victory. Today the Sheraton Blitz is a firmly rooted tradition, a tool that others might wisely try.

Besides engineering and sales, other staff activities are maintained in Boston to provide assistance when this is needed. Our newest supporting service, under the direction of Frank Petrie, was created to provide intensive training for all Sheraton employees. The hotel industry has been slow to attain the perfection travelers expect from the domestic airlines, and hotels can rarely match the charm and glamour provided by pretty airline stewardesses. Sheraton decided to consider this deficiency.

Frank, who was formerly associated with the aviation industry, perhaps visualizes lovely feminine sirens, garbed in stewardess uniforms, adorning our registration desks. This, however, I doubt will come to pass, for Sheraton's desk clerks are a highly prized asset. The absence of the accustomed greeting from behind a registration desk, a touch of friendliness so many cherish, could undo much of the good will millions of dollars in advertising have sought to create. However, seeing Petrie in action is an informative experience. Managers, as well as top Boston brass, often participate in his interesting meetings, and our personnel enthusiastically receive his glowing descriptions of the greatness of our country and the benefits of our free-enterprise system. He explains the advantages of those little extra constructive efforts, not only to the workers themselves, but also to hotels and to the public we try to serve. These exhortations, never aimed at employee unions, are an exciting inspiration.

Petrie's goal is to foster in Sheraton employees that pride of accomplishment which adds so much to the enjoyment of one's daily work while also improving the prospects for advancement. Many of those interested in Sheraton's progress are discovering that, even if transactions such as buying a Beaconsfield hotel on a shoestring and selling at a million-dollar profit are spectacular, training and motivating twenty thousand Sheraton men and women to advance themselves, their company, and thus the economic strength of their nation can be even more exciting.

On returning from a visit to our Sheraton-Carlton in Washington, Frank Petrie once commented on the limited opportunity that hotel afforded for plying his usual trade. Training its able personnel in the value of courtesy was like trying to teach science to Albert Einstein. A popular bellman at the Sheraton-Carlton, one who perhaps enjoys a speaking acquaintance with more celebrities than almost anyone in the nation's capital, expressed the situation succinctly when conversing with our director of personnel training. "You see," admitted the perceptive bellman, "we already is a plush outfit."

2

At times people ask what has contributed most to Sheraton's progress during twenty-two years of hotel operations. It is naturally a difficult question. If pressed for an answer, I believe it would be, "Finding ways to measure results."

In the field of mechanics, tools for determining performance, such as gauges, meters, and scales, are readily available. Science leans heavily on such instruments for providing information. Business must also measure the performance of companies, of departments, or of various individuals, and many aids for such measurement are already at hand. Daily, monthly, and annual financial reports are constantly in use. But these rarely provide all information needed to measure what managements may seek to accomplish.

Sheraton's statistical department is trying to fill this gap. It is headed by John Wood, a man skilled in marshaling data required for graphs, charts, comparisons, statistics, and other devices for evaluating company performance. Interpretation, however, is not an exact science, and errors sometimes arise or overlooked factors cause distortion. But if a company's "batting average"—its ratio of useful to unwise decisions—is high, progress is usually satisfactory. Measuring performance frequently provides the most direct path to making constructive decisions.

Nearly a year ago we selected twenty-two categories of activities that gave promise of opportunities for improvement. In each instance means were at hand for measuring the progress achieved.

"Operation Pay Dirt" was the name we gave this program, for we were to dig deep for possible profitable veins. With the public demanding that prices stay down, with twenty thousand Sheraton workers asking for higher pay, and with fifteen thousand stockholders—the almost forgotten investors whose dollars financed the business—clamoring for more dividends, management must constantly find means for increasing company earnings. Operation Pay Dirt gave promise of discouraging waste while attempting to expand the volume of sales.

Each of the twenty-two Pay Dirt activities came under the jurisdiction of a different Boston executive, most of these juniors not theretofore exposed to opportunities for creating measurable results that could demonstrate their executive skills. Each project was assigned a theoretically attainable goal. If all objectives are reached, we may salvage or create a million and three-quarters extra dollars. But the value of the program may exceed the actual tangible dollars sought, for it may develop latent executive talents in twenty-two future Sheraton leaders, an even more important accomplishment.

The smallest of the Pay Dirt projects seeks to save fifty thousand dollars a year. If this is achieved, none but the utility companies should complain, for this project attempts to reduce by three million kilowatt-hours the annual consumption of unneeded electrical energy. Lights in storage rooms, for instance, must be extinguished when not actually required. Smoothing out peak electrical loads that add to so-called "demand charges," or substituting lower-horsepower motors for ones of excessive capacity, could help the cause. Since this savings program started, we find lights in our home-office corridors more promptly extinguished when closing time is reached. If similar attrition in unneeded kilowatts is achieved in all the hotels and office buildings, we should easily exceed our optimistic expectations.

A more ambitious objective followed the discovery that repainting hotel rooms, which is necessary every two and a half years, was either done by outside contractors or accomplished inefficiently by a hotel's own employees. Newer stopwatch techniques mean Sheraton managers, armed with modern time-study data, can now place painters economically on their hotel payrolls and can determine with precision the required output per worker, and the number of these needed to provide every hotel room, once each two and a half years, with necessary attention. Figures compiled by statistician John Wood point to probable savings of two hundred thousand dollars a year, thanks to the miracle of item number four on our Operation Pay Dirt chart.

These savings of two hundred thousand dollars could provide a reduction of two cents a day per occupied room in the price we must charge the public; or else they could mean a wage increase of a half-cent an hour for twenty thousand workers. Should the savings instead be added to earnings, fifteen thousand shareholders, even after the tax collector received his due, could expect two cents more a share, or a tenth of one per cent larger return on the market value of their investment. These figures may seem trivial. It is management's task to magnify them by seeking ever more opportunities to discharge its obligation to labor, owners, and the public.

Each of the twenty-two Pay Dirt projects is well under way, and once a month statisticians record with impressive red lines on master Pay Dirt charts the progress toward our objective. As results are periodically tabulated, I believe junior executives, especially those destined to achieve outstanding success, watch the red lines on the performance chart with the enthusiasm more often accorded baseball statistics when the major-leagues season is on. Recent advances in the red lines on our Pay Dirt chart suggest ninety-five per cent of our million and three-quarters goal is likely to be reached.

Nearly every proposed Sheraton activity is examined carefully to see if results can readily be measured. Projects that permit accurate determination of progress are more likely to receive management approval. But saving waste and promoting sales, no matter how effective, must be supplemented by other means if maximum results are desired. Some of these can be quite interesting.

3

For hotels to be profitable it is essential that money spent in dining rooms and cocktail lounges finally reaches the hotel coffers. To insure this desired sequence, we sometimes recruit professional "shoppers," but definitely not too often. Once they are recognized, their usefulness approaches zero.

In cocktail lounges these pseudo-guests often work in pairs. One may sit in a distant corner, interested only in the contents of a glass reposing in front of him. The other, an apparent stranger, enters later and orders some drinks at the bar, leaves the money with a generous tip on the counter, and calmly staggers out, taking no heed whatsoever of the cash register, or whether it responded to the financial aspect of the transaction. The seemingly disinterested man in the corner, often to the dismay of an erring bartender, was actually quite observant. Such research by teams of shoppers often reveals how little a manager can take for granted if he is really anxious to succeed.

Perhaps one reason hotels so often did poorly in the past was that managers were far too certain that "this could never happen here."

While many Sheraton Hotels are constantly being modernized, upgraded, and rendered more efficient, new ones are frequently added to the chain, for all of us are eager to see the company grow. No matter how many hotels comprise the Sheraton system, we are always anxious to see gaps filled in—to see hotels acquired in cities where Sheraton was not previously represented. More hotels make possible greater specialization in our central supervisory organization; they mean more opportunity to channel business to other hotels in the system, and more central purchasing and increased budgets for national advertising. The company truly thrives upon expansion.

XI.

More Hotels for Sheraton

A N important addition to the Sheraton family came in 1954, when the Palace Hotel in San Francisco became the Sheraton-Palace. Even the name "Sheraton" with a small hyphen attached nearly sparked a revolution in the city of the Golden Gate, for the Palace had been a part of the local tradition since the early decades following the great gold rush.

The original Palace, erected in the eighteen-seventies, was surely in its day the greatest hotel in the world. Built literally out of the silver nuggets wrested from the Comstock Lode, it was far too large and magnificent for the youthful city that surrounded it. It would have been difficult in those days to find a world celebrity unfamiliar with at least some of its magnificent suites.

Into the great garden court, glass-enclosed and fitted with magnificent crystal chandeliers, were driven the victorias or broughams of the day to discharge the elite of San Francisco. We even hear that in those early lusty days an overpass connected, perhaps indiscreetly, one of the hotel's floors with a residence across the street; but that any impropriety was involved is stoutly denied by descendants of the early owners.

The original builders of the Palace were unusually foresighted in planning for the hotel's protection should disaster ever strike. Suspecting a possible geological fault, they had anticipated the danger of fire following some especially troublesome temblor. The possible threat of broken water mains in the wake of a disaster could mean fighting flames with no suitable water supply. To meet even this contingency, the builders of what was to be the world's finest hotel had taken, they thought, quite adequate precautions. Constructed of strong materials, the hotel should withstand the fiercest of earthquakes, but as an added measure, underneath the hotel some indestructible tanks were installed, capable of holding a million gallons of water. The Palace was to be immune to earth convulsions and any possible aftermath.

On April 18, 1906, the San Francisco holocaust broke out. At the time it was doubtless one of the worst catastrophes in recorded history, the damage reaching a half-billion dollars at a period when the word "billion" still commanded respect. The foresight of the builders of the Palace paid off. Though heavily jolted by the shattering shock, the magnificent structure was essentially intact, and prided itself on serving breakfast—with some complications, to be sure—on that disastrous morning. Confusion had reigned as illustrious guests converged, clearly somewhat bewildered, upon the famous lobby. Present among these was Enrico Caruso, clutching some treasured possessions. He had been less meticulous, it seems, about saving other necessaries—such, for instance, as a pair of pants.

As the hotel recovered from the lethal blow which shook the very bowels of the earth, and as the flames farther downtown relentlessly rushed onward, the owners could be grateful for the foresight of the builders. City water, as expected, gave out, but the hotel's million gallons remained intact. Not even advancing flames should endanger a structure so meticulously planned. But her ever-cautious designers had not foreseen everything. Downtown municipal buildings were in the path of the fire, but their builders had lacked the foresight of the planners of the majestic Palace, and water, available in the stricken city only in the reservoirs of the great hotel, was seized by the city fathers. Fortified by the declaration of martial law, they could take what they wanted. The priceless waters from the cisterns of the great Palace were carefully carted away in a futile attempt to stem spreading downtown flames; and so the noble Palace became a sacrifice to the growing devastation.

Following the destruction of this once famous landmark, a new and even greater Palace arose from the ashes of its predecessor. The new hotel, once again provided with enormous underground reservoirs, was endowed with an even more extravagant garden court, though one no longer accessible to the vehicles of its distinguished clientele. Nearly all the Presidents from Teddy Roosevelt through Truman occupied its resplendent Presidential Suite, just as earlier Presidents frequented the one in the original Palace. A grand piano in a corner of the present Presidential quarters still responds at times to strains of the "Missouri Waltz" as interpreted by Presidential fingers.

After Sheraton acquired the famous Palace, Molly and I spent a night there, much impressed with the historical background and that of its eminent predecessor.

"How did you sleep?" Manager Edmond Rieder inquired as we came down the following morning.

"Very well," we assured him cheerfully.

He seemed surprised. "You say you slept well?" he asked, looking somewhat dubious, so we inquired, "Why?"

"Oh," said Rieder, "I only wondered. You see, you slept in the bed in which President Harding died."

Although the shock to San Franciscans of seeing the name Sheraton attached by a deliberate hyphen to their greatly cherished Palace can have fallen but a little short of causing the havoc of a second earthquake, nonetheless business was picking up. Our predecessors, we felt, had been more intent on maintaining the traditions of the past than the vitality of the profit-and-loss statement. When those innovations known as advertising and sales promotion burst upon the hotel world, rumor had it that the former Palace management felt it should never stoop to such questionable devices, and anyway "One must not let competitors know the Palace needed business."

Bob Hope, I believe it was, gave us some welcome though unsolicited attention. Having just returned from England, he was asked in a television interview how he had found things in London. Casually he remarked that nothing had really changed. The royal palace had not yet become the Sheraton-Buckingham.

Making the Sheraton-Palace pay involved further embroilment with tradition. The principal remaining bastion of the full French cuisine, exemplified by the superb service in the Garden Court, was producing valuable publicity. Gourmets like Lucius Beebe could wax magnificently eloquent in the elite magazines over the prowess of Lucien in preparing such formidable delicacies as *Poitrine de Pintades sous Cloche*. But even the golden flow of highly prized publicity could not stem the tide of mounting deficits arising from an unwillingness of San Francisco gourmets to sustain on a financially feasible level this relic of a bygone gastronomic age. Amid editorial wails from a quite vocal press, understandably reluctant to see an era of splendor disappear, names of dishes once associated with great French chefs were beginning to yield, on the Garden Court menus, to lamb chops and string beans. We may have participated in a near-fatal thrust at one of San Francisco's treasured traditions, but, if committing this indiscretion was inescapable, it at least partially restored some needed luster to the hotel's once meager monthly earnings reports. With ever higher wages demanded by thousands of Sheraton employees, and the public unhappy over rising room rates, it is no longer possible to maintain all the costly traditions that sentiment once dictated. Harsh economic facts relentlessly require recognition.

Much attention, of course, was focused on delicate public relations in San Francisco, as well as in other cities where Sheraton was acquiring new hotels. Intrusion of a hotel chain into such a touchy matter as operating a local hostelry was always likely to be suspect, and maintaining good community relations was necessarily an important consideration for us. But while we were mindful of the urgency of such problems, other matters also demanded attention if growth was to be encouraged. Further acquisitions must be considered. Expansion was often the responsibility of Bob Moore, now chairman of our board, and devising unorthodox approaches to opportunities for new acquisitions was one of his many delights.

2

On one occasion Bob Moore's approach to the question of expansion was at least original in our business world, for he borrowed from Aristotle's techniques to further the fortunes of Sheraton.

A priori reasoning, a cherished device in the Aristotelian repertoire, is often thought of as belonging to the world of eminent philosophers bent on making difficult the life of struggling college students. However, reaching conclusions by deductive processes from a given collection of circumstances is not restricted to philosophical scholars probing the reaches of the human mind. It has also served more tangible ends—several million dollars' worth, to be precise. Bob Moore, a dozen years ago, buried himself in one of those forbidding financial compilations known as Standard and Poor's manuals, which contain financial data covering almost every significant American corporation—not even excluding those in bankruptcy. It was one of the latter that caught Bob's attention as he looked over the huge volumes. Using the *a priori* approach, he deduced that opportunity was knocking. By merely examining the financial statistics of a now obscure company, especially earnings figures which were very red, and by reading of its shrinking activities, he concluded that here was an enterprise that could arouse thoughts of possible corporate marriage.

The not too reluctant potential bride Bob had discovered was the U. S. Realty and Improvement Company. Early in the nineteen-twenties it was a speculative favorite, an enterprise of considerable magnitude, but more recently its affairs had fallen on somewhat unfertile soil. The great depression had taken a heavy toll. Bob wrote the receiver, presenting a daring program, without even seeing the properties involved. The two companies, he suggested, could be merged by assigning a quarter of the shares of the combined companies to former U. S. Realty shareholders; the balance would go to Sheraton. Active negotiations followed, and a plan was approved by the courts. Soon the U. S. Realty assets were a part of the Sheraton system. Some tax benefits, added assets to work with, and an opportunity to improve the earnings of the former U. S. Realty properties—all these advantages, worth millions to Sheraton, were the results of perusing an obscure financial story of a nearly forgotten company. A similar approach may perhaps have been followed by a former schoolmate who once attended Noble and Greenough in Boston with me. Royal Little of Providence, Rhode Island, made impressive financial history by creating his Textron empire.

3

Among recent additions to Sheraton's group of hotels was one of which we had often heard. It was the French Lick Springs Hotel, currently the French Lick Sheraton, and eventually, should we dare to shorten the title further, the Sheraton-Springs Hotel. This property is in Southern Indiana and dates back to an era when Senator Tom Taggart was the proud owner. The latter, a pronounced dry when in Washington, was not averse to seeing his hotel venture prosper, and gambling flourished at this famous resort. But after the Senator's death, less happy days ensued. The famous hotel, foreclosed upon because of a disposition to omit necessary interest payments, languished for years in the unhappy possession of one of New England's great insurance companies. Seventeen hundred acres of land, the makings of an artificial lake, a shooting range, bridle paths, sulphur baths for curing all known ailments, and finally two championship golf courses—all these attractions were almost forgotten. Without the magnetism of a Tom Taggart, augmented by the lure of games of chance, the large brick buildings were nearly deserted.

Back in the days of the hotel's former splendor the purgative properties of the local mineral waters were heavily exploited. To meet the inevitable reaction that the makers of Pluto Water, which is still bottled on the premises, practically guaranteed, rustic structures were erected in proper profusion at appropriate intervals along the paths frequented by elderly guests. These small but necessary havens, dedicated no doubt to Chick Sale, were always equipped with the symbol of a half-moon crescent cut in the upper half of the door. Under the influence of Pluto, it was assumed, lightning was sure to strike, and under such circumstances there was little time for spotting an available refuge not previously bolted from within. Accordingly, the custom evolved among elderly guests, always armed with walking-canes, of hanging these tokens of occupancy outside the privy doors, handles hooked in the conveniently provided crescents. Thus an unoccupied sanctuary could readily be spotted. For years the management had prided itself on having sufficient retreats to preclude any calamities, but eventually an emergency did arise. An evil genius, perhaps a political opponent, somehow acquired a quantity of walking-sticks and hung them, one by one, on all unencumbered cubicle doors. Unsuspecting guests on their accustomed morning stroll suddenly faced a series of most catastrophic disasters bearing vivid testimony to the infallibility of the little Pluto Water flasks each guest room so thoughtfully provided.

Sheraton's original investment in the six-hundred-room French Lick Hotel was small, little more than a million dollars for a hotel that must once have earned nearly that much each year. Remodeling, air-conditioning, and modernizing the premises to attain the needed luxury rating cost many times the purchase price, but the investment was worth while. Our rule of two dollars in value from each dollar of improvements was not violated, for the hotel is once more a great success. Its objectives, however, have changed. Few guests today are interested in cures, or in seeking fortunes at nonexistent gaming tables.

Doubtless General Manager Connolly can still assure prospective guests who are victims of any suspected ailment that the hotel's sulphur baths will effect miraculous cures—particularly if occupancy is running low; however, the principal business is now conventions. These include business gatherings and other kinds of meetings far from city distractions, where the latest sales pitch or some similar corporate objective can be disseminated on a mass-distribution basis. During the summer months, when, despite new air-conditioning installations, group meetings tend to fall off, a hotel-inspired midwestern Jazz Festival and later a more intellectual Music Festival bring thousands of Midwesterners a taste of the arts the East heretofore sought to monopolize. Such leading performers as Duke Ellington and Arthur Fiedler have both been major attractions. The Sheraton-Springs Hotel—as we hope it will someday be

[133]

called—is definitely one of the brighter stars in the Sheraton constellation.

4

An experience we often look back upon with considerable pleasure was the acquisition in St. Louis of the former Jefferson Hotel, now the Sheraton-Jefferson. The Hilton Company, with two hotels in that city, wished to avoid controversy over possible diminished competition and decided to sell. Our experience with our chief competitor was most friendly. Mr. Hilton, who personally took charge of negotiations, we found charming and a tough though eminently fair "opponent." When the deal was finally closed and the details all agreed upon, we discovered among the hotel's inventories, paid for according to the terms of the contract, though presumably without Mr. Hilton's knowledge, quite a few copies of *The Silver Spade*, an interesting book recounting the achievements of our industry's leading figure. The new Sheraton-Jefferson manager, doubtless of Scotch derivation, must have felt his investment in *The Silver Spade* should henceforth pay dividends to Sheraton. As long as the supply lasted, guests would find on their night tables, as an added attraction at our St. Louis hotel, a free copy of *The Silver Spade*, recounting the glories of Conrad Hilton, courtesy of the Sheraton Corporation of America.

One more reference to Conrad Hilton will not, I hope, sever friendly relations. Bradford Washburn, Boston's famous scientist and mountain-climber, once came to the Hendersons' for dinner bearing a mysterious gift. Removing the ribbon and wrapper, we saw a box with a beautiful glass cover. Inside was a lethal-looking object mounted with the skill to be expected of one who headed our Boston Museum of Science. Much larger than a cockroach and seemingly far more ferocious, the creature inside, to our chagrin, was finally identified as only a praying mantis. The inscription inside proclaimed: "Captured by Bradford Washburn on the Bedspread of a New York Hilton Hotel." Unfortunately the date was included, but we hoped no one would recall August 31, 1954, as the occasion of the exuberance of Hurricane Carol, a wicked maiden that may have wafted this curious creature from some uncouth Caribbean island into an open New York hotel window. Had the date been more graciously omitted, I might have divided with Brad Washburn the kingly ransom that so priceless a possession might have brought within reach.

XII.

Hotel Managers

NOTHING is more important to the success of a hotel than the skill of an able manager. Selecting managers by means of screening can eliminate some unlikely prospects, and attendance at a prominent hotel school such as the one at Cornell University can add measurably to the prospects for success. But even the most effective training and the most minute screening can never guarantee the outstanding performance, nor assure that spark of genius, that distinguishes so many of our able managers. Trial-and-error is our best mechanism for providing an effective guide, but this procedure is not infallible.

A pitfall of trial-and-error lies in the possibility that managers, when carrying out assignments, may achieve exceptional results —either good or bad. If these results were due to unusual though perhaps unrecognized circumstances, they could give rise to unwarranted conclusions and cause serious injustice to a manager or possible heavy loss to the company. Some former Sheraton managers who later were most successful in other hotels furnish convincing evidence of occasional flaws in our trial-and-error technique.

Once, under the harsh dictates of trial-and-error, a Sheraton manager "resigned" because the hotel he directed was making less than the desired progress. After some months of idleness, probably spent in contemplating the mysteries of certain corporate actions, this manager was invited to return to Sheraton at a substantial advance in salary and at a more important hotel. Despite understandable reluctance, he accepted the job, and for years the relationship that followed was most profitable. The feelings of this able operator were perhaps partially assuaged when he heard of the difficulties his successor encountered in the hotel where results had disappointed us.

Although occasional injustices occur—rarely now, we hope—the existence of such hazards is compensated in part by the generous incomes able managers command.

The unprecedented growth of Sheraton during twenty-two years is a singular tribute to outstanding managers, men performing brilliantly for the benefit of fellow employees, the traveling public, company stockholders, and government tax collectors—all with a stake in good management. The care we devote to selecting managers is characteristic of a competitive free-enterprise economy, a system sensitive to pressures and incentives for accomplishment. Perhaps our care in choosing these men whose talents are so vital to effective utilization of human, physical, and financial resources, is a telling argument against socialistic economic systems in which politics, favoritism, and the doctrine of seniority rather than ability are too often yardsticks for managerial promotions.

Among managers with a niche in Sheraton's Hall of Fame, Ralph Freeman is high on the list. For many years he managed our Park Sheraton Hotel on 56th Street on New York's West Side. Prejudiced as we are, we have rarely bracketed this hotel in matters of prestige with the stately Waldorf Astoria, yet under Ralph's able direction it came surprisingly close to rivaling that famous East Side establishment on the basis of "cash flow." This term, as the reader may discover, we use in preference to "reported earnings," for it puts Sheraton, with a tendency toward high depreciation reserves, in a more favorable competitive light. Cash flow we define as reported earnings with depreciation added back. Parenthetically, our recent audits show Sheraton as enjoying the highest cash flow ever recorded by any hotel system.

Ralph Freeman died recently while still quite young, and his death was a personal as well as a corporate loss. Gone was an important asset, though one not recorded on the balance sheets. That Sheraton quotations on the stock exchange failed to dip a point or two when Ralph died simply confirms a lack of omniscience on the part of stock-market investors.

Attending his wake in the undertaking establishment of the faith he had just adopted was a memorable experience, and the large attendance marked the high esteem of his friends. His estranged wife, unknown to most of us, was present. Bigwigs, municipal and from the business world, attended. Pathetic, modestly sitting in a corner, engulfed in heartrending sobs, was a lovely yet lonely young woman clad in very somber black. Later, when the generous proceeds of company life-insurance policies were ready for distribution, legal rigidity precluded taking account of the touching drama witnessed in that tragic funeral parlor.

While Ralph Freeman managed the Park Sheraton in New York his most illustrious guest was Eleanor Roosevelt, who occupied a suite for several years. Due to frequent television broadcasts from her Park Sheraton address, the hotel's prestige began to rise, doubtless even among Republicans. Mrs. Roosevelt was especially liked by members of the staff, to whom she was always gracious. On one occasion, at Christmastime, the extent of her generosity may have exceeded her calculations. Christmas trees are grown on the Roosevelt Hyde Park estate, and word went out that any employee who wished might receive such a gift from the much-admired former First Lady. Perhaps she was thinking in terms of thirty or forty employees, the number usually visible to most of the guests. Actually hotel employees resemble icebergs, six-sevenths of them being usually below the surface, mostly remaining unseen. I suspect it surprised Mrs. Roosevelt when close to eight hundred Park Sheraton men and women accepted her generosity.

Another event occurred at the Park Sheraton many years ago. Elmer Boswell, a Sheraton senior vice president spending the night there, was heading for the elevators to retire when he observed a commotion near the popular Mermaid Room, where joviality usually reigns until early-morning hours. Music of recording orchestras from a slowly rotating platform, together with other customary adjuncts to a successful supper-room atmosphere, was providing pleasure for the patrons. A guest, as occurs on rare occasions, had enjoyed himself beyond the limits of normal tolerance and was being escorted to the sidewalk with whatever "persuasiveness" the occasion seemed to demand. Elmer, observing the somewhat indelicate scene, approached the uncooperative guest and coaxed him to a mezzanine office rather than see him abandoned to a cold and inhospitable sidewalk. Strong coffee, supplemented by some fatherly words, effected a prompt revival, and the guest, realizing his indiscretion, became most apologetic.

Strangely enough, on the following morning—for the indiscreet reveler turned out to be a guest—he came down looking for Elmer. "I want you to know," he told our vice president, "I will never forget your kindness." And in this he kept his word. As head of a large organization, he personally booked at various of our hotels, from companies with which he was affiliated, more than a half-million dollars' worth of group business. Elmer, I suspect, gladly concedes that the Boy Scout approach pays surprisingly large dividends.

Another candidate for recognition among Sheraton's able managers is Albert Fox, who heads the Sheraton-Belvedere in

Baltimore. His notable success, we assume, comes from achieving the pre-eminence of an impeccable perfectionist. Even a pin lurking on a lobby Oriental rug (other hotels use broadloom) would prompt Albert to stoop and remove it. As a result, each employee, usually a mirror of the manager's character, can be counted on to emulate his meticulosity. The Sheraton-Belvedere is a testimonial to the mousetrap theory, for its manager for years has been aware that careful attention to details can beat a path to his registration desk. Few travelers to Baltimore, we fondly assume, fail to tender the accolade for perfection to the hotel headed by Albert Fox.

However, as the years went by, occasional flies appeared in the Albert Fox ointment, ones that must often have led the sometimes harassed perfectionist to consider his green copper roof as a possible taking-off place for a jump. Unions and the N.A.A.C.P. were his principal *bêtes noires*.

Some years ago the unions, organizations not always accorded a welcome mat when knocking at the doors of Baltimore hotels, suddenly discovered an entering wedge. Sheraton, with other hotels in more "pliable" territory, could occasionally be argued with, whereas competing Baltimore hotels could better insulate themselves from unsolicited encroachment. Because of this greater vulnerability, Sheraton was the first to succumb.

Albert Fox, on learning the unions had won their election, must have contemplated his corner on the mansard roof. Though doubtless expecting the end of the world, he apparently decided to wait and see if his worst fears would be confirmed. To his great surprise, perhaps because higher wages made his men more willing to work, fewer employees on shorter hours actually produced more, and the Belvedere annual balance sheet continued to reflect the progress to which, under Fox's able direction, all had become accustomed. The copper roof was probably forgotten, at least until the next crisis loomed.

The next emergency, actually, was soon to reach a crucial stage.

A company plan to discourage waste in its food operations was designed to recapture a million dollars a year. Known as a system of "pre-control," it demanded accurate forecasting of food covers needed in the days immediately ahead. Under the rigors of this plan, should two hundred *filets mignons* be required to embellish some lush banquet, the time-honored custom of providing fifty extra portions to preclude a danger of shortage would now come to an end. Not that there was any doubt the extra portions could be used; the question was, with kindhearted chefs and hungry employees at hand, by whom? Henceforth, under the dictates of pre-control, five extra *filets mignons* would suffice.

The objective of pre-control was to reduce the food cost percentage, that crucial ratio of cost to sales, by at least two percentage points. With a yearly volume of fifty millions in our total food operations, two percentage points would mean a cool million dollars. Even Uncle Sam could happily cock an ear; he takes fifty-two cents in taxes from every dollar we earn.

Albert Fox reacted to this pre-control "nonsense" perhaps as warmly as a sixteen-year-old girl might respond to her first stolen kiss. He was horrified. Gourmets are understandably suspicious of schemes to reduce the cost of food. The higher echelons of those seeking culinary perfection are traditionally fearful of devices that could tarnish a hard-earned reputation for gastronomic pre-eminence. Reluctantly Fox capitulated, though doubtless with deep misgivings, and the pre-control system was introduced in Baltimore. A year later, noting that Belvedere food sales were still on a high plateau and that costs had fallen by the prescribed amount, we gingerly asked how the system was working. Were there any serious complaints?

"Well," Mr. Fox conceded reluctantly, "not from the guests." From an unexpected source, however, trouble had come. The garbage collector had canceled his contract. The pigs, he complained, were no longer satisfied.

Fox's thoughts must have turned for a third time to his hotel roof when the N.A.A.C.P. took an interest in his operations. Those who contemplate troubles in Little Rock should not forget Baltimore. Sheraton, in accord with other leading hotel systems, had adopted a liberal policy on matters of racial equality, but Baltimore remained a stumbling-block. That city, still a barrier to N.A.A.C.P. aspirations, was naturally a citadel many were eager to crack. A few disturbing incidents when bars were momentarily lowered suggest progress on this sensitive front could perhaps be achieved more surely by advancing more slowly. And so I suspect Fox still maintains clear the approaches to his roof. However, despite difficulties, real or imagined, which often seem to beset him, Albert Fox has made the Sheraton-Belvedere one of the nation's great hotels.

Years ago, when we bought the Wendell Hotel in Pittsfield, Massachusetts, an important part of the transaction was a desk clerk included among the assets of that enterprise. Young, attractive, and able, Lloyd Carswell was soon singled out by Elmer Boswell for promotion. Elmer had a keen eye for potential managerial talent.

After promotion from desk clerk to assistant manager, rapid-fire advances followed. From assistant manager to resident manager, traditionally the number-two command, came next, and soon Lloyd Carswell had the title of general manager. A series of transfers to ever larger hotels followed, and when the new Philadelphia Sheraton was completed, Lloyd was its general manager. To progress from an unknown desk clerk in a small hotel to the head of one of Sheraton's newest and one of the world's finest took Lloyd little more than eight years. Presently in Honolulu, he is now directing our four newly acquired Waikiki Beach hotels.

Lloyd has the unusual talent of combining the attributes of a genial host with the acumen of an able business administrator, a combination rare in the hotel industry. The days of the charming Boniface popular with all but those who view the financial reports are rapidly coming to an end. He has gradually given way to the highly trained hotel executive skilled in directing a complex business enterprise. Established in Philadelphia only a short time, the Carswells became accepted by all segments of top Philadelphia circles, including, no doubt, the Main Liners, a circumstance that certainly did not handicap a large metropolitan hotel. History will perhaps repeat itself in Honolulu.

Another manager sharing with Carswell a reputation for ability as a businessman enjoying great popularity is Ed Crowley, boss of the former Town House of Los Angeles—now, no doubt to Ed Crowley's remorse, the Sheraton-West. Ed's friendship with leading Texas oil tycoons, his acquaintance with most top political figures, his rounds of golf with those bearing some of the most fabulous names in Hollywood, and his intimate acquaintance with leaders in the sports world mean that Sheraton-West guest registers usually resemble a compilation of Who's Who in the nation's newspaper headlines.

Not far from Los Angeles, the famous Huntington-Sheraton at Pasadena is headed by Steve Royce, its former owner and now the general manager. Steve, I am convinced, has the widest circle of friends among socially prominent Americans of any man in the hotel business and doubtless vies with James Aloysius Farley for high honors in the field of wide acquaintanceship.

Another Sheraton manager who has risen high in the company's top echelons by becoming boss of one of our leading hotels is Douglass Boone, a collateral descendant of Daniel Boone and head of Chicago's Sheraton-Blackstone Hotel. That Douglass Boone attained this high stratum in Sheraton's eminent hierarchy never ceases to amaze us at our Boston company headquarters. Not that there was ever a question of his technical skills; as a hotel man he possesses flawless credentials. The surprise at his notable progress comes from other considerations. In a company so heavily imbued with a lingering Harvard bias, which even permeates our board of directors, it was astonishing that an Eli from Yale could infiltrate a major activity and reach a top position. This was especially inexplicable when one considers the shabby treatment Yale often accords Harvard when it is unaccountably in possession of better football teams. My head is bowed in penitence as I record that Douglass Boone, a former Yale athlete, is a brilliant Sheraton manager, as well as host to Presidents and Presidential aspirants when political conventions take over Chicago.

Maurice Lawlor once headed Boston's Sheraton-Plaza—actually it was still called the Copley Plaza at the time. I happened to meet him one day in his lobby when I had just emerged from the barber shop, the possessor of a fine new haircut. It was shortly before Christmas, the day Lawlor had set aside the main ballroom for an employees' Christmas party. He asked if I would join the fun.

Several hundred were in attendance, including friends and relatives of the employees. An orchestra provided dance music, and there was entertainment between waltzes and fox trots. Lawlor had enjoyed a good year and was expressing his appreciation to those who helped achieve these happy results. I suspect the profusion of mistletoe suspended at strategic points was a measure of the manager's gratitude.

I must have seemed somewhat lonesome amid these gay activities, for soon a charming young lady, evidently under compulsion of the Christmas spirit, assumed the role of a self-appointed hostess and, taking me for a new employee, graciously suggested we dance. Perhaps it was a Leap Year. At all events the music was pleasant, and the newly installed electric dimmers were providing the prescribed atmosphere. My agreeable companion and I were doing very well, dancing and then watching the acts put on by the more talented employees.

"Which department are you from?" my lovely partner asked.

Remembering my haircut, I said casually, "I'm from the

barber shop." Feeling an obligation, especially at Christmastime, to a new employee, she obligingly began outlining the advantages and pitfalls of the hotel business. In the midst of this indoctrination came the climax of the festive ceremonies, the presentation of a bronze plaque to the employee with the longest service record, a doorman who had been spinning the revolving doors for nearly forty years. Maurice Lawlor addressed this veteran of the hotel's front entrance as my pleasant companion and I happily looked on.

"To present this plaque to our oldest employee," the manager was saying, "and to commemorate this auspicious occasion with some appropriate words, may I call upon our Company President, Mr. Ernest Henderson."

There was no escape. I had to mount the platform, but not without a fleeting glimpse of the now disillusioned companion who so generously befriended the "new hotel barber." I never saw her again, but I fear her faith in humanity was somewhat shaken.

Maurice Lawlor, the former boss of the Sheraton-Plaza, who is now assisting in the task of revitalizing a more recently acquired hotel, and some fifty other Sheraton managers are all, it is fair to say, doing an outstanding job for the company. We went to great lengths to "discover" them, and our care in measuring their performance, promoting them from time to time to larger and more important units, and giving them recognition for outstanding achievements is perhaps the principal key to the company's notable growth. Trial-and-error, despite some limitations, remains our ultimate test for managerial pre-eminence. When the right man is in charge of a Sheraton hotel, lines on the monthly performance charts usually begin to curve majestically upward. If Sheraton should lose even one of its many able managers, this could be costly to its persistent progress.

XIII.

Hobbies

I F AN abundance of hobbies were a key to a successful business career, Sheraton would now have even more hotels. When it comes to hobbies, we have more than our share—nearly a dozen at present. Actually most hobbies are useful in nearly any business, and I never hesitated to capitalize on them. Outside interests often draw together people infected by a common addiction, such as collecting antiques, boating, bird-watching, or one of the many other ailments to which hobbyists can fall prey.

Although hobbies are often a common denominator bringing people closer to one another, there is a striking exception to this otherwise valid theory. It is the taking of photographs, a virulent disease through most of the stages of which I have passed. Three-dimensional pictures, home movies, processing and enlarging color prints by means of dye-transfer processes, making full-sized lantern slides for projection—all these manifestations culminated in a single ultimate achievement: taking black and white pictures of people. I was to learn, however, that this did not always mean making friends, though it frequently influenced people—adversely, unfortunately, in most instances. This is how I made my most important discovery: that persons never admit to themselves that they have changed one iota in the preceding five years.

I observed that whenever I presented an enlarged picture to almost any acquaintance, particularly to a lady past the age of twenty, I would be forced to cross off one more from a shrinking circle of friends. Should a group of five appear in the picture, each would mention the excellent likenesses of all the other four. Finally I discovered an antidote for the relentless attrition among friends exposed to my camera lenses—a cure that is fortunately infallible. I now wait five years before developing my pictures. Since I achieved this brilliant strategy, my photographic prowess is again acknowledged by those portrayed, though they sometimes express surprise at the youthful appearance of others seen in these delayed-action enlargements.

I am a great admirer of Edwin Land, inventor of the Polaroid Land Camera, which is famous for making excellent pictures in just sixty seconds. The next time I see him I shall offer a suggestion. Despite the great success of his nearly instantaneous process, I shall recommend he forthwith discard it. I will point out the added millions that could be his with a film requiring five years to process.

Hobbies are like a seasoning that gives zest to the pleasure of living. An especially cherished pastime of mine, actually a delightful vice, is collecting large cents. These are the big copper pennies, somewhat larger than a silver quarter, struck from 1793, when the United States first minted coins, until 1857, when the more familiar small cents were substituted. My ambition was to have a really good specimen of each. A fairly complete collection, including a few major die variations, calls for some hundred coins. Their value depends on the rarity of certain dates and on the scarcity of some die variations, but especially on the state of perfection of the coin itself—whether signs of wear or damage have appeared. Finally significant is the quality of the patina that the passage of time produces. A valuable large cent with a superb olive-green tint can be quickly ruined by efforts of inept collectors to "improve" their treasured coins by polishing with ammonia or other chemicals intended to restore the initial copper shine. The damage, of course, can be undone, but this requires patience—perhaps as much as a hundred years' worth.

The really valuable dates in the "uncirculated" or "extra fine" categories, such as 1799, 1804, or 1823, bring many hundreds of dollars from eager collectors. Other dates are far less costly.

My most interesting coin is in excellent condition, though not among the rarest. It is actually one of the first to be struck, back in 1793. Since no American die-cutters were available in the days of the young republic, a German expert was sent for to cut an American die. He was asked to engrave the words: "United States of America" near the outside circumference, but in this he partially failed. Having left insufficient space for "America," he settled for "Ameri.," omitting the last two letters. The Ameri. coin, as it is presently called, was our first attempt at a national currency. One of these cents rated "extra fine" is now worth some two hundred dollars, twenty thousand times its original face value.

Coin collectors often carry a lucky coin or two, and I, of course, am no exception. I have a Spanish "piece of eight" the size of a silver dollar. These coins, with the exception perhaps of the ones hoarded by Captain Kidd, were often cut into eight equal segments resembling slices of a piece of pie. Two of these, representing a quarter of the coin, were known as "two bits," an expression still descriptive of twenty-five cents in today's language. Few people realize that the value of our American dollar was originally measured by the silver content of Spanish pieces of eight.

Another interesting coin shown at a numismatic exhibit at our Sheraton-Fontenelle Hotel in Omaha was a rather large one, weighing perhaps fifty pounds. Made of coral or some similar substance, it was two inches thick and some eighteen inches in diameter with a large hole through the center. The inscription on its face indicated that the Pacific island of Yap once had price controls; the purchasing power of the coin was specified. It could buy a quarter-acre of land, a twelve-foot canoe, ten thousand coconuts, or one wife. Molly thinks I should exclude such a coin from my collection to make sure I would not spend it.

Another interesting hobby resulted from the discovery that Bob Moore had become a "rock hound," more scientifically known as a lapidary. Not to be outdistanced by a partner in so intriguing a venture, I too became one of these and boast a cellar full of grinding-wheels and miscellaneous polishing compounds. Included in my assortment of accessories is a diamond-rimmed saw with jewels around its circumference. These are so small that, even when the blade turns at sixteen hundred revolutions a minute, a finger placed on the whirling edge feels only a smooth surface; yet a solid rock of agate, a piece of opal, or perhaps a chunk of jade can be cut into various shapes with relative ease. Polishing is a tedious pursuit but, when mastered, produces beautiful semi-precious stones suitable for cuff links, earrings, or other interesting items. To become a lapidary takes patience, but rewards are high when measured in satisfaction.

Five or six years ago, remembering days of World War I when as a Navy radio operator I had to learn the code, I decided I might become a licensed amateur operator. This would require the necessary quota of theory, and the ability to juggle dots and dashes with sufficient aplomb to turn out thirteen words a minute by means of the international Morse Code.

Driven by curiosity, I took the exam. Amazingly, I passed. I was now a radio ham. All I needed was some necessary equipment. Several hundred thousand amateurs are scattered throughout the world, most of these in the U.S.A. Each has a distinctive set of call letters. I am W1UDY. The W stands for the U.S.A., and the "one" represents the New England states, the first of ten American districts.

From a mail-order advertisement I purchased a five-hundred-watt transmitter—half the allowable maximum power. When this massive object arrived in Lincoln, Massachusetts, I had already secured receiving equipment through a local source, and it was in operation.

I began to hear calls from various parts of the world when atmospheric conditions permitted. Amateurs would call CQ from distant lands, usually in English, though sometimes tinged with Spanish, Italian, and sometimes Japanese accents. CQ is a general call telling others a contact would be appreciated.

Installing the transmitter was a major project. The language of the instruction book, discussing the loading of circuits, commenting on various kinds of emissions, dealing with electronic rectifiers, pentodes, etc., seemed to have little relationship to the vocabulary of decoherers, silicon detectors, or rotary spark gaps familiar in my younger days. However, the struggle to tame this great monster, a brute that could reach the far corners of the earth, was now under way.

When the dozen or more tubes finally emitted the requisite glow, and a battery of meters resembling the cockpit of a DC 7 showed the prescribed deflection, it was time to try the microphone. "CQ," I ventured daringly, disguising as best I could my acute nervousness. I listened for a possible reply, hopefully perhaps from Baghdad or from some equally exotic corner of the globe. No response. Nothing. Repeating these timid CQs produced the same results: exactly and precisely nothing.

When a broadcast receiver breaks down, nearby service men are usually on call. Not so with ham radio. Practitioners of this exclusive art must themselves be experts; it is far beneath their dignity to consider professional aid. In my case the manufacturer, fifteen hundred miles away, could render little help. Instructions kept arriving, but the technical language now current was almost useless without a dictionary to translate factory admonitions into the more familiar language I knew back in 1917. However, I went to work. Five times I disemboweled this monster and somehow reassembled it. Parts sometimes were left over, but such minor problems caused me no undue concern. Each time, when all was again in readiness, I uttered once more the hopeful "CQ," but still there was no response. Months had elapsed—involving more effort, perhaps, than would have been needed to add another unit or two to a growing hotel chain, had I directed the same energy into such more productive channels. Regardless of obstacles, I was determined to make this object perform.

The sixth attempt revealed a hidden compartment supposedly immune to trouble. A seemingly useless wire hung there, unhappily suspended in space. It had become loosened perhaps in transit from Iowa. I soldered the offending conductor and restored the components to their respective positions. Again I turned on the great transmitting tubes. Once more I ventured the magic "CQ," followed by my own call letters. Turning the receiver dials to the selected frequency, I was promptly overwhelmed. Five or six stations answered all at once, recalling the old-fashioned party phone line of earlier days. All were directly on my frequency. They were calling W1UDY.

Awestruck by this fearsome development, and momentarily speechless, I gathered the needed courage. Cautiously I replied to W1UAR, some thirty miles distant; his signal was the clearest. It was Burt Davies, head of a large leather tannery. Subsequently, often accompanied by his wife, Burt frequently visited our Lincoln, Massachusetts, home, and for years thereafter we maintained interesting two-way conversations over our microphones, usually on Sunday mornings. Dozens of amateurs, some as far distant as Pretoria, South Africa, or perhaps Edinburgh, Scotland, would break in with interesting comments; they too could hear Burt tell colorful tales of hunting in the Rockies or of pursuing an elusive bear in the great Canadian Northwest.

[151]

These amateurs were "reading the mail," as this form of "eaves-dropping" is known among hams.

Confirmations in the form of QSL cards would verify distant contacts. Such cards addressed to W1UDY from many corners of the globe attest to two-way conversations with some sixty different countries, including some behind the Iron Curtain. The greatest distance reached should theoretically never exceed twelve thousand miles, that being halfway around the world. This would seem to disqualify my boast of a contact sixteen thousand miles from Boston. Not so, for on one occasion a conversation with a Johannesburg ham, not at that moment possible at a distance of eight thousand miles with antennas beamed to the southeast, could be achieved by rotating the antennas by remote control a hundred and eighty degrees. Thus I established a two-way conversation by propagating the radio waves the long way around the globe.

It is something of a paradox that short-wave signals, traveling only in straight lines, can go around the world. Radio waves can accomplish this seemingly difficult feat because, when heading for the horizon, they strike the so-called ionosphere, that region some two hundred miles above the earth now being populated with Sputniks and Explorers. The ionosphere, consisting of what might be called partially broken-down molecules, actually acts like a mirror. It reflects the waves down to the earth, which in turn bounces them back to the ionosphere. These "leaps," jumps of about two thousand miles, mean that, to reach Johannesburg by way of the northwest, radio waves must be reflected back and forth seven or eight times, even though traveling only in straight lines.

The language of the ham is colorful, dating back to days when spelling out words in dots and dashes placed a premium on brevity. An oft-recurring phrase, "the girl friend," became the YL, short for "young lady." In the course of evolution, a wife became the XYL. These "ex girl friends" are apparently not offended by this seeming calumny. Many YLs and XYLs are themselves licensed radio hams.

I can testify to occasional international flirtations by way of short-wave radio by revealing my "affair" with Costa Rica's glamorous Evita. She was an XYL, but that was no drawback; her husband never objected, provided her contacts were kept at a distance of two thousand miles; besides, Evita's husband, a traveling salesman, was often far from home.

Evita's glamour was of course far beyond question. One can always tell by their lovely voices. I'm afraid, however, in this instance my charming though unseen Costa Rican beauty was perhaps a little fickle. I still hear her occasionally conversing with a W6, a Pacific Coast ham, who is now the recipient of the endearing sentiments, expressed in slightly broken English, of which I was once the fortunate beneficiary.

Hams address one another by their first names. So it was, on a summer day in Dublin, New Hampshire, that I found myself talking to Herb. He was a W8, and so I inquired if that meant Cleveland, where W8s abound. "No," said Herb cheerfully, though I thought his nose turned up perceptibly. "No," he repeated, "Shaker Heights." This evidently put me in my place, especially since Herb, hearing I was in New Hampshire, decided I must be a country farmer. Politely he inquired how the crops were doing.

"Fine," I replied in my best New Hampshire drawl.

Thus Herb and Ernie in "QSO" talked back and forth for quite a while. I learned he was building a boat. Recalling the story current in the Boston papers at the time, telling of a man who had built a boat in his basement only to find it too large for the cellar door, I recounted it to Herb. Due to a minor miscalculation, the side of the house had had to come down.

"Oh," said Herb, "no trouble like that." His boat was in Detroit, and would be completed the following Saturday. In fact, he explained by way of his short-wave equipment, he was taking some of the boys to Detroit for the occasion. A dinner to mark the event would be held at a Detroit hotel.

Becoming more interested, I cautiously inquired, "Which hotel?"

"Oh," said Herb, "you can't keep track of the Detroit hotels." Formerly, he said, it was the Book Cadillac, but some fellows from Boston had taken it over and had changed the name. Unable to resist, I told Herb I knew the manager, Neal Lang. I suggested Herb should look him up, and Neal Lang would see that all went well.

Changing atmospheric conditions ended this contact on the twenty meter band. However, two days later an urgent long-distance call came from the Sheraton-Cadillac in Detroit. Neal Lang was on the line. He seemed a bit confused. Seven hundred people, he explained, were dining in his ballroom. Most of them had come by special trains from Cleveland to participate in the launching ceremonies of a twenty-thousand-ton ore boat. One of the steel-company heads, a company with a subsidiary which built the vessel, was asking about a friend in New Hampshire, a farmer named Ernie.

A further incident that summer was a contact with a Japanese student in Nagasaki. With notable lack of tact, observing it was the twelfth anniversary of the troubles visited upon that Japanese city, I inquired if the young man had perhaps been there twelve years earlier.

"How could I have been?" he replied in comprehensible English, putting me, I thought, properly in my place.

It was understandably a delicate subject. Although the Hiroshima affair was perhaps justified as a means of shortening the war, this reasoning hardly applied to the second missile, conferred upon Nagasaki.

Fortunately my Japanese friend forgave my lapse of discretion, for he was soon complimenting me on my impeccable Japanese, basing his conclusion on my single word of greeting. I had said, "Good morning" in his own language, using the one word that constituted my entire Japanese vocabulary. "Good morning" in Japanese is pronounced "Ohio."

"Ohio," by the way, though the sun was sinking on the western horizon, was the correct salutation. Not only was it morning in Nagasaki, but actually the morning of the following day, since Japan lies beyond the international date line. Stranger still, we could both see the sun at the very same moment, even though on different days according to our respective calendars. A setting sun in New Hampshire would be rising at the same time on the following day ten thousand miles to the west.

If doubts still linger that the world is round, these radio contacts should dispel them.

Amateur radio operating can have its more tangible benefits. I was once in contact with a station in Berlin when an American priest in Germany, hearing a Bostonian was on the air, wanted to say hello. I was talking from Lincoln, only a few miles from Boston, and the priest had relatives in nearby Malden. What was their phone number? I asked, and in a moment had them on the line. With the telephone held close to the radio, I brought the voice of the American priest to his relatives in Malden. A two-way conversation followed, all the way across the Atlantic.

The American reverend father, expressing his gratitude, wondered how he could show his appreciation. Not in the least shy, I mentioned how useful a German couple could be in our Louisburg Square home on Beacon Hill, where we were soon to move. A few months later Hans and his pretty young bride appeared at our door. They took excellent care of the Hendersons for over a year, and then set out to carve for themselves a career in this land the Germans call "one of unlimited possibilities." I am sure no other hobby pays more welcome dividends than those we can trace to our ham radio activities.

There are, however, other pursuits in my assorted list of hobbies. Among these is yet another cherished indiscretion. I like to write songs.

Songwriting, though pleasant, is a rather unremunerative hobby. Thirty years ago, devoid of any needed qualifications, I started to write a song. I believe even now it may not be quite completed. During these many years it has been subjected to the immutable forces of evolution. I evolved a dozen different lyrics in a vain hope of catching the public fancy. Technically, this song belongs to the genus "popular music," though this of course is a misnomer. It could hardly have been less popular, and after thirty years, despite the many variations, it still awaits a nod from a most reluctant music-publishing industry, whose members seem blissfully unaware of the golden opportunity they have neglected. I still await amends from the Hit Parade for many years of indifference. But even if publishers, at least in my biased opinion, seem remiss, there have been some minor triumphs.

Once on a moonlight night at Daytona Beach several couples, after dancing at a hotel we once owned there, joined Molly and me in our car. We headed for the miles of immaculate beach on which automobiles are permitted to drive. Far from visible civilization, with the sea air in our nostrils, we enjoyed the near-tropical setting. Stars were shining with a vigor strange to Northerners, lighting the ocean waves as they fell on the beach. In this eerie Florida atmosphere, enhanced by charming company, I reached for the switch on the automobile radio. The local station of a national network was playing Leo Reisman's dance music from the Persian Room in New York's Plaza Hotel, an important unit in Mr. Hilton's empire. Suddenly familiar strains came over the air—"Clarinda," one of my twelve variations. At the conclusion Reisman expressed hope that the composer, head of a competing hotel chain, might be listening in.

I hasten to add that whatever virtue might lie in the name Clarinda did not stem from any prior emotional involvement, but rather from the circumstance that emphasis on the syllables matched the desired rhythm.

Another song, instead of taking thirty years, needed only two or three days to write. It bore the title " 'Twas in the Night," and got off to a good start, though I nearly missed hearing it. Word had come that Arthur Fiedler had been cajoled into including it in the program of one of his Pop Concerts at Symphony Hall. Unfortunately he selected a night when I would have difficulty in returning from a speaking engagement at Saranac Lake in the Adirondacks. With no conventional transportation available, there was still a last resort, a one-man plane-rental service. The one man, sadly enough, had just suffered a prolonged siege at the controls and did not wish to relinquish a well-earned rest. I had an idea. As a former Navy pilot, I could still perhaps operate a plane. The regular pilot could sleep in the rear seat, snoring as much as he pleased. He was probably thinking of World War II rather than the earlier unpleasantness with Germany when wondering whether an ex-Navy pilot could safely fly his plane, for had he known thirty-five years had passed since my flying days, he might have hesitated. However, he gladly consented. He slept better, it seemed, with only the roar of motors in his ears rather than bedlam at home generated by screaming children.

The Saranac speech completed, we took off at once, heading straight for Boston. It was a beautiful summer night. Halfway there, Monadnock Mountain loomed before us. While the pilot painlessly dreamed, I made a minor detour, passing over our newly acquired Dublin house sitting on the side of the mountain. The house and the seventy-foot steel short-wave tower were clearly visible. Fortunately my taxi pilot awoke as we approached the Boston airport, otherwise my ambition to hear an orchestra seventy pieces strong play my song at Symphony Hall might have been imperiled. With the pilot's help, we landed safely.

Once I arrived at Symphony Hall, it was hard to deny the

thrill of seeing my name on the concert program, bracketed with Brahms, Gershwin, and other legitimate composers. The fact that Arthur Fiedler may have partially crossed his fingers during this segment of the program, or that his judgment was even mildly swayed by the circumstance that the performance was in part a tribute to Sheraton, I simply ignored. The fact remains that all who believe they can write a tune, and this may include half our population, can expect an agreeable thrill if they are able to find an orchestra and an audience of twenty-five hundred willing to be exposed to music of their own composition.

"Come with Me" and an attempt at a hymn are my only other entries for future glory, either of this world or of the one to come. The latter composition was sung in our small Episcopal church in Dublin. It sounded well—so well, in fact, that I fear I may someday discover a counterpart in some existing hymn. I expect to skim the pages of our hymn book at some future date to make sure no other stands between me and possible perpetuation among contributors to ecclesiastic harmony.

Songwriting is a pleasant hobby, though one to be shunned by those unwilling to face frequent disappointments.

Hobbies in general can be exciting and of course provide needed relaxation. However, there are other "extra curricular" activities in which many of us, in varying degree, participate—if not always actively, at least at times from the sidelines. Politics, a nearly universal interest of most American businessmen, is one of these. Although the subject is necessarily controversial and therefore highly dangerous, it seems nonetheless inevitable that some paragraphs here expose my favorite prejudices and beliefs. The coming chapter, one that might doubtless have been better omitted, has been indiscreetly retained.

XIV.

Some Comments on American Presidents

D ESPITE an aversion to politics, I have met several recent Presidents, and in some fortunate instances our hotels were privileged to serve as their hosts.

Before we acquired our present Boston hotel, Woodrow Wilson was one of the Copley Plaza's occasional guests. Lindbergh and Cardinal Pacelli, who later became Pope Pius XII, had, in common with President Wilson, added to the hotel's luster. One of our first managers, when the hotel became Sheraton property, while chatting with a newspaper reporter, observed a rusty room key lying on his desk. The manager casually mentioned it might have been the one President Wilson walked off with thirty years before. The following day an account of the belated return of the Woodrow Wilson key was a front-page story in most of the nation's newspapers. Free publicity is always welcome, since hotels are naturally eager to keep their names before the public.

Woodrow Wilson, though he took us into war with Germany, was, I felt, a dedicated statesman and made a real effort, though it was unsuccessful, to keep us out of war. I was never quite so sure the same could be said truthfully of Franklin D. Roosevelt.

Truman, in many ways, I liked. Perhaps I may be prejudiced; he often visits Sheraton hotels, which accounts for the piano kept in his honor in our San Francisco Presidential Suite.

Herbert Hoover, though he was doubtless one of our great Presidents, we of Sheraton must write off as an almost total loss. Bill Chadbourne, a director of our Park Sheraton in New York, was a good friend of Herbert Hoover, and we met the former President at a dinner party in his Park Avenue apartment. President Hoover, whom I had the honor to sit beside, surprised us with his knowledge of our industry. Thus we learned of his partiality to a competitor: he is a director of the Hilton chain. Despite this affiliation, we are happy to learn, he sometimes takes a suite at one of our Washington hotels.

Once, shortly after we acquired the Astor Hotel, word came that President Eisenhower would visit New York City and would stay at what had just become the Sheraton-Astor. No suite was adequate for this momentous occasion, and, with only a few days to prepare, fast action was required. A wall separating two suites was quickly removed, providing a living room of more spacious proportions. Then came the matter of decor. As dedicated disciples of the famed eighteenth-century furniture designers—we could hardly have been otherwise, since Thomas Sheraton was one of these—we naturally settled on the elegance of that once golden era. Honors were divided between Sheraton and Chippendale. A chair done in the latter motif bore an engraved silver plate—authentic, we hoped, in view of its cost—proclaiming it one of President Washington's former possessions. Highboys and blockfront desks, a Sheraton settee, and other examples of that great age of craftsmanship were hastily assembled. Several eighteenth-century prints of how the well-dressed golfer looked in the latter seventeen hundreds adorned the walls. Our decorators performed admirably, though they unfortunately requisitioned my favorite Curtis wall clock made in Concord some hundred and eighty years earlier, at about the time Paul Revere was galloping in the general direction of that famed Massachusetts city. I had purchased the clock personally at a Park-Bernet auction, hoping it would become the central theme of our Louisburg Square living room. To my dismay, our decorators turned against me my own favorite admonition: "Remember, the company's interest always comes first."

A personal letter from President Ike thanking us for the attractive arrangements is a highly treasured possession, though I am still mildly uncertain whether even this priceless memento quite fills the gap on our Boston living-room wall. The Astor was later sold, or rather "exchanged"—as stamp collectors trade stamps—for the former Ambassador Hotel, now the Sheraton-East. My hopes of ever regaining my Curtis clock are growing very dim.

President Roosevelt occasionally stayed at our earlier St. Louis hotel, before the days when the Sheraton-Jefferson entered the Sheraton orbit. Although an admirer of many of the Roosevelt domestic achievements, I was often plagued by the fear "political expediency" was overemphasized during his many administrations. This apparent need for sacrificing to the dictates of expediency when seeking political goals was a matter of much concern to me.

I recognize, of course, the wide appeal of most Roosevelt policies to many Americans, particularly the underprivileged; but I am also aware that Roman emperors found it profitable on occasion to pursue a similar course. In the case of the Roman emperors, popularity was achieved by granting the multitudes much that was wanted, for nothing. The later downfall of the once eternal city, however, suggests that the price for political popularity is sometimes rather high. The softening of the moral fiber of the great Roman populace doubtless hastened the collapse of a once flourishing empire, thereby inaugurating a thousand years of dark ages.

I am mindful of the advances made in some of the Roosevelt

administrations, but I question if an end always justifies the means.

I met F.D.R. in Europe, before the days of his physical affliction, in rather unusual circumstances. During the great German advance on Paris in July 1918, the exodus from the French capital to points south strained all means of transportation. Two of us Navy pilots had received orders to proceed to Italy. Conscious of the French delight in excluding fresh air from overfilled trains, we sought refuge from the summer heat on the roof of our railroad coach. From this vantage point we could really enjoy the world. War or no war, France was beautiful.

Approaching the border town of Modane, we were passing through the Alpine foothills, where the scenery was breathtaking, but it was not to last for long. An unexpected hazard suddenly loomed, rushing towards us at some sixty miles an hour, or, more likely, the equivalent in French kilometers. It was a tunnel. There it was, its dark opening almost filled by our forward coaches, leaving what seemed only inches between the cars and the ceiling. Flattened on our noses, we hoped to make it.

The passage seemed interminable. All was in utter darkness, and there was scarcely even space for the volumes of smoke from the great locomotives ahead—two were provided because of the magnitude of the great Alpine inclines. However, daylight finally returned, and we discovered that apparently each particle of soot our engines could blast from their ferociously belching stacks had encrusted itself in great opaque layers either on our faces or on our uniforms.

As we pulled into Modane and clambered down from our hazardous perch, an officious guard detained us. Unable to determine whether, beneath the soot, we were white or black, friends or foes, he refused to be hurried, and as he deliberated, our train pulled out. On board were our possessions, identifications, and in fact everything we owned on the European Continent. Clearly we were now in trouble.

Eventually our guard, prying through layers of soot, discovered sufficient corroborative evidence to establish our American identity. Grudgingly he accepted our story and at last released us. Nearby on a platform was a well-dressed individual, handsome, erect, unmistakably a distinguished American civilian, accompanied by several aides, who seemed much amused by our awkward predicament. My soot-covered companion, Clyde Palmer, recognized him as Franklin D. Roosevelt, Undersecretary of the Navy.

Despite the unusual occasion of our meeting, we found F.D.R. cordial. It was the only time I met him personally. Earlier meetings with Presidents Taft and Wilson in New Hampshire had been under somewhat more favorable circumstances.

A year after our experience at Modane, I had the difficult burden of bringing to Clyde Palmer's family in Melrose, Massachusetts, the tragic details of the fatal airplane crash of their only son.

Years after, when Roosevelt was President, I was to wonder whether he was not largely responsible for the unfriendly attitude toward business so widely held during his administrations. Despite these misgivings, I was forced to concede that some unsound business practices were expeditiously discouraged by the almost promiscuous damning by Roosevelt of nearly all engaged in commercial pursuits, a technique which, perhaps on grounds of political expediency, he seemed unduly to relish. Unfortunately painful scars were inflicted, and some of these still persist. Many persons even today take pleasure in thinking ill of those who conduct the nation's business affairs.

Rebellious intellectuals, many of whom apparently dislike an economic system stressing the tangible to the disadvantage of their own contribution to society, had their embers of discontent fanned at times into a burning reddish glow, apparently by

President Roosevelt. He seemed to seek an emotional rather than an objective response, skillfully obscuring the fact that wealth must be produced by creating productive capacity before becoming available for the less tangible services intellectuals were offering—all this, perhaps, for personal political motives.

Assumptions that gave plausibility to the theory that businessmen were saturated with greed, corruption, and a disdain for human values were often predicated on relatively isolated instances of evils present in the business structure. By dramatizing the sins of occasionally unscrupulous exploiters, political advantage could be gained. Roosevelt's unprecedented third and fourth terms testify to the eagerness with which some, perhaps those less well rewarded for their contributions to society, often seized upon the suggestion that others higher in the economic scale achieved success through resort to unethical practices.

Although later strongly opposed to Franklin Roosevelt, I did not reach this conclusion as a result of his attacks on business. I could understand an urge for political scapegoats, even though Hitler also used the scapegoat technique, to be sure in a far more objectionable form. I did not question Roosevelt's crusading for the underdog, and I agreed the underprivileged needed a champion, though, as has been seen, I could not accept fully the thesis that Roosevelt's concern for those of lesser means was wholly independent of political expediency. It was clearly good strategy to appeal to the prejudices of ninety-five workers in a hundred-man factory, even at the expense of the five executives who may have made the operation possible. Had the numerical ratios been reversed, I question whether Roosevelt's solicitude for a mere handful of workers would have reached the same proportions.

I strongly approved the creation of agencies such as the Securities and Exchange Commission, which required full disclosure of pertinent financial information, and I likewise welcomed the enactment of social-security laws long overdue in this country. Although undestandably the financial community resented at first the creation of the Securities and Exchange Commission, the passage of this New Deal legislation marked an important advance. Grudgingly, I give the credit to F.D.R. If today the possible repeal of the S.E.C. should come to a vote, few if any in the financial community would be likely to cast their ballots for its demise.

Legislation in the Roosevelt era to curb financial excesses naturally brings to mind questions raised today by new curbs on labor unions. Although such legislation naturally faced opposition from those directly concerned, I venture a prediction that workingmen will be among the first to concede the benefits from such laws, especially if greater responsibility comes to their union leadership.

Contrary to a still lingering belief, most American business executives today are intensely interested in the welfare of workers and are likewise responsive to the interests of the public, if for no other reason than that success in business virtually requires this attitude.

Despite a feeling that Roosevelt used businessmen as political scapegoats, my 1936 ballot was cast for him. Later I regretted this indiscretion, but not because of his domestic policies.

It was Roosevelt's international program which troubled me most. I was never convinced that France, Britain and the United States might not have escaped the Second World War and its very painful ravages had F.D.R. exercised the restraining hand of statesmanship, rather than pursuing what may have been an unnecessarily belligerent policy that seems to have made a world war inevitable. I felt that Roosevelt's dislike for, and lack of understanding of, Germany actually encouraged at least some of the evils that developed under Hitler, and that Communism in Russia was really world enemy number one.

I have long felt, though this view is still most unpopular,

that many of the Nazi strong-arm manifestations so violently distasteful to us were, despite their unpalatable nature, actually the sole brand of backfire that could prevent Communist domination of the Germany of 1933. The Germans, according to this view, were forced to use the Communists' own unsavory devices to kindle the kind of backfire which alone could prevent an otherwise certain Communization of Germany, and therefore ultimately that of the whole of Europe. This interpretation, which I believe has never been effectively refuted, was doubtless understood in Washington but withheld from the American people, perhaps because of the violent political impact on some crucial Eastern states of certain totally unrelated though properly despised Hitlerian racial doctrines. These were perhaps blinding us to the more vital though less emotionally arousing European developments.

It seems to be a psychological truth applying to heads of state that, if they are damned for certain reprehensible acts, they must therefore be held automatically wrong in every other move they ever make. This unfortunate concept apparently rests entirely on emotion rather than on reason, and accordingly represents an impediment to the adoption of a wise foreign policy. The concept of "guilt by association," though roundly condemned nowadays, did apparently account for many difficulties faced by such men as Francisco Franco when Nazi aid was brought to bear in the Spanish Civil War. Not the merits of questions at issue, but rather the character of the support received, may at least partially, though perhaps subconsciously, have been the basis for judging that unfortunate conflict.

I always feared that Roosevelt, so deeply enmeshed in domestic politics, was perhaps more aware of forty-seven electoral votes from New York State, obviously vital in national elections, than of the need for exercising the international statesmanship which might have prevented a major world war. Our present difficulties with Russia, more critical perhaps than those of prior international involvements, could conceivably have been avoided.

In other words, a few million dollars' worth of emotionally charged and heavily outraged feelings in this country, caused by the insane stupidity of an obviously unbalanced Austrian paper-hanger, was evidently not weighed in the scales of infinite wisdom against nearly a trillion dollars' worth of devastation, human destruction, and world misery to be wrought by World War II.

It should perhaps be remembered that even in this country we can have in a Southern state a governor not always noted for his devotion to one of our own minority races. Should this governor somehow have reached the White House, could this have justified a foreign power in risking a trillion-dollar war costing millions in lives? Comparisons, of course, are odious; yet they do sometimes arouse some quite sobering thoughts.

It was my feeling that Roosevelt, as head of the world's most powerful nation, when he failed to exert a restraining influence on world affairs for the preservation of peace, was appraising the stupid acts of a misguided corporal on an emotional rather than on a reasoned basis, thus playing directly into the hands of the Russian Marxist revolutionaries.

Recently I was asked by the president of a Boston historical society to address the members of his organization on the subject of America's participation in two world wars. A speaker apparently had given out and a substitute was urgently needed. I protested resolutely. My views were unpopular, unorthodox, and far too controversial. I pointed out that my theories could not always be proved and that at all events emotions always outweighed facts where foreign wars were concerned. He paid no attention whatsoever; the need for a speaker must have been acute. The thoughts expressed on that occasion, explain perhaps in part my disagreement with much of our past foreign policy.

These thoughts on international events are presented in the Appendix. They may throw light on what may have been the most daring hoax in recorded history, involving millions of lives and hundreds of billions of the world's wealth. Essentially they tell the story of a diabolical plot hatched by three powerful world figures dedicated to an ambition only a world war could gratify.

XV.

The Story of the Lusitania

I

THE sinking of the *Lusitania* was one of the more sensational historical events which paved the way to our entry into the First World War. Early in the nineteen-twenties some remarkable light was shed for me on this interesting subject by a Boston doctor named Andreas Christian who lived on Beacon Street. He told me a story about the *Lusitania* so fantastic that for years I could scarcely give it serious thought, but more recently, new developments have brought it to mind.

The doctor in the early twenties told me how in 1915 he had engaged passage on what was the *Lusitania*'s fatal voyage. As bookings were quite heavy, he had been asked to share a stateroom with a friend, an American naval attaché. However, after noting the well-remembered German embassy advertisements warning that since munitions were carried on British passenger ships they were subject to submarine attack, Dr. Christian canceled his passage. The American naval representative, proceeding on government business, sailed on the voyage, survived the sinking, and later returned to this country. It was his story that Dr. Christian recounted.

On the evening before the last day of the fatal voyage, the Navy men speculated on the time the *Lusitania* would enter the so-called "war zone," where submarines were known to operate. Under military secrecy, no information was offered by the British ship, but the American attaché estimated that by eleven at night the crucial longitude line would have been crossed. This he determined by calculating the speed of the ship by counting the number of vibrations per minute, a figure that would correspond to the revolutions of the propellers.

Although I no longer recall the number of revolutions that represented various speeds, let us say that eighty revolutions was the speed at which, for economy purposes, the ship proceeded in safer waters—say, eighteen knots. Since the vulnerability to torpedo attack would fall sharply at the vessel's top speed of twenty-five knots (perhaps ninety-two revolutions a minute), the Navy man awaited signs of this increased speed as a verification that the danger zone had been reached. To his surprise, at approximately the expected hour, the revolutions, instead of accelerating, suddenly dropped, indicating a slower speed, one at which the great *Lusitania* would be almost a sitting duck for a carefully aimed torpedo. Equally strangely, the usual precautions of blacking out portholes on entering the war zone were mysteriously neglected. Finally, the invariable custom of pursuing a zigzag course, the accepted means for confounding enemy submarines, was omitted.

The next morning the big ship, still afloat, approached the Irish coast, still proceeding at less than eighteen knots, a most dangerous circumstance according to the trained judgment of the U. S. naval attaché.

Suddenly the torpedo struck.

Following the explosion, and for the first time during that fatal voyage, the engines were advanced to "full steam ahead." This would assure the sinking of the ship in only a few minutes, rather than in the hour or two that would have been normal had the engines come to a stop.

This story was so strange I kept it to myself for years. Not long ago, sitting at the chief engineer's table on a British transatlantic liner, I became acquainted with this ship's officer and recounted to him my astonishing tale, expecting, of course, a vehement denial. Surprisingly, he acknowledged that a secret board of inquiry had confirmed nearly all these allegations but explained the apparent enigma by claiming that false instructions received by wireless from a German-owned Telefunken station on Long Island caused the disregard for normal precautions. The explanation, I felt, was preposterous, since no captain could have been fooled by such ridiculous instructions. Confirmation of the circumstances of the sinking, however, was disturbing.

Recently, at the Harvard Library, I searched for literature on the subject and was surprised to find in the May 1935 issue of the *American Mercury* magazine, twenty years after the sinking of the great vessel, an article on the *Lusitania* commenting on the official British inquiry in 1915 (when war hysteria was at its height). The hearings had revealed the dangerously slow speed of the vessel and its failure to zigzag, though questions regarding the blacking out of the portholes were disputed. Whether such precautions were taken is doubtless ascertainable. The damaging part of the article, however, was the revelation of inconsistencies and contradictions in the captain's testimony and the obvious efforts to "whitewash" the proceedings. Obliquely, the author referred to the possible conclusion that the sinking was a "plant" to bring America into the war. Will the complete *Lusitania* story ever be told?

Did history perhaps repeat itself on December 7, 1941, as suggested by Admiral R. A. Theobald in his *United States News and World Report* article of April 2, 1954, or by the eminent and scholarly Professor Beard of Columbia in his book on Pearl Harbor? Both implied that concentration of our Pearl Harbor fleet in a militarily indefensible position, after repeated warnings by high Navy brass, was a planned invitation to a

Japanese attack. Could this have been done to bring us for a second time into a world war?

Not only the sinking of the *Lusitania*, but also the murder of the Austrian Archduke at Sarajevo in 1914 and the subsequent Belgian atrocity stories may have been machiavellian schemes to mold public opinion, an important objective in times of war. This was a part of the subject of my address to that Boston historical society. To my great surprise, it was quite well received.

Perhaps the events preceding that world-shattering murder at Sarajevo were equally masterminded by individuals with axes to grind, in order to influence the course of world history.

2

The question may well be raised at this point what connection there could be between events at Sarajevo, and Pearl Harbor and what happened to the *Lusitania*, and the building and expanding of a large hotel enterprise. Actually the connection may be closer than might at first appear.

In the matter of significant historical events that altered the course of history, not one person in a hundred seems willing to examine the evidence which could determine whether currently accepted versions of these are accurate. Most of us prefer to rely on emotionally oriented convictions and seem little interested in knowing whether public opinion was perhaps prostituted. When emotions run high, the subconscious satisfaction in thinking ill of the objects of our displeasure often deprives us of objectivity, a quality equally needed when assessing events of history or when directing the destinies of a large corporation. There are many instances when to disengage one's action from the dictates of emotional responses is vital to the successful conduct of a business enterprise. As an illustration, few of us ever question the integrity of those with whom we have long been associated; yet hidden breaches of faith so fantastic that few would believe them possible do at times occur. Instances of untrustworthiness have occasionally confronted us. In aggregate, losses stemmed through the exercise of "skeptical cynicism" have reached high in the millions during the years we have been in business.

To mention but a few incidents none believed could happen, there was the case of a prominent citizen in a position of trust in one of our larger hotels. Active in social and civic affairs, he was a member of various scientific and cultural societies, a man everyone regarded highly. The annual cost of operating his department, however, exceeded by thousands of dollars a month that of similar departments in other Sheraton Hotels. Costs were steadily mounting, and no amount of probing could explain the discrepancy. Finally we secured the department head's "resignation." That was many years ago, but ever since some six thousand dollars a month have been restored to the earnings of the hotel in question. An avalanche of protests from prominent citizens, condemning us for our "outrageous" action had to be taken in stride. We never lodged any charges, for "defamation of character" countersuits are hard to defend. We had no proof, but we were very pleased indeed with the savings that followed this helpful "resignation."

Another instance of hidden costs that baffled our engineers had to do with the master meter measuring steam from a local utility company. When all attempts at a solution of the problem of excessive steam consumption failed, we installed an extra meter. Skeptical cyncism paid off. Fifty thousand dollars a year, we verified, was the cost of steam the hotel never received, a surcharge former owners doubtless had paid for a considerable number of years, perhaps because of a blind faith in the accuracy of existing utility-company meters.

In almost any business, I am sure, the conviction that "this could never happen here" presents a great potential hazard. Those who accept explanations at full face value, whether historical events or possible business losses are involved, may be burying their heads in the sands of delusion. A skeptical attitude, though not always justified, could be the key to a company's success, or perhaps a factor in preventing involvement in a future world war. Facts rather than emotions furnish the better guideposts, despite any violence that may be done to our cherished convictions.

My lukewarm fondness for our wartime foreign policy, though not shared by most Americans, can perhaps be better understood if one gives thought to these paragraphs on skeptical cynicism. They explain in part my difficulty in accepting all political actions at their full face value. I find it hard to believe that wars, because they were fought and won, were necessarily inevitable, or that the alternatives would always have been as disastrous as our "feelings" seemed to suggest.

Perhaps, however, we can now turn from this unhappy subject to another that may also be of possible interest.

XVI.

Comments on the American Economy

I

Obviously I believe in our free-enterprise system. It has treated me quite generously. I realize, of course, that this characteristic alone can hardly justify its existence, and that the masses of Americans must also benefit if what we call "people's capitalism" is to survive. Being understandably prejudiced, I have endeavored to weigh the evidence as to the merits of our economy with more than ordinary caution.

During much of the past century American business evolved much as did the fictional Topsy; it just grew. For several decades following the Civil War, rapid industrial expansion took place. Little thought in those days was given such matters as "social justice," and the lot of the farm worker must have been harsh indeed, for there were plenty of applicants for factory jobs, despite miserable pay and long and grueling hours. The number of immigrants who came here to compete for these factory jobs in a distant "promised land" suggests conditions in Europe were even worse.

Although much has been said about the greed of employers during the early days of industrialization, our initial empire-builders did provide the ingenuity, skill, and courage necessary to make this country prosper. Before industrial expansion began, activities such as fur-trading, handicrafts, and agriculture were among the few devices for creating wealth in this land. The demands of our people were necessarily small, and goods to satisfy their wants correspondingly limited.

As the factory system developed and more goods began to appear, the articles produced suddenly became the new necessaries of life, creating an ever rising standard of living. I have always felt that critics of the long hours and poor working conditions of early pioneer days should not consider these hardships a reason for condemning the economic system under which we live today. Industrial activity, in order to expand, required the creating of capital in a world largely devoid of this commodity. This was accomplished by resort to low wages and long hours, which gave an opportunity to make profits. Builders of businesses simply had to make money so that factory expansion and purchases of machinery, necessary elements in the development of better jobs, could be financed. Even the old "robber barons" of the late nineteenth and early twentieth centuries, though in retrospect they may outrage our sense of social responsibility, doubtless in their day laid the foundation, through the accumulation of wealth, for today's American industrial leadership.

J. P. Morgan arrived upon the American scene when the more flagrant economic abuses were already beginning to yield to regulatory legislation. Although looked upon by contemporaries as a great financial idol, Morgan already today, at least in some classrooms, is being held up as a symbol of ruthless greed. Surely it is unwise to measure leaders of a former era by the yardstick of a later age, for accepted standards can differ from those of yesterday. Our own concepts of right and wrong are indeed subject to the laws of evolution.

As our knowledge of economic affairs widens, and our national wealth expands, we can begin to enjoy the luxury of shorter work hours, of a wider distribution of the wealth created by growing productivity, and of giving thought to a better understanding of the dignity of man. Before we could consider the modern concept of social justice, we had to create the national riches which made possible thought about this subject.

J. P. Morgan and the elder Henry Ford, both frequently damned by pseudo-liberals, probably contributed more than any others in history towards the creation of national wealth and made possible in our day terms such as "the rights of working-men." The sharp condemnation of these two industrial giants, perhaps because they retained a few odd millions, mostly, to be sure, reinvested in further tools of production, may in part be due to a trace of that jealousy which affluence sometimes inspires. I wonder how many critics have added even a thousandth part of what Ford or Morgan contributed to our present national prosperity. I wonder how many of these detractors have provided a single highly paid job for each thousand of those offered by the Ford Motor Company, the United States Steel Corporation, or some of the other industrial giants still known as Morgan companies. It does seem that we fail at times to place the proper emphasis on matters that really count.

We are all gradually learning that mass production, capable of turning out vast quantities of valuable goods is our one great mechanism for adding to the nation's assets and therefore to its wealth. The process of production fortunately has further value, for it can translate our people's labor and skills, by far our greatest resource, into needed wages and income.

The more our productivity is channeled into creating assets having a long life—factories, machinery, and housing, for instance—the faster will be the rise of our total national wealth. Unfortunately consummables, having a relatively short life, add but temporarily to our aggregate of national assets.

If we wish to continue to be the richest nation in the world, we must continue to outproduce all other nations, especially in

[177]

the field of goods with a long span of usefulness, and, if possible, those which further accelerate our productivity. Thus we may build up the wealth to support, when needed, high taxation and higher living standards. Thus we can create added savings to provide factories and tools for new and even better jobs essential to our expanding population.

There are doubtless many who naïvely believe the mere printing of money, or the raising of wages without a corresponding rise in productivity, can add to our national wealth. Obviously they are wrong. But when billions of dollars of goods are mass-produced by industry through the process of translating our abundant labor and skills into tangible products of great value, then we are literally pumping added wealth into our economy, wealth that can, among other things, finance the enjoyment of those intangibles which, though not in themselves wealth-producing, nonetheless enrich our civilization.

It is essentially this same economic concept, that of emphasizing the need to increase a company's own net worth, that has differentiated Sheraton from many other companies, organizations often more interested in creating immediate earning capacity. Sheraton's unusual approach accounts, we believe, largely for its almost unique growth record among companies listed on the New York Stock Exchange. Sheraton seeks to pump added value into its corporate properties rather than to emphasize immediate earnings that can be presently enjoyed.

In our struggle today with Russia we find that country, supposedly a "people's paradise," while in the process of creating capital needed for industrialization, following closely the practices of early American industrialists, those individuals often thought of as nineteenth-century economic tyrants. Russia today is paying incredibly low wages, just as did our own first railroad pioneers. In both instances accomplishments have grown out of the sweat of many toilers. Early American tycoons, however, used most of the profits wrung from poorly paid workers to further the expansion of growing enterprises. Those were days of great American economic development.

In Russia today the government, with its virtual stranglehold on industry, controls a business monopoly far vaster than what we in America call "big business." However, the Russian government, unlike American employers, has an added tool to enforce austerity upon underpaid workers, a device to augment further profits from the people's toil. By establishing a monopoly which eliminates competition, the Russians can control prices and often fix them at exorbitant levels. This procedure, similar to imposing a national sales tax perhaps as high as a hundred per cent, further penalizes Russian workers when they consume the goods they produce. The willingness to exploit workers in a manner reminiscent of our own early industrial plunderers makes Russia a danger to our free world of today.

The vast profits arising from the control of workers' pay permit Russia large expenditures for subversion and enormous sums for spreading discontent among the world's populations. These profits provide means of undercutting and disrupting world export markets. They make possible granting strategic loans at artificially low interest rates to governments amenable to this brand of bait. Furthermore, profits from controlled prices and wages can also accelerate, as was done in America by our own early exploiters, the further production of national wealth. Such expansion of industrial capacity under normal circumstances would be eminently desirable. In the hands of a government taking advantage of its own people by holding its workers in thralldom, insulating them from knowledge of the outer world, and using controlled newspapers and an Iron Curtain, this economic power is of concern to all the free world. When deception, purges, controlled law courts, intimidation, and rule by resort to exile or worse provide the basis, then such a wealth-creating mechanism is a serious menace.

Statistically, at her present rate of expansion, though her output is now but forty per cent of ours, Russia may require only a dozen years to catch up. If in the early seventies a Russian autocracy is still enforcing austerity on her people and we in America continue to dissipate the wealth we produce on unduly luxurious living standards, we will almost surely lose the Cold War. We may then face the threat of being only one more among the satellites revolving around Moscow. Khrushchev may make valid his boast that through economic expansion he will "bury us."

It was the advent of mass production, largely fathered by men like the elder Ford, that gave impetus on such a vast scale to the creation of wealth in America. It is owing to mass production that we can create living standards which permit American workers to enjoy so much of what a few generations ago was often beyond the reach of the wealthy—or even of kings and queens, for that matter.

Since wealth must be created before being distributed, perhaps more recognition and encouragement should be given industry for bringing to America the blue ribbon of financial supremacy. True, Russians may rival our military might, but this they do only by denying workers what we call necessities of life. America owes much credit to industry for creating wealth not only in sufficient abundance to maintain, through taxation, large military and governmental expenditures, but also to meet a continuous, and at times perhaps unwise, clamor for ever higher living standards.

To produce the wealth required to do these things, and still provide means for financing its own expansion, has been a gigantic task imposed upon American industry. But the difficulties have been needlessly magnified by some destructive forces impeding industry's ability to create all the wealth free enterprise is able to produce.

One of these corrosive forces is the inefficiency, looseness, and occasional corruption sometimes present at various levels of government. Unnecessary political extravagance is a burden that the productivity of industry or the wealth which it produces, is called upon to meet, usually through excessive taxation.

Then there is the ever present desire of workers, and executives too, for that matter, for the immediate enjoyment of all and sometimes more than all the fruits of their labors. This is especially true in instances where workers, utilizing the coercive pressures of their unions, continually demand higher pay. Since we are all a part of a democracy, it is politically expedient to encourage us in the belief that we are entitled to the immediate enjoyment of more and more luxuries that might perhaps better be postponed for the greater national welfare. Other countries, excepting some under dictatorships, seem beset by similar pressures from those preferring immediate benefits to enforced austerity. This is an unfortunate characteristic of a democracy, for it limits the channeling of profits into further expansion of productive facilities which could later augment our national wealth.

Finally, besides waste in government and the desire for wage increases, there are losses from duplication, inefficiency, featherbedding, and restrictive provisions imposed on employers. There are such matters as shutdowns from strikes. It is largely obstacles such as these that limit the full production of wealth by free enterprise.

If such impediments to productivity were removed, more wealth would be available for a major national need, that of better education, a field where the Russians are apparently outdistancing us.

Teachers, many of them critical of businessmen, have not always realized that wealth created by industry is usually the basic source of taxation through which school budgets are normally financed. Industry is indeed a goose that lays, directly or indirectly, education's golden eggs. A teacher's more legitimate target when he is dissatisfied with his lot might be the all-powerful labor unions demanding wages so high that little is left for the tax collectors from whose levies education is usually supported. Excessive wage costs of course also impede the expansion of business, which could otherwise create in the future more taxable wealth capable of caring for some of tomorrow's educational burdens.

I wonder how many critics of business realize that a company such as Sheraton, with sales of a hundred and fifty millions a year, pays out annually sixty millions in wages and employee benefits, leaving only three millions, or one-twentieth of the amount represented by wages, for dividends to shareholders. In other words, for each dollar paid shareholders, twenty dollars go to employees. Profits percentagewise are surprisingly low. This is why taxable earnings of industry fail to provide, among other things, satisfactory school budgets. The Russians, by inspiring artificial austerity and by curbing unions, solved their perplexing teacher-salary problems, though the means of accomplishing this feat are not always emphasized in their propaganda.

2

Although we Americans have not gone far enough in training our youth, and are soft as to hours of work and niggardly in our scale of remuneration for educators, there is one area where education is receiving excellent recognition. This is in the field of executive training.

Junior as well as senior executives in greatly increased numbers are now going back to school and taking refresher courses in various subjects. This is an important development of the contemporary business world. The popularity of courses for executives that require from a few days to several weeks of training each year is indicated by the experience of the American

Management Association. This non-profit group has enjoyed a growth in attendance at its business-training sessions from seven thousand participants ten years ago to the present rate of seventy thousand annually.

Enthusiasm for the value of education—undergraduate, post-graduate, and adult—has led me to put my convictions into practice, and for several years I attended summer courses conducted by A.M.A. at Colgate University. Among them were some open only to corporation presidents, in which twenty-five to thirty heads of companies took part. Among the participants were heads of large industrial companies, of railroads, and of other enterprises providing tens of thousands of jobs. If our own experience was typical, many companies are making greater progress because of information gathered by their presidents at these worth-while conferences.

Turning again to our American economic system, and the value of wealth derived from the production and distribution of goods, I would like to point out that high productivity is what imparts strength to our American dollar and gives it its stature in the marketplaces of the world. Should our factories ever shut down completely, or should their output be significantly curtailed, our currency, now the envy of the civilized world, would soon begin to soften. Despite disagreement among certain eminent economists, I think it is fair to suggest that the more we encourage production, the greater will be the wealth we can distribute among those entitled to share in its blessings. It is to our national productivity that we must look if we are to retain the luxury of being a democracy with all its freedoms, while at the same time maintaining our accustomed living standards.

3

Worries over Russian competition, though justified by the threat of her expanding rate of production, did not preclude our enjoying a visit from some Communists sent here by Mr. Khrushchev. A short time ago Molly and I were asked to entertain six or eight young Russian editors for tea at our home on Louisburg Square. They were visiting this country as guests of the State Department, and seeing a few Boston homes was considered a suitable supplement to their proposed itinerary. We invited some leading Boston capitalists to welcome these guests from behind the Iron Curtain and found introducing the heads of some large New England corporations to the young men from Russia an amusing experience. The visiting editors, both cordial and agreeable, did not seem to mind too much if occasionally we mildly pulled their legs. Some spoke English, while others preferred to use an interpreter.

Paul Clark, chairman of the board of the great John Hancock Life Insurance Company, and a valued Sheraton director, was one of the men we presented to the visiting Communists.

What did Mr. Clark do? they wanted to know.

"I work for thousands of Americans, many of them working-men," Paul explained, evidently thinking of his many employee group policies. "I work for people who want life insurance."

"You," said a Russian, looking at Paul's distinguished appearance and taking in the impeccable cut of his coat, "you are working for thousands of workingmen? We thought you were a capitalist."

Later they turned to me, after admiring our living room, the polished walnut Steinway, the crystal chandeliers, and several mid-eighteenth-century relics of the age of Sheraton and Chippendale, and inquired what I did. Remembering an experience with a streetcar, I admitted my skill in operating one of these.

[184]

Observing the renewed interest this evoked in our Oriental rugs and the ancestral paintings on the wall, I quickly added, "Here in America, of course, workers are very well paid." The Russians convened a hasty caucus, but after a moment's deliberation concluded I was joking. They burst out laughing, and all was promptly forgiven.

We soon discovered the youthful Russians not only possessed good voices but could be coaxed into offering the "Volga Boat Song" for the benefit of all present. They were somewhat astonished, on reaching the concluding measures, to hear their song reproduced in high-fidelity stereophonic sound. We had recorded their voices with dual microphones, creating the three-dimensional effect of a Cinerama production. If conceivably in 1914 I helped initiate World War I through that unforunate ten-mark gold piece episode, perhaps on this occasion I atoned in part, for in a small way we may have mitigated the pressure for World War III. The Communists finally left, having obviously enjoyed themselves. We were never sure, however, that the stereo sound reproduction in the home of a streetcar conductor ever made the Russian newspapers.

4

While offering comments on the American economy, may I introduce a rather controversial subject, that of executive salaries?

Perhaps there are times when businessmen do receive excessive remuneration, but fortunately there are safeguards to discourage abuses. Stockholders and directors with a voice in these matters are not often silent if executives are overpaid. The cleansing forces of competition can also help "drive to the wall" companies whose heads are treated too generously or may lack requisite managerial talents.

A recent study which compared Sheraton's top executive salaries with those of the heads of nearly a hundred companies of similar size, indicated our top brass was in the lowest group of all. Since under S.E.C. regulations such information is public knowledge, it is betraying no confidence to mention that no salary paid Sheraton's top officers exceeds fifty-eight thousand dollars. The president of a major Sheraton subsidiary, however, does somewhat better, drawing more than double this sum. Since he contributes to company earnings many times his compensation, his salary as well as the tab for his private plane are actually an excellent investment, not only for his company and its workers, with jobs depending on able leadership, but also for his customers, the large automobile companies, which have great confidence in his management.

Shirley Murphy, a charming *gentleman*, despite the slightly feminine tinge at times attributed to his name, is the president of this Sheraton subsidiary. The company, formerly Thompson's Spa, Inc., once operated a chain of Boston restaurants. We purchased it under the illusion that familiarity with hotel food operations would qualify us for reviving the faltering enterprise. Discovering our error, we disposed of the restaurants, changed the corporate name to Thompson Industries, and negotiated a merger with a concern headed by Shirley Murphy that made stainless steel stampings for automobile companies.

Although it is a far cry from the beautiful counter girls that in the days of Thompson's Spa helped make Boston famous, to the chromium-plated fender strips now adorning many Chrysler and General Motors fenders, or to the stainless-steel window frames on many of today's Fords, nonetheless this transmutation did mean converting the ghost of a dying restaurant chain paying quite meager wages into a lusty employer of several thousand highly skilled workers receiving millions in remuneration.

The success of this majority-owned company provides an interesting illustration of how important is the payment of whatever salaries it takes to retain the interest of men who can direct and manage a company successfully. There are of course many that will never concede that any large salaries are justified, yet I am strongly convinced America would lose one of its best mechanisms for generating prosperity should it fail, as perhaps has England, to attract through the medium of incentives the talent and know-how which makes companies prosper.

Some of the large salaries paid by our great American corporations often reach a level of several hundred thousand dollars a year, but such compensation would rise even higher were our industrial geniuses paid more nearly in proportion to their contribution to American industry. Executives of companies such as General Motors, even if their flair for production, marketing, or finance was wholly disregarded, could perhaps, through their ability to avoid costly mistakes, more than justify their seemingly high salaries, from the viewpoint of shareholders, workers, and public, for all have a stake in the ability of those who guide the destinies of a business. Actually, of course, highly paid executives retain little of their apparent compensation; most is taken by the tax collectors.

Many of us are familiar with the lotteries so common in European countries and realize that these would lose much of their appeal should the top prizes be reduced to a modest level. Perhaps, in the same way, were salaries to be sharply reduced, the incentive to qualify for top executive positions might also be impaired. With sixty-five million jobs in this country, should not the top "prizes" be rather high, especially when salaries for able administrators often represent the most profitable single outlet for available corporate funds?

Financial incentives which encourage the building and expanding of industry are clearly the basic force which creates more jobs for others, more taxable incomes for Uncle Sam, and more goods to satisfy our needs. Financial incentives are a cornerstone of national prosperity and should, when possible, be encouraged—business-baiters to the contrary notwithstanding.

It is regrettable that, while five- and six-thousand-dollar-a-year executives are usually quite plentiful, those entitled to ten or perhaps twenty thousand a year are harder to find, and any who can earn fifty thousand or more a year are exceedingly scarce and hard to locate. Able management is perhaps the key to America's greatness, and should surely not be discouraged because critics fail to understand the complexities of our economic system.

But now perhaps we can leave this materialistic subject and consider a totally different question, one that is far more abstract.

5

I would like to suggest an excursion into the realm of fantasy, an imaginary trip to Utopia in search of paths leading to a better nation. It could be an intriguing voyage, and, no matter how unlikely of fulfillment may be certain proposals for meeting our national problems, worth while. Our founding fathers, gentlemen of great perspicacity, were, after all, not necessarily omniscient, and we at least have the benefit of hindsight.

Presented herewith are twelve problems that face the nation and some "politically inexpedient" ideas for meeting them. The major problems might be listed as follows:

1. The large number of workers frequently unemployed.
2. Inflation's inroads into the value of the dollar.
3. The lack of incentives to lower prices for goods produced.
4. The failure of democracy to provide voting power commensurate with responsibilty.
5. The tribute exacted by political expediency.
6. Occasional lack of integrity among certain lawmakers, public officials, and others on the public payrolls.

7. Lack of integrity "audits" in business.
8. Excessive power of coercion and occasional instances of corruption in labor unions.
9. The conflict between liberalizing foreign trade and meeting just complaints of those injured by foreign competition.
10. Failure to gear the capital-gains tax to maximum government revenue consistent with minimum hardship to business.
11. The need to reduce and eventually perhaps eliminate recessions and depressions.
12. The need to encourage employee profit-sharing plans by making these attractive to business corporations.

The road leading to Utopia is obviously rough. It would doubtless require changes in long-accepted traditions. Concepts of democracy might have to be altered. The chances for finding solutions may be small, yet they are worth considering if Khrushchev is to be forced to swallow his threat.

TWELVE STEPS IN A NATIONAL REORGANIZATION

1. Solve the unemployment problem by substituting for existing jobless benefits a government-sponsored educational program. The unemployed would receive payment, at perhaps half the rate of existing wage scales, for increasing their knowledge or skills. Funds so expended could create an added national asset, for the potential of our work force, our most valuable "raw material," would be increased. The human asset on our national balance sheet would more than offset such costs.

2. Minimize inflation due to rising wage costs by regulating pay increases that do not reflect increased productivity. Give the Federal Reserve Banks or some other nonpolitical bodies power

to establish regional wage boards to pass on wage adjustments before they become effective.

Inflation, in many respects the same as a general sales tax, adds cumulatively each year to the burdens of all consumers. Some workers, of course, gain on balance—but only by robbing Peter to pay Paul, a form of coercion clearly not in the public interest.

3. Provide tax incentives to encourage manufacturers, distributors, and retailers to narrow margins of profit and thus increase their volume of sales. This should add to productivity and therefore to national prosperity. Everyone, theoretically, could gain.

4. Give corporations the right to cast ballots in elections on the basis perhaps of one vote for every five or ten jobs maintained, so that economic merit may carry more weight in national elections. A corporation, though still outvoted five or ten to one by its own employees, could at least have a feeble voice in matters affecting its interests. This should benefit industry, the goose with a near monopoly on the production of the nation's golden eggs.

At the historic Boston Tea Party, the principle of taxation without representation was roundly condemned, yet business concerns, providing nearly a third of the nation's tax revenue and indirectly, through jobs provided and wealth created, far more, are not allowed a single vote. This contrasts with Communist practice, where big business, in this instance the Russian government monopoly, apparently has the exclusive vote. In Russia, one dictator can presumably make all crucial decisions, especially if the opposition was adequately liquidated.

5. Educate the nation to the need for long-range rather than the often more appealing short-range goals. Publicize the importance of subordinating political expediency to the nation's long-range welfare, and discourage votes that rest on narrow popular prejudice. Permit the government to advertise in newspapers or on TV so that educational and other long-range needs may be stressed.

6. Demand absolute integrity among politicians, lawmakers, and public officials and establish an agency to enforce such rectitude, using powers similar to those of the S.E.C. in the now purified realms of finance. Clothe this agency with the right to administer truth drugs and lie-detector tests, should such procedure benefit the welfare of the nation. Integrity tests should of course be limited to actions subsequent to the effective date of this program.

7. Require companies to provide, in addition to financial audits, integrity tests for employees in "sensitive positions." Such "personnel audits" would likewise not apply to prior indiscretions. Lie detectors could be useful, despite the massive outcries that would be certain to arise. A few hundred dollars' worth of annoyance would result, but benefits might be measured in the billions. Actually, "irregularities" under such circumstances would almost immediately cease, for there would be little incentive to indulge in nefarious acts if retribution was necessarily close at hand.

8. Enact whatever legislation is needed to prevent abuses in labor unions. Integrity tests might be surprisingly useful in many instances.

9. Set up a central authority for such groups as the textile industry, which suffer from foreign competition. A form of "industrial soil bank" could receive duties collected on competing imports and use such funds for taking out of production (and placing in "mothball" reserves if needed) surplus facilities no longer required; as an alternative the funds could subsidize the injured industry. Since we recognize the right of eminent domain when land damage is involved, why not compensation for industries harmed by national policy? Once the principle is recognized, further tariff reductions could strengthen our ties with other friendly nations.

10. Establish a new category of "extra-long-term" capital gains for assets held more than five years. Such gains should be

taxed at half prevailing rates for assets held six months or more. The Treasury Department would agree, I am sure, that millions of additional tax dollars could come from transactions involving capital gains which otherwise would never occur, bringing extra needed revenue to the government. Business could in this way become more prosperous, thereby adding to the nation's financial strength. Taxing "artificial" and unreal profits resulting from price increases due to inflation would then no longer constitute an unjust form of capital levy.

Unfortunately our legislators, too often slaves to political expediency, must usually bow to workers, who are usually dominant among the voters. Our lawmakers have to—or believe they have to—be responsive to the emotions of the masses. Accordingly it often happens that proposed changes in our laws, no matter how desirable from the viewpoint of the government and the nation, must be shunned lest business might somehow benefit. It is a quaint human frailty to conclude—erroneously, of course —that whatever helps "the other side" necessarily hurts us. I assume it is unlikely that the capital-gains levy will be reduced.

11. Eliminate a principal cause of recessions and depressions by limiting wide changes in the level of security prices as measured by so-called stock-market averages. This device for controlling recessions relies on the theory that billions in security dollars (a principal reservoir of the nation's liquid wealth), when created or wiped out in great stock-market movements, are a major factor in developing business cycles. Resolute action could offset large swings in the general level of common stocks. This would supplement the more conventional methods now in use, such as controlling bank credit and interest rates.

12. Provide a substantial federal income-tax credit as an incentive to induce companies to qualify with the Treasury Department for employee profit-sharing plans. Much of the cost to the government would be recaptured on increased employee

[192]

earnings, and from rising productivity due to a better understanding by employees of their stake in American industry.

Allow the President to appoint a qualified authority to supervise this "national reorganization." Labor, management, and education might be represented, perhaps with a limited voice in the conduct of this authority.

The total cost of this ambitious program might be met through imposition of a limited federal sales tax. Five per cent might suffice, a very small burden if measured in terms of the immense prosperity that could result. However, it is hoped that all requirements for progressive taxation, *however drastic* these may have to be, should come exclusively from graduated federal income taxes. Otherwise voters would always expect the "other fellow" to pay the entire cost.

Perhaps a Congressional convention could study the merits, in the light of nearly two centuries of experience, of a change in our basic concept of democracy and of our American economic system as it has evolved since it was first envisioned by our founding fathers. It would be strange if at least some opportunities for improvement did not emerge from a new and scientific reappraisal.

If the apparent shortcomings of our economic way of life can be rectified, virtually everyone, except perhaps the makers of red ink, should gain, for a wave of prosperity greater by far than anything yet imagined would surely sweep this land. Our standard of living could rise even higher, outdistancing by an even greater margin that of any other nation. Then the inherently superior free enterprise, released from artificial shackles, could ignore Communist competition, even though that competition is supported by enforced austerity.

Political expediency, unfortunately, will make it exceedingly difficult to give serious consideration to this rocky though interesting road to Utopia.

As we take account of these many economic facts of life, I hope at the very least we will be able to discover one thing: that hard work efficiently accomplished, rather than featherbedding and duplication, is the real key to expanding national prosperity.

Perhaps our English vocabulary is deficient because of the lack of an anonym for the word austerity. Perhaps we should coin such a word. *Luxurosity* might serve the purpose.

Labor leaders and politicians make heavy capital out of promises to their constituencies of "luxurosity," while austerity to them is an evil to be shunned—except perhaps in times of national emergency.

It seems to me there is a historical background in the ancient rivalry between Athens and Sparta. The former was evidently allergic to the disciplines and austerity practiced by the Spartans; yet Athens eventually succumbed during the Peloponnesian war.

Rome in the fourth century discovered to its discomfort that history can repeat itself. Luxurosity as practiced by the Roman Empire was no match for the tougher barbarians to the north.

We, a people fond of luxuries not ordinarily available to any but the elite in Russia, are threatened by the power of a heavily disciplined Russian economy. It seems worth our while to calculate the risks that this situation presents. Can we permit in this instance that history should once more repeat itself?

The progress of any country depends largely upon its major resources. These consist essentially of the skills of its workers, the effectiveness of managements, the abundance of available raw materials, the existence of wide markets, and a supply of capital to provide needed tools and equipment. However, economic advantages of this nature are in part counteracted by inefficiency, corruption, unnecessary extravagance, as well as by the pressures for luxurosity. It is the sum of favorable forces, reduced by the extent of crippling elements, that determines a nation's economic growth—two or three per cent a year for the United States compared with allegedly three to four times this rate for the U.S.S.R.

Politicians have often reaped political advantage from the masses by permitting the impression to exist that heavy spending programs financed by high taxes on the wealthy classes constitute a sort of "Robin Hood" activity in which the well-to-do are robbed for the benefit of poorer people. Actually it seems to me the nation's workers are the ones who pay most dearly for municipal extravagance, costly benefits, and obstacles to efficiency sometimes imposed by labor organizations. I believe ultimately it is not the wealthy people who are primarily hurt by an unfavorable business climate. Business has to succeed even in areas where unduly heavy taxation and other obstacles to the operations of a business exist. People usually have to have jobs to support their families. Accordingly wage levels inevitably adjust themselves to the realities of a prevailing business climate. Large local life-insurance companies, for instance, must compete with other similar companies in different parts of the country. These companies provide jobs for many thousands of clerical workers whose compensation depends in part on the cost of doing business in any given locality.

If the cost of doing business in Boston is higher than in New York, because of taxes, welfare burdens, union restrictions, etc., the difference is almost sure to show up in lower wage rates paid insurance clerks in Boston. This differential may amount to as much as five or ten dollars a week per employee—a high though unseen tribute exacted by those responsible for unnecessary burdens imposed on employers of labor in some regions.

The Russian economic system expands under direction from the top. It is based on regimentation with controls aimed at increasing production and productivity. Under our free-enterprise system, we rely largely on natural incentives. The lure of economic gain is expected to attract sufficient funds into investment channels to assure a gradual expansion of our own production facilities. Since New Deal days, however, high taxation of larger incomes—those ordinarily providing funds for investment in industry—has tended to dry up these sources for financing the expansion of productivity.

The graduated system of taxation may be—at least to some extent—justified from the point of view of social justice. However, if it is continued, other sources of investment funds must be created by providing necessary incentives. This should be the free-enterprise substitute for the Russian centralized controls.

Much, though not enough, has already been accomplished through incentives created by our government. In Puerto Rico, for instance, where industrial development was backward, accompanied by much unemployment, corporations were attracted by the granting of ten-year exemptions from income taxes. These incentives created a virtually explosive expansion in industrial activity that produced tens of thousands of new jobs in Puerto Rico.

Government tax incentives are currently being applied in a manner that solves partially the problem of attracting more funds for investment. Tax incentives encourage the growth of great company-sponsored pension and employee savings funds. These growing aggregations of investment capital, largely a device for encouraging savings by employees, represent a most constructive trend. Unfortunately the utilization of these funds does not always serve the greatest need of the nation—the expansion of industrial capacity. Here again the government could provide further incentives to directing such funds into the most desirable channels.

Young and growing industries are especially in need of investment funds for expansion. These companies, however, are usually precluded from consideration by the large pension funds, which are usually administered by banks unwilling to take any risks whatsoever. Bankers fear the possible loss of the profitable custodianship of these large aggregations of capital. However, insurance companies—basing their safety on the reliability of vital statistics tables—have become successful specialists in the field of risk taking, since every life-insurance policy is obviously a risk. If pension funds could be given an incentive to take intelligent risks in the field of investments, especially in instances where national economic expansion is involved, they could render a greater service to the country. The premiums in the form of higher interest rates available on less "seasoned" loans should more than compensate for an added risk. Some form of insurance for such increased risks could be helpful in our objective of meeting competition from a controlled Russian economy.

There seems to be a close relationship between expansion of savings and investments, on the one hand, and industrial expansion. If this is so, an increase of productivity calls for the transfer of more of our national income to investments. Total investments in this nation amount to perhaps a trillion dollars. An extra thirty billions a year could theoretically add three per cent more annually to our industrial capacity. This increase would make it harder for the Russians to catch up with our present economic lead.

In other words, enlarging the scope of employee pension and savings funds and liberalizing investment policies of the ultra-conservative bankers administering these funds could provide a powerful weapon for the conduct of our economic war against the U.S.S.R. by encouraging the expansion of our productive machinery.

Of these various solutions I have outlined to meet our economic ills, the program for controlling business cycles is disputed with especial vehemence by most leading economists. I have therefore amplified this concept in a subsequent chapter, and presented it in greater detail in the Appendix. The subject, perhaps the most vital the nation faces, deserves careful thought, since none of the nostrums yet advanced by economists has solved the dilemma. With common-stock prices again penetrating rarified atmosphere as measured by so-called market averages, the possibility of a new and catastrophic depression in the visible future cannot be wholly excluded from calculations.

If the antidote to a new depression is to be the unleashing of vast amounts of purchasing power by creating unbalanced budgets, easy credits, and other devices which presumably can and probably will stem an incipient depression, then the stimulating monetary forces may make exceedingly costly inroads—through the path of inflation—into the foundations of our economy.

Having completed our imaginary trip to Utopia, let us now return from the realms of the theoretical, and consider once more some rather practical questions. One of these deals with the daily tasks confronting a corporation executive.

XVII.

Duties of a President

AMONG the duties of a company president is meeting corporate obligations to the public, to employees, and to shareholders. To emphasize this need, Sheraton directors recently adopted a resolution which appears on the official records. It reads:

"The principal objective is to operate Sheraton hotels as efficiently as possible in order to produce maximum earnings consistent with the highest standards of business ethics. This means giving recognition to the rights of workers who make the success of the company possible, as well as meeting the obligation to render outstanding service to the public." Fulfillment of this mandate is the first duty of our president.

Within the framework of this directive there is a further ambition—to expand company activities when possible, for through growth we can best discharge our responsibilities to those eager for advancement, and create new opportunities.

Our sales volume is approaching two hundred million dollars a year. Improving the earnings by one and one-half per cent of this sales volume each year is not an unrealistic goal for a management desiring progress, and can be achieved by greater efficiency, reduced waste, a larger volume of sales, or such devices as the Operation Pay Dirt program. This one and one-half per cent, besides absorbing some portion of the cost of annual wage increases, or relieving somewhat the pressure for room-rate advances, could also help finance, at least in part, the expansion of the business. With rising population curves, new job opportunities are needed to prevent future unemployment. A sum equal to one and a half per cent of sales over a year's time would amount to approximately ten thousand dollars a day.

tors recently adopted a resoultion which appears on the official

This figure of ten thousand dollars, then, is a rough measure of the added income that the president, using the skills of his executive organization, might consider a suitable daily objective. There are, of course, bleak days when, after long hours and effort, little is accomplished. At other times, ideas may "click," and opportunities for large savings may be within reach.

Recently an ambition to capitalize on the value of nearly a million outstanding credit cards resulted in a plan, adopted almost on the spur of the moment, to form a Sheraton Central Credit Card Club. The cost of incorporation was only a few hundred dollars, though access to Sheraton's credit-card files was a valuable asset. Sixty days later we exchanged the credit-card company for securities of the Diners' Club worth several million dollars. Utilizing such resources obviously paid handsome dividends.

An important advantage of multiple-hotel systems comes from economies inherent in group operations, and it is one of the president's duties to capitalize when possible on these opportunities. To accomplish this objective, we often test local publicity campaigns, incentive programs for desk clerks, new systems of food control, or other promising devices, in a single hotel. If the idea fails, it is quickly discarded. If successful, it can usually be adapted to fifty other hotels. If we "lose" we lose only once, but if we win, the benefits are often multiplied many times, and may be perpetuated for many years.

In the operation of a business enterprise, errors of omission are often more costly than those actually made. An important responsibility of a president is to hold down, when possible, losses which arise from neglected opportunities. Once during the depths of the depression we were offered the Empire State Building for five million dollars, only a half-million of this to be in cash. Timidity discouraged us from asking our Boston bank for the needed loan, though in retrospect I am sure the money was available. Today such a half-million-dollar "equity" in the Empire State Building would be worth thirty millions or more, sixty times the cash requirement once indicated, an illustration of the miracle of leverage as well as the magnitude of possible errors of omission.

I believe it was H. L. Mencken who once shrewdly observed that it is not the things we do but rather what we don't do that we eventually regret. I confess a profound admiration for the controversial Mencken, particularly when casting longing glances at the majestic dimensions of the Empire State Building.

Another duty company presidents often face is raising capital for expansion. Outstanding senior debt, we believe, should not exceed half the fair market value of the real estate held. This is a safeguard against the ravages of possible future depressions. However, since the value of hotels is proportional to their earnings, when we increase the income through greater efficiency or by other devices, it is usually possible to raise additional funds by selling more debentures, provided the total outstanding senior-debt ratio remains conservative.

Marketing additional securities once presented some unusual problems, for real-estate bonds had fared badly during the great depression, and even twenty-five years later investment bankers were still perceptibly gun-shy. Cautiously, some five years ago, an investment banking firm, together with a small group of underwriters, marketed a modest issue of Sheraton debentures. Three millions were offered, and the issue, perhaps surprising the bankers, was a substantial success, leading soon after to a more ambitious offering.

The timing, in this second instance, was less propitious, for rising money rates were pushing bond prices down, and then a recession added to the difficulties. Fortunately, prejudice against real-estate bonds was diminishing, partly perhaps because Sheraton common shares (adjusted for stock dividends) and debentures as quoted in *The New York Times* had been reaching new highs during the 1957–58 recession, and partly because Sheraton has been one of the top performers since the days of Pearl Harbor, among the more than twelve hundred companies listed on the New York Stock Exchange, surpassing by several fold even such paragons of growth as International Business Machines Company during that period of time.

The interesting record of hotel-company securities in the recent market recession, a phenomenon in which shares of a worthy competitor shared, may account to some degree for the greater respect now accorded our industry by a once skeptical financial community.

During the frenzied nineteen-twenties hotels were apparently built not as much to fill existing needs as to provide real-estate bond salesmen with securities to meet an almost insatiable demand for such investments. Top-heavy debt structures, lack of emphasis on managerial experience, overvalued properties, and lack of economic need for many buildings financed by unsound bond issues contributed to a precipitous collapse when ill winds of a depression started blowing in the nineteen-thirties. Rent controls of the Second World War froze hotel rates at those depressed levels brought about by the "overproduction" of the nineteen-twenties and the depression of the nineteen-thirties. Thus the industry's ills were perpetuated through most of the nineteen-forties. Fortunately, at least some of the difficulties of past decades are no longer likely to recur.

Two years ago we organized a subsidiary to distribute Sheraton "income debentures," a security with a noticeable resemblance to preferred stock. These, being debt securities, have the significant advantage that the interest payments are tax-deductible and only half as burdensome as comparable preferred-stock dividends. Financing with income debentures unfortunately is somewhat unfamiliar to most investment bankers and few, if any, have distributed such issues except in reorganizations. However, our financial trail-blazing has been productive. We recently marketed an issue of fifteen millions of these income debentures, a substantial portion going to several of the country's largest and most prominent investment trusts.

A second offering, one that literally set the financial community aghast, consisted of seven-and-a-half-per-cent capital income debentures. This seemingly magnanimous interest rate is almost unprecedented among better-known successful companies. Actually, we consider it an indication of strength rather than a confession of weakness. There is a custom prevalent among many corporations of issuing junior debt securities with a more conventional interest rate, but supplemented with conversion privileges which are in effect a call on some common stock. Sheraton, as a major growth company, found this more usual approach far too costly compared with the alternative of offering a somewhat higher interest rate.

Some five years ago, when we first marketed an issue of debentures with warrants to purchase Sheraton stock—a device similar to a conversion privilege—the warrants served as a bonus to implement an unrealistic interest rate. They alone are now worth more than the entire issue of debentures originally sold. That is, it would cost nearly seven million dollars today to repurchase at prevailing prices the debentures and their warrants, for which little more than three millions was originally paid. When we contemplate this costly financing, we realize it might have been cheaper to issue debentures calling for thirty per cent interest

back in 1953, rather than ones with warrants to purchase Sheraton common shares.

Actually, seven-and-a-half-per-cent interest on capital debentures is not too burdensome, for these interest payments, all
tax-deductible, actually cost less than would dividends on a three-
and-three-quarter-per-cent preferred stock, since the latter are
not tax-deductible.

With large issues of company securities in the hands of investors, the need occasionally arises to address financial analysts, a
recurring duty of many company presidents. When undertaking
such activities, I always tried to put these awesome financial
experts in a receptive mood to prepare them for the heavier fare
inevitably awaiting them. A few favorite Sheraton stories serve
this purpose. One tells of an experience several years ago in
Dallas, Texas. When that city discovered that Houston, an
invidious rival, had acquired the new Shamrock Hotel, in an
uproar it determined to rectify an intolerable situation. It must
have a new hotel of its own, and we were urged to assist in the
solution of this crisis.

Three of us arrived in Dallas after an all-night flight, landing as the sun began to rise. Most of the city was still asleep,
but newsboys were on the streets. Large black headlines in
the morning papers greeted us. Reading them in a glow of
pleasant surprise, we were astonished at the cordial reception
being accorded us. They said that an Eastern hotel chain was
contemplating a Dallas hotel. Our pride in the spectacular headlines diminished when we read: "Large site already selected."
This we considered a little premature. After all, we had only
just arrived. Further on we read: "The new hotel will be
a Statler."

Although stunned by this revelation, we nonetheless proceeded to a hotel where reservations had been arranged. Irvine
Shubert, our general counsel, and Bob Moore were along. We
had a pleasant suite, though a critical Sheraton eye might have

detected occasional deviations from accustomed Mary Kennedy specifications. As our mission was obviously in vain, we planned our return journey. We stopped at the desk for our account and were told it was forty dollars. A little steep, I thought, while reaching for my wallet, a somewhat unaccustomed gesture since even in those days few cities lacked a Sheraton hotel.

"Just a moment," the clerk reminded us. "It's five P.M., two hours past our check-out time. Eighty dollars." Again we hesitated, but only for an instant. After all, why should we object if a hotel demanded "adequate" rates? Counting out the money, we remembered Gene Eppley, a fellow director from Omaha come to Dallas at our invitation. Owner of a group of Midwest hotels, Eppley knew Texas well and could have assisted in selecting a site.

"May we have Mr. Eppley's bill?" we asked of the pleasant young clerk.

"Sorry, sir," was the courteous reply. "We can't charge Mr. Eppley anything for his room. You see, *he* is a hotel man."

Another story I enjoy telling security analysts—for good measure if the first fails to thaw their defensive armaments—has to do with the General Brock Hotel at Niagara Falls, Ontario, now the Sheraton-Brock Hotel.

The General Brock was a part of a transaction that included the Mt. Royal in Montreal, the King Edward of Toronto, and several other Canadian hotels. On the day we took title we drove to Niagara Falls to inspect the impressive General Brock, which overlooks this famous natural wonder of the world. A pleasant manager with a somewhat British accent greeted us cordially, and began to show us around. He pointed out the luxury suites with great pride, and we were duly apprised of the famous members of the royal family who had honored the General Brock. Presently we asked who the general was for whom the hotel was named. The manager apparently did not hear, so we tried again.

"Just who was General Brock?" I repeated with slightly greater emphasis.

"Just a moment," the manager interrupted, pointing to the magnificent panorama. "From here you have an even better view."

"But who," I demanded, this time with real determination, "was General Brock, and what made him so famous that a hotel was named for him?"

Seeing no escape, the manager finally broke down. "General Brock," he admitted with reluctance, "was the general, back in 1814, who chased the Americans out of Canada."

As an addendum to this story, I enjoy telling the security analysts how for a time we were dismayed at the earnings of the Sheraton-Brock. Why, we wondered, with honeymooners so plentiful, were the exquisite accommodations not in greater demand? I then explain how an alert efficiency expert found a clue. All the rooms had boasted new twin beds. Today, nearly always filled to capacity, the Sheraton-Brock has mostly large double beds.

Besides the president's duty to keep financial analysts informed and, hopefully, interested in the potentials of our industry, there are other responsibilities under the heading of public relations. Company executives must participate, when asked to do so, in worth-while community activities, and the president is no exception. Thus it came to pass some years ago, when the Greater Boston Chamber of Commerce, doubtless in desperation to find a successor for a retiring president, turned to me, I promptly accepted and served for a year. I lacked the talents and experience required, but fortunately William Bird, a near replica of a human dynamo, was well equipped as managing director to carry most of the load.

Although momentous events occurred during my year with the Chamber, the truth, a carefully guarded secret, was that most of the achievements had previously been sparked by effective actions of various Chamber committees. Though my own contributions were small, the education I received was very real. Among other things, I learned of the accomplishments of such civic organizations in combating legislation adverse to the economic interests of the area, their work in attracting new business to a community, and their contribution toward long-range planning for the region's advancement. The work of the Greater Boston Chamber of Commerce, financed on a relatively small budget, must actually have been worth tens of millions of dollars a year. The constant battle waged by the Chamber of Commerce for constructive long-range programs, in contrast to political and labor pressures for immediate benefits, is not sufficiently recognized in most American communities.

I may be wrong on this point, but it seems to me this difference in emphasis often, though of course not always, reflects opposing views of Republicans and Democrats; the former are more often seeking a longer-range and less popular approach, while the latter are more likely to be concerned with the immediate consumption of the wealth the nation produces. Although both points of view have staunch support, it is understandable that business interests place more weight on future benefits than on the immediate consumption of the fruits of free enterprise. This difference, I suspect, accounts largely for the present status of Republicans as the minority party.

Another civic activity followed my year with the Greater Boston Chamber of Commerce. I became president of the World Trade Center in New England, an organization modeled after International House in New Orleans, which takes credit for raising the tonnage of its great Mississippi port from eighteenth to second place among seaports of the nation. The port of Boston, a great shipping center in the days of clipper ships, is now relatively stagnant, enmeshed in political, labor, and rate problems which currently deprive Boston of much of the opportunity for growth which a great ocean harbor normally contributes. To solve some of the pressing problems in a program to regain some of New England's lost international trade is one of the many objectives to which the World Trade Center in New England is dedicated.

Struggling with political and labor problems affecting the economy of this region presents some baffling challenges, but the task is not hopeless, for Boston is gradually learning what cities like Cincinnati, Pittsburgh, New Orleans, and St. Louis have already discovered—that businessmen, legislators, labor leaders, and eventually educators too, must work together shoulder to shoulder, contributing their respective skills and experience, if great American metropolitan areas are to escape the deadly erosion presently being visited upon so many municipalities. My association with civic activities has been interesting and rewarding, and I am confident organized effort to increase international trade in the six New England states will eventually have significant repercussions in a New England renaissance.

Besides occasional civic duties, a corporation president has many other obligations. By no means least among these is the requirement for occasional crystal-ball gazing, for it is usually the president who must forecast, for company guidance, coming economic trends.

As an illustration of the need for viewing the future, there are instances when some doubt may exist as to continuing economic stability, and plans for expansion may require modification. Then, if an expected slump does not come, normal progress will have been unnecessarily interrupted. To gauge the future, Sheraton uses a simple economic indicator, one that has proven most reliable, though often belittled by leading economists—the level and general trend of security prices.

Our theory of forecasting economic trends is based on the assumption that minor fluctuations in business that occur normally often become magnified into serious recessions or depressions by changes in the level of security prices which they *cause*.

The theory rests on the assumption that the amount of liquid wealth in the country, much of it represented by the market value of common stocks, often determines if certain large transactions will take place. Common stocks constitute the largest single reservoir of the nation's liquid wealth.

Since common stocks at any given time are readily exchangeable—practically overnight—for cash, changes in their general level affect our economy much in the same way as do changes in the "supply" of currency or bank deposits. No quantity theory of money that fails to give a proper "weighing" to all reservoirs of "potential purchasing power," including the value of marketable securities, is likely to have real significance.

When the total of "liquid dollars" represented by common stocks rises or falls significantly there is of course a psychological impact, but more importantly, a change in the level of security quotations often determines whether the means are at hand to finance the purchase of a house or a business enterprise, or for other activities where cash in the bank or the equivalent in security dollars is a requisite. A change in market value of stocks may affect materially not only the availability of the needed purchasing power, but also the borrowing capacity of millions of people whose wealth is a factor in our economy.

A recent study by our Henderson Foundation, though not completed, indicates that some automobiles, and a fairly substantial number of expensive homes, are financed by means of the purchasing power inherent in common stocks. When, as occurred in August 1957, precipitous declines in common-stock values wipe out up to five and six billions of stock-market values in a single day, liquid wealth is swept away and available potential purchasing power is reduced. Our company, convinced that such destruction of values would be translated into a declining level of business activity, curtailed by many millions its budget for projected alterations and improvements. For all American corporations such attrition in business activity doubtless reached high in the billions. With the threat of a depression, cash would have to be husbanded.

This phenomenon of retrenchment became widespread toward the end of 1957, and business indicators started turning appreciably downward. However, we guarded against the impact on Sheraton. We were convinced a severe recession would follow the precipitous drop in market averages. Falling security prices, we felt, were causing, rather than predicting the extent of, the recession.

Similarly the strength in security prices during the early months of 1958, following a previously established and necessary foundation for recovery in the form of several months of relative market stability, clearly indicated an approaching improvement in business conditions during the last half of 1958. When common stocks in April 1958 rose from their trading range, starting once more on an upward course, it was virtually certain business indices would follow upward, despite the widespread skepticism expressed at the time. The sharpness of the rise in security prices had virtually guaranteed an equally sharp rebound in business activity.

I have presented a further outline of this theory in the accompanying Appendix. It attempts to explain why a country like Russia, where common stocks are unknown, is relatively free of cyclical phenomena. It points out that in European countries, where common-stock holdings, though less widespread than in our country, do exist, cyclical disturbances strike with less severity than is customary here. In America it is often the common stock rather than the French family sock that serves as repository for much of our available liquid wealth.

Not until we adopt some device, either as suggested in the Appendix or in some other form, to control major market swings can we expect to free ourselves from the devastation of major business cycles. This is the conclusion my theory seeks to establish.

For more than twenty-five years I have crusaded for the acceptance of this view of the major cause of business cycles. Prominent economists are conspicuously skeptical, many openly ridiculing the theory that a changing level of security prices can seriously affect business activity. More recently, confronted with ever more convincing evidence of the significance of this relationship, some of the nation's economic experts are beginning to give some credence to these conclusions. Eventually I hope the theory will be widely accepted, paving the way, perhaps, for the control of the greatest of our economic ills.

Besides cyclical troubles that often beset us, there are other problems occasionally facing American corporate enterprises. Sometimes we of Sheraton try, perhaps with unorthodox tools, to deal with some of these.

XVIII.

Sheraton's Ten Commandments

A NUMBER of troublesome ills often plague our corporation. To ward off a few of these, we have sought at times to build up a degree of corporate immunity to at least some of the more insidious ones. For this we have devised a company "Decalogue," a collection of "thou shalt nots" dedicated to all those connected with Sheraton. We believe fewer guests would visit our hotels each year had we not sought actively to discourage many transgressions by formulating our own private Ten Commandments.

Our first and greatest admonition is: "Thou shalt not throw thy weight around, however irresistible may be the urge to do so."

This first commandment arises from the occasional need to dissuade some newly created third vice president from demanding, when visiting Sheraton hotels, that brand of super-service more properly reserved for a Persian potentate, or perhaps some freely spending oil tycoon. Sheraton executives from the president down are expected to reflect credit on the company rather than display, on the mere strength of their Boston credentials, the temperament of a celebrated chef or a famous prima donna. I admit that my personal efforts at enforcing this regulation are often thwarted by the irrepressible desire of managers to show off some glamorous presidential suite or a newly decorated "room of tomorrow." Actually, I rarely escape deferential treatment, such as the ever recurring basket of fruit with the manager's card attached, a custom originally designed to impress some visiting V.I.P. At any rate the fruit is genuine—I tasted it once.

Hotel managers do not often realize how much sweeter would be the music in the president's ear should the official greeting express regret that "unfortunately the Presidential Suite is occupied." Since these luxury accommodations usually bring from fifty to a hundred and fifty dollars a day, inroads of such magnitude into the hotel's potential profits do injury to the memory of my Scotch forebears—and besides, there is no danger of losing my own patronage, even without such attention.

In one instance I thought I observed with propriety the amenities of the commandment that forbids the throwing of one's weight around. After concluding in New York one evening the lengthy ritual which vested in Sheraton title to one of the better known Midwestern hotels, I arrived the next day in the lobby of this newly acquired property to meet our general counsel. An attempt to reach him on the house phone met with no success whatsoever, for the hotel had not recorded his arrival. Knowing he had checked in the night before, I was understandably annoyed. Near the desk stood two immaculately attired males in the morning coats readily recognizable as badges of high hotel rank. Observing that their deliberations concerned the baseball scores, yet remembering our first commandment, I turned to them most politely. Was either, perhaps, an assistant manager? Clearly irked by this intrusion, shaking their heads in negative gestures, they pointed to a much encumbered desk clerk who, I was to understand, would help me when the queue of prospective registrants had been accommodated. At that crucial moment the former president and general manager of the hotel appeared in the lobby. Recognizing me, perhaps from pictures in the trade press, he greeted me with cordial deference as the new owner of this multimillion-dollar establishment. "These," he said, turning to the gentlemen with the striped pants, "are your two assistant managers."

I have rarely seen more unhappy expressions on two rather red faces.

Our second Sheraton commandment relates to a quite different subject, that of receiving gifts. This commandment proclaims: "Thou shalt not take presents from those seeking thy favors. Beware of those who bear gifts."

We often find it strange to learn how many people wishing to do business with our company suddenly discover a need to shower us with costly tokens of affection. Such attention is most common at Christmastime, but can also be shown on almost any other occasion.

To discourage favors for the gratification of our people, we mail a polite note each year just before Christmas to our many suppliers, suggesting with distinct firmness that the recipients observe our rule of no gifts. Despite these timely reminders, costly items still frequently appear. Rather than embarrass the thoughtful sender, we suggest the favored employee relinquish to a specified company vicepresident the particular offending object. It is eventually auctioned off, the proceeds contributing to an occasional extra outing sponsored by the employees' welfare fund.

I do not wish to suggest our particular brand of "halo" necessarily outshines such accouterments ordinarily displayed by others. It simply means that adherence to our second commandment often saves us a great many dollars.

Few practices are more destructive to successful hotel operation than countenancing valuable donations. This applies especially to gifts by purveyors to those who buy food for hotels.

The insidious angle is the excessive cost to a hotel in relation to the trivial amounts of generosity usually involved. For example, the extra cost of food for some large hotels has sometimes reached a quarter of a million dollars a year due to only a relatively few dollars of a supplier's proffered largesse.

Many years ago, when attending an out-of-town banquet, I sat next to the head of a large food company whose customers were schools, clubs, hospitals, and hotels. He told me that forty per cent of his company's accounts depended in varying degree on favors extended by what he called his "gratuity department." He contended it was an evil most suppliers deplored, but also acknowledged that the loss of a major percentage of a company's sales volume could easily prove fatal. Today, twenty years later, I hope, at least in part owing to efforts of the larger hotel chains, an appreciable reduction in this once widespread custom has been achieved.

A third commandment, owing its origin to some unfortunate experiences, proclaims to all our managers: "Suffer not thy wives to gratify a yen to decorate Sheraton hotels. May wives render unto their husbands what is rightfully theirs, but unto Mary Kennedy that which is in her domain."

Once I visited a small hotel of ours on Wood Street in Pittsburgh, before we purchased the William Penn, now the Penn-Sheraton Hotel. Hearing Mary Kennedy had been there shortly before, I assumed the manager would soon show me his newly decorated rooms. As I expected, this ritual was presently under way, but the results were unexpected, for the color combinations were most distressing. Torn between loyalty to our lady vice president responsible for Sheraton decor and the evident need for admitting her failure, I explained with what tact I could muster that even the ablest in the art of decorating should be allowed an occasional lapse. However, I said, since our manager had been clearly let down, our otherwise sacrosanct third commandment might perhaps this once be suspended. Hereafter, should he so desire, the manager could choose the colors himself. At this he turned visibly pale and finally decided to confess. He had misplaced the Kennedy colors, and those in the newly painted rooms were all of his own selection.

A fourth commandment, beamed at Sheraton desk clerks, warns them in solemn tones: "Thou shalt not dishonor a confirmed reservation, lest thy days be short in the job thy company giveth thee."

Desk clerks are not infallible, of course, and errors do at times occur. However, there is often scholarly doubt whether more than a fraction of the guests turned away for lack of reservations, who invariably claim they wired in advance, actually did so. More often the subterfuge of claiming a prior confirmation only reflects the prospective guest's mild oversight in attending to this seemingly trivial detail.

Occasionally, though fortunately at rare intervals, a group does retain rooms beyond an agreed-upon date of departure, an emergency leaving desk clerks as well as others in authority in an acute state of distress. Though we usually provide a factor of safety so that desk clerks can cope with these painful situations, there can be, and unfortunately sometimes are, instances when hotels are overbooked. Sheraton prides itself on the rare incidence of such catastrophes; though if lightning does strike, we try to console ourselves, at least in part, with the knowledge that for each customer thus alienated, and presumably transformed into a sworn enemy, perhaps two new guests have been garnered after being exposed to a like indignity by an erring competitor.

Once a major misfortune, clearly beyond our control, occurred in Washington during the Second World War, when Washington hotels were heavily booked in advance. We received from the White House an "invitation"—a euphemism for "command"—to provide forthwith at least forty rooms. Winston Churchill, on an unannounced mission, had arrived in the capital, accompanied by a sizable entourage. Forty irate businessmen who on that occasion automatically joined the ranks of displaced persons destined for the proverbial park bench—or perhaps, even worse, for some rooming-house accommodations—doubtless never forgave us. We could not even advance a legitimate alibi, for the Churchill visit, we were warned, was "classified." The patronage of these forty angry individuals, I suspect, has since been enjoyed by Conrad Hilton.

Our fifth commandment can, we believe, elevate perceptibly the efficiency of any hotel. It decrees: "Thou shalt not give orders to an underling without making fully clear the exact purpose thereof."

We are firmly convinced subordinates will accomplish considerably more if reasons for the tasks imposed upon them are made crystal clear. The belief that "subordinates are there to do or die, and should never ask the reason why," has no place in Sheraton's operating concepts, just as the old adage, "Papa knows best and never need explain," has little more to commend it than a handful of gravel in an automobile gear box.

Our sixth commandment prescribes: "Thou shalt duly recall that the virtues of those running small hotels may be the vices of those guiding larger establishments."

This commandment was borrowed from our friend the late Edward A. Filene, the great department-store magnate, who applied this differentiation to retail establishments. Filene was the curious, though not unique, combination of a genius who could create one of the nation's greatest specialty stores and a visionary who could almost wreck the same enterprise.

His dogma that the virtues of a small shopkeeper are the

vices of larger operators is especially applicable to hotels, and doubtless sprang from the genius side of his nature. In shop-keeping, as Filene called his trade, as with innkeeping, which occasionally designates ours, the small operator excels by person-ally supervising all minute details. In large hotels, however, ability to delegate authority is often the principal requisite. Success depends more on talent for selecting, training, and inspir-ing department heads, for these must bear responsibility for carrying out details of a successful large hotel operation. It is upon department heads in such hotels that the work falls of supervising food and beverage matters and those relating to front-office procedure, the boiler rooms, elevator maintenance, and perhaps the selection of talent for a supper room, should the hotel be among the few still offering evening entertainment.

One of Sheraton's able managers of a small hotel caused some acute headaches when subsequently promoted—as seemed eminently logical—to a large luxury operation. Only those skilled in the art of delegating authority seem to achieve real success when managing larger properties.

Our seventh commandment, is properly a crucial one. It stipulates: "Thou shalt not demand the last 'drop of blood' when effecting a business transaction."

This restraint, we feel, pays off in the millions. Despite the temptation to drive a harsh bargain, sharp dealings rarely seem to pay; they too often misfire, allowing others to secure the wanted signatures on crucial dotted lines, and scars of battle from such encounters frequently preclude later profitable trans-actions. Most Sheraton hotels have increased so much in value in recent years that a few dollars' leeway in the negotiations, though seemingly vital at the time, could have little present significance. This does not mean we are "soft" in our negotia-tions, but it does imply that the words "Take it or leave it" are rarely uttered during these delicate sparring matches.

Furthermore, we do not believe in losing an opportunity through stubborn refusal to appreciate an opponent's point of view. Sheraton frequently has first call when a hotel—or a chain of these, for that matter—comes on the market, suggesting that observing our seventh commandment pays satisfactory dividends.

Our eighth commandment admonishes waiters and other technicians of the spud and the bean, functionaries whose skills so often determine the popularity of a hotel. It demands: "Thou shalt not permit the escape of those fleeting degrees of Fahrenheit so essential to a customer's delight when he is exposed to delicacies on a hotel menu. May unending torture pursue a kitchen staff that suffers beans to be boiled beyond a specified limit."

The ninth commandment is for all in authority: "Thou shalt not make decisions based on a 'feeling' that some action may be called for." Sheraton decisions must rest on firmer foundations; careful calculations, or knowledge of the facts, are demanded. Trial-and-error may occasionally be acceptable, especially if results can be gauged with an open mind, but banned to the far reaches of hoteldom's Siberia are decisions resting on "hunches," rules of thumb, or conclusions reflecting our emotions. Far better to rely on that sterner stuff emerging from a ubiquitous company slide rule.

When decision-making is difficult under our prescribed approach, we sometimes use another technique by assigning to all favorable and unfavorable aspects of a suggested course of action what we call a dollar "price tag." By this dollar tag, we mean an estimated value in dollars and cents for each advantage and disadvantage associated with a given project. By adding the plusses and minuses, despite the hazards of approximations, we usually secure valuable guidance for making constructive decisions. The wisdom of this profitable approach may be illustrated by reference to certain obvious pitfalls in some of our emotional responses.

People, for instance, can become greatly aroused over lurid crimes involving appealing victims; yet they may give little thought to a theft of some vital military secret. The former may involve injuries which a few thousand dollars of compensation would readily cure, while the latter might cause losses high in the millions of dollars. An innocent victim with an emotional appeal, such as a child at the bottom of a well, or an individual falsely accused, often produces great headlines in our sensational press, while lesser space may suffice for a far more significant event. Too many decisions, unfortunately, are affected by an emotional impact; too few by solid reasoning, despite a disparity in the dollar "price tag" that could have revealed the discrepancy.

The tenth and necessarily last commandment—since precedent precludes variation—is: "Thou shalt not explode like a firecracker when an underling falleth into error, lest perchance it be thou who erred by not providing proper guidance."

Even our top executives, I am sure, should occasionally ponder this commandment, for a subordinate will rarely err sufficiently to arouse his superior's wrath if the latter has properly instructed the hapless potential sinner by warning of hazards that might confront him.

I hope Larry Appley of the American Management Association, that august body that shares with the American Medical Association the initials A.M.A., will approve this collection of commandments, for many will conform, if I learned my lesson well, with current A.M.A. gospel.

XIX.

Building New Hotels

DURING its first twenty years as a hotel company, Sheraton depended for growth on the purchase of existing hotels. We tried to make these profitable by redesigning, modernizing and re-equipping them to operate more efficiently and to attract a growing volume of business. In March of 1957 we blazed a new trail by opening our first brand-new hotel, the nine-hundred-room, sixteen-million-dollar Philadelphia Sheraton, equipped with all latest facilities and provided with banquet accommodations for three thousand guests.

Many of our strongest supporters, among them important stockholders who had seen their shares rise a hundredfold in value, were now in an uproar. Doubtless they consulted their newspapers daily, fearful lest the market value of Sheraton stock should now begin to crumble. On learning that our forecast of earnings for this Philadelphia venture had indicated red ink, they must have been even more convinced that Sheraton was losing its financial mind, embarking perhaps on a program of erecting white elephants for the edification of a once successful management. They must have forgotten that we too have an interest in the future of the company.

Predictions of red ink, to be sure, were correct, but this particular color on our financial pages can be misleading, for, strangely enough, it can be profitable to a business such as ours. Under the revised revenue laws enacted some years ago to permit double depreciation on newly constructed buildings as an incentive for creating more jobs, the extra deductions often absorb all taxable income. This can postpone for several years the time when the tax-collector eventually appears. Temporary freedom from income taxes for companies in the "red" makes ownership of new buildings especially desirable during the early years, when added cash for fast debt-reduction is helpful.

A second factor favoring construction of new hotels is the generous financing often available, an advantage arising from the willingness of local banks and financial institutions, usually alert to civic needs, to assist when new hotels are needed.

Sheraton built its Philadelphia hotel on the basis of forecasts of potential available earnings before deductions for depreciation. Such annual earnings, we calculated, would reach a million dollars. The first year's operation actually produced a cash flow of one per cent above original estimates, and, since "accelerated" depreciation eliminated taxable earnings, we were able to apply the entire million dollars to the repayment of loans which civic-minded banks had advanced. The hotel, though "in the red," was actually very profitable.

Unfortunately, with high rates of depreciation, the tax benefit is eventually used up, and higher than normal taxes may be expected in later years, a factor Uncle Sam doubtless contemplated when according seemingly magnanimous treatment to owners of new buildings. In all probability, he will eventually fare very well, for during coming years large amounts of cash earned in Philadelphia will enable us to pay down much of the outstanding indebtedness, which means tax-collectors ultimately should do better than would normally be expected. With lower deductions each year for depreciation, as this fleeting antidote to taxable earnings becomes "used up," and with lower deductions for interest costs as debts are paid down, the

U. S. Treasury eventually should more than make up for a delay in collecting its share of prospective earnings.

There are many who benefit from the incentives to new construction created by the 1954 Revenue Laws, with their provision for "accelerated depreciation." Among those benefiting from our Philadelphia venture are the hundreds of construction workers who built the hotel, the five hundred or more employees who operate it today, and the members of the traveling public who enjoy its accommodations.

Even competing hotels suffered relatively little, for added conventions attracted to the City of Brotherly Love helped to offset losses from new competition and brought extra business to Philadelphia merchants. Even the nearly forgotten school-teachers of Philadelphia may conceivably share in the benefits— yes, even teachers, though doubtless unaware, have a real stake in their city's new hotel. Real-estate taxes of more than two hundred thousand dollars a year are collected on it, a supplement to the resources from which school budgets are largely derived.

The government too, as I have said, will eventually win, for someday it will collect taxes on an enterprise that otherwise might never have come into existence. In addition, of course, the government received payroll taxes from the millions paid workers during the period of construction, as well as income taxes on the profits of builders and suppliers who took part in the erection of the Philadelphia Sheraton.

Members of Congress deserve lasting credit for their wisdom in enacting legislation in 1954 to liberalize the tax laws, creating the incentives that produced so many desirable repercussions. And yet how often people criticize laws that seem to favor commercial activities, without weighing the benefits that labor, municipalities, the government, and the public derive from assistance given private enterprise.

Designing our Philadelphia hotel was a project of especial

importance for which Sheraton convened its managers and home-office executives years in advance. Nearly all managers at times think: "If I should ever build a hotel, this is what I would do differently." Here was a chance to erect a structure reflecting the combined judgments of our whole organization. The end product of this synthesis of opinion was a beautiful hotel, attaining a new level in luxury, built for several millions less than experts predicted would be required.

Despite all the experience available, however, some errors did enter our calculations. The original elevators, designed to meet normal needs of a fully occupied hotel, were adequate for ordinary use. But we had booked many large conventions, and had somehow overlooked the frequent back-and-forth visiting between floors they would involve. The extra load was too much. We needed two more elevators to correct this oversight, and the cost, due to the omission from the original plans, was close to two hundred thousand dollars. But Sheraton will not cry over spilt milk. Other calculations designed to save money had lowered costs by millions compared with occasional losses from estimates that backfired. A poker player may lose some dimes occasionally by misjudging the value of his hand; yet if he wins most of the time, he considers himself fortunate. Sheraton follows this philosophy. Stakes may be somewhat higher but losses are actually very rare.

In keeping with the traditions of our industry in opening new hotels, when our Philadelphia Sheraton was completed a three-day celebration was decreed by our public-relations department. It was to be a "triduum of festivities," according to the engraved parchments serving as invitations to prospective guests. We wanted the celebration to be commensurate with the significance of the occasion and arranged for the inevitable planeload of Hollywood celebrities, for if we neglected this adjunct to a hotel opening, who would believe we were ready for business?

Joe Pasternak of Hollywood, engaged at the time in producing *Ten Thousand Bedrooms*, his screen version of the vicissitudes of an American hotel operator opening a unit in Rome, appeared in Philadelphia with his leading lady, Anna Maria Alberghetti. A bevy of Hollywood stars accompanied them. Hearing Anna Maria sing, to say nothing of an exciting dance with her, proved beyond question that, no matter how much an Italian Ambassador could add to the glory of his country, friendly relations with the land of the former Caesars could never be more graciously cemented than by a few more Anna Maria Alberghettis.

Somewhat more costly but equally glamorous, at our Philadelphia opening, was a dance with one of my all-time favorites. Looking only a few years into the past and remembering Fred Astaire and Ginger Rogers on the screen, I recall wondering, "Who would not give a fortune to be in Fred Astaire's shoes?" Joe Pasternak could contrive such miracles. We had just tendered him a check for ten thousand dollars as Sheraton's gesture toward Hungarian Relief, in appreciation of his presence in Philadelphia with the Hollywood great that accompanied him. Joe, too shrewd in matters of public relations to overlook further dividends from the check he held, announced to the brilliant assemblage in the great ballroom: "Ten thousand dollars for Hungarian Relief will be paid for a single dance with Ginger Rogers by the President of Sheraton Corporation. Will the orchestra please play a fox trot?" The next few moments proved conclusively that even the wildest dreams, ones against whose fulfillment a-million-to-one odds might have been offered by Lloyds of London, do somehow at times come true.

A Perle Mesta ball, a series of gala banquets, a presentation of highlights of the festivities on a Dave Garroway television show transplanted for three days to Philadelphia—all these were climaxed by the arrival of "Paul Revere." Reaching the hotel on horseback, he had covered the three hundred and thirty miles from Boston, clad in correct Colonial attire, courtesy of the "made to order" department of Brooks Brothers. The route, through rarely used back roads in Connecticut, had been duly researched by a committee of top authorities on Paul Revere headed by author Esther Forbes and Admiral Samuel Eliot Morison. The original of this re-enacted ride was an authentic though little-publicized mission that brought to Pennsylvania news of the famous Boston Tea Party as well as word of Revolutionary plans being made by early Boston patriots. On this more recent occasion the modern Paul Revere brought with him a historically exact replica of a silver Paul Revere bowl as a tribute to Philadelphia's Mayor Dilworth. The original had been fashioned by the man famous for his skill in distinguishing, to the discomfort of King George the Third, the difference between one and two lanterns when displayed in the steeple of Boston's Old North Church. Paul Revere, besides his equestrian achievements, was also a silversmith of note.

The cost of the Philadelphia extravaganza was high, reaching up into six figures; yet, as was verified by our fondness for putting "price tags" on our activities, the expense paid off in good measure. The value of television and radio time, newspaper and magazine space, calculated in terms of paid publicity, exceeded by a wide margin the cost of glamourizing the launching of this brilliant venture.

I am afraid, however, the proposal made to the people of Philadelphia on that not always solemn occasion is not too likely to bear immediate fruit. In the Philadelphia *Inquirer*, following one of the many banquets, these comments appeared:

In accepting the citation Henderson said the opening of the hotel is a fitting link between Philadelphia and Boston, one existing since Colonial Times:

"On this occasion may I propose a modern symbol of friendship and unity. We have read in the headlines of many corporate mergers. I, too, have one to propose. It may not be ratified at once by our respective legislatures, or necessarily binding forthwith on both communities."

Henderson said his proposal was to merge Philadelphia and Boston into a single great municipality so that "jointly we will be as large as any city in the nation. . . . The new metropolis," he said, "could be Philabostonia." A motion calling for this resolution was made and duly seconded. It was unanimously carried.

New Yorkers, I am afraid, need not be unduly alarmed. Many more resolutions will doubtless be needed before "Philabostonia" overshadows their momentarily threatened city.

When the days of celebrating drew to a close and guests began to leave, Eph Catlin, a vice president of the largest Boston bank, accompanied by his beautiful wife, graciously said good-by, thanking us for the pleasant occasion. "Everything went so well," he said politely. "Almost nothing went wrong"—this latter perhaps a mild exaggeration. "Well," he volunteered on further reflection, "there was a minor incident, one you should perhaps know about.

"Last night, while dressing for the Navy League Ball, we heard voices in the bathroom of our beautiful suite. Cautiously we opened the door. No one was there, yet with high-fidelity reproduction we heard a husband—perhaps in some distant corner of the hotel—telling 'Marge' she must hurry with her shower; they would be late for dinner. Every ripple in the tub was audible."

Eph, tracing the sound to a ventilator grill, mounted the side of the tub and, lips at the aperture, probed the possibility of a two-way transmission.

"Marge," he whispered daringly, "never before have I seen you look so beautiful."

A moment of silence followed, interrupted only by the sound

of a cake of soap falling into the water. A two-way communication, Eph concluded, was established.

The success of the Philadelphia hotel was contagious. We soon started the construction of five more new Sheratons, and spectacular hotels in Dallas, Texas, and Binghamton, New York, opened recently. Portland, Oregon, followed shortly. A major addition to the Sheraton Towers on North Michigan Avenue in Chicago and a motel in the suburbs of Baltimore are under way— the latter on the theory that motels, except in larger cities, can offer real competition. The conclusion "If you can't lick 'em, join 'em," has apparently won Sheraton recognition.

XX.

General Philosophy: Beliefs and Theories

I

IN SOME respects I am a maverick, for I apparently like to
support unpopular causes. In one instance, however, I
seem to be safely on the side of the majority. I have no
sympathy for certain views of Albert Einstein and others who
belittle the making of money.

Einstein, perhaps like Edward A. Filene, may have combined
great genius with a distinct trace of impracticality. His position
as a notable sage is not in dispute, but his opposition to acquiring
possessions perhaps sprang from a lesser segment of what could
have been a dual personality. My criticism of him, and of
others who perhaps fared poorly in the worlds of commerce or
production, is not based purely on prejudice, though a vestige
of this affliction is doubtless present. My disagreement rests on
more cogent arguments.

Earnings, except when coercion is present, are essentially
rewards for providing the public with what it wants and will
willingly pay for with its hard-earned dollars. Subject, of course,
to competition, the greater the desire for certain goods or
services, the more the public is willing to pay for these. Accordingly a man earning less than he is able to earn may be offering
fewer, inferior, or less-wanted services than those he could
provide.

As an illustration, the number of dollars a data-processing device attracts depends largely on what else is available for these same dollars in similar or perhaps different fields. If more dollars seek the products of the maker of some electronic device than flow to the works of a poet, the discrepancy doubtless stems from a greater demand for the output of the former. The poet may be a greater genius than the purveyor of Univacs, but this is beside the point. In a "democratic" economy, dollars have freedom of choice as to how they will be spent. The poet may well dislike this feature of our economic system, yet he should not blame free enterprise for possible public apathy for the wares he has to offer.

Thus, if the poet commands only a small income compared with that of the producer of electronic giants, this doubtless reflects the unequal value buyers place on the products of each. A Univac may save thousands of man-hours, releasing these for other use, and this accomplishment will naturally attract more dollars than gravitate to an area of more limited demand.

Although surprisingly many people consider money unimportant, believing even that a stigma should attach to earnings exceeding minimum needs, fortunately there are valid arguments belying these questionable conclusions based perhaps on prejudices that may bear a trace of those well-known grapes that sometimes lack in sweetness.

Here are some reasons for questioning an attitude critical of large incomes:

An individual whose earnings are modest, perhaps because he is rendering less-wanted services, may be spending fewer dollars than he would if he enjoyed a larger income. He may thus be holding down a potential demand for goods—that economic force which makes jobs for other people.

Since Uncle Sam receives, on a progressively rising scale, income taxes on all but the lowliest incomes, an individual could be thought of as shortchanging Uncle Sam when he is earning less than his maximum potential. Criticism of heavy spending may have possible merit, but this need not imply that small earnings are a virtue. Persons with larger incomes than needed fortunately have agreeable alternatives for disposing of the surplus. Charitable and educational institutions clamor for funds. How much better if Einstein, rather than condemning our way way of life, had applied his magnificent talents to creating larger earnings which, though he did not want them, could have been directed into charitable or productive channels.

Another choice is open to people who prefer a modest scale of living—excluding, of course, those with a leaning toward masochism, or who enjoy rationalizing their lack of prowess in the commercial world. Those espousing austerity could easily invest extra earnings in enterprises providing needed jobs or producing goods others could use to advantage. With so many uses for extra earnings, it seems almost sinful to limit financial incomes, especially when this means curtailing useful services.

Perhaps too often the individual who deplores an ambition to accumulate wealth, a commodity so often helpful at least in one's old age, may be among the first, through lack of financial perspective, to become a public charge or a burden to an uncomplaining relative. Should not those allergic to financial gains suffer at least momentary pangs of conscience when they contemplate the cost of our national budget or the drain on the public purse for defense or education, and realize others must provide the tax dollars they fail to contribute toward meeting these necessary expenditures?

I believe the case for meager earnings is especially weak when it means denial of one of the greatest of human satisfactions, contributing to worthy charitable causes. Taking everything into consideration, lowered demand for goods clearly reduces job opportunities, indirectly diminishes needed tax revenues, and limits investments which could stimulate industry.

Expenditures for the public good would inevitably shrink if

Americans earned only what was required to satisfy minimum needs. Who can question that our industrial leadership and our high standard of living rest largely on the investment of funds that the nation worked very hard to accumulate.

I certainly wish our churches and other uplift institutions would raise a great outcry against the wickedness of earning less than one's maximum capacity. Exhortations to avoid the evils of riches naturally have an emotional appeal, but such unsound theories have no factual basis; they rest perhaps more on jealousy or on rationalizing an inability to perform more remunerative tasks. They constitute a dangerous poison coursing in our national veins.

What is true of individuals with respect to the virtues of earning-power is equally true when applied to business enterprises. We have always eagerly sought to increase our own company earnings, and occasionally we have observed how others tried to achieve similar commendable goals. An interesting example is described in the following section.

2

In our quest for better values at ever lower cost, we once discovered a valuable source of table linens in Belfast, Northern Ireland, where a manufacturer could care for a large proportion of our extensive requirements. Fifty hotels must have a quarter-million yards of linens to serve seventy-five thousand food covers a day. Belfast accordingly received sizable orders bringing much-needed American exchange into the dollar-starved sterling orbit. Our purchasing office, on establishing this connection, was curious to learn how a single North Ireland supplier could handle so much business while his local competitors were seemingly out of the running. The answer indicated a lingering prejudice against large-scale operations, and also pinpointed the contrast between

European and American concepts of the function of a business enterprise.

The Belfast textile merchant, a dozen or more years before, had made a survey of American textile machinery in order to render more nearly automatic the production of his linens and attract a larger share of the available American market. He needed several hundred thousand dollars to convert his plant to American mechanized standards. Although lacking the necessary credit, he somehow persuaded his local financial institutions to advance the needed funds, and soon the newly streamlined plant was in operation.

With new machinery, a single worker could produce what had once required five men, and most of the employees understandably feared for their jobs. Would four out of five be forced to seek work elsewhere? This possibility had been widely rumored by those opposed to a change in economic thinking. Actually things turned out quite differently. With a better product at lower prices, export orders were expanded, shipments reached ten times their former volume, and an increased labor force, double the original number, was needed to man the new machines. However, the story does not end here. Quantity-production economies made possible higher remuneration. The growing business was soon paying double the former wage scales, and even office help was receiving more for shorter hours of work. Of even greater significance to a nation short of dollars, a commodity useful when buying American goods, Belfast was attracting a growing stream of coveted U. S. dollars, those vivid symbols of high American productivity.

The rewards to this maker of Irish linens were apparently very meager. Ninety-five cents from every dollar of augmented earnings, normally the incentive to trigger expansion, was taken by British tax collectors, gentlemen apparently dedicated to the theory that no one should earn more than John Bull considers sufficient. Perhaps an even greater shock to this instigator of higher wages, more abundant jobs, and more American dollars, was the attitude of his fellow citizens in Belfast. His neighbors began to shun him, for he had dared to challenge the ingrained customs of centuries. To the unions, too, he was a sworn enemy, for he was "upsetting" labor markets. The rewards for Americanizing a somewhat impoverished area were clearly very few.

3

The problems posed by labor unions in Belfast differed somewhat from those which unions present to businessmen here in the United States. My criticism of labor unions is not based on their quite proper interest in high wages. These are of course desirable, provided they are accompanied by high productivity. Unfortunately demands for higher pay are sometimes accompanied by a desire for less and less work, a trend which weakens the national economy, and impairs our country's position in its quest for world markets by causing prices to rise unduly.

How much more constructive would be attempts by unions to raise wages through efforts to increase productivity, which they could accomplish either through more efficient work or by reducing waste and duplication. This approach would justify higher wages on an economically sound foundation without requiring price increases that rob workers—and others too—of the full value of their money. If a sales tax is bad, as labor economists generally suggest (actually with doubtful validity), how much worse is an inflationary price spiral due to insufficient emphasis on productive efficiency. Since workers often receive some ten to twenty times in wages what is ordinarily paid in dividends to shareholders, it would seem that they have a much greater stake in productivity than do in fact the owners of the business.

Of course wage increases that are passed along to *all* consumers in the form of higher prices create a temporary advantage for some workers, even though depreciation of our currency is involved. This, unfortunately, is an "unearned" increment levied by coercive pressures exerted by some at the expense of others.

The argument that wage increases should come out of profits, though frequently advanced, is usually unrealistic, for the long-range effect on future jobs could be decidedly harmful. The curtailment of profits normally available for expansion can reduce future job opportunities, as well as affect, perhaps, the outcome of our economic struggle with Russia.

The often-heard argument conveniently enunciated by labor economists that higher wages are the best means of expanding purchasing power has only limited validity. The extra expenditures by workers that follow generous pay raises usually go for momentary pleasures or goods that are soon consumed and add but temporarily to the sum total of our national wealth, whereas corporate earnings reaching investors, or those which remain in the business, are usually plowed back into further tools of production, in whose benefits future workers may again share, presumably also in the ratio of ten or twenty to one.

These economic facts are hardly grist for the mill of most labor leaders, who are usually intent on short-range goals, but certainly they deserve more attention than is presently accorded them.

I would like to venture a prediction that someday a new type of labor leader will emerge, a labor statesman willing to advocate harder work and more production, rather than shorter hours, featherbedding, duplication, and strikes. I predict that working-men themselves will gladly support such enlightened leadership. Workers, according to our experience, are far more conservative and "sound" than they are believed to be by their own leaders, who seem to feel a constant compulsion to obtain for their members something for nothing. As soon as far-sighted union chiefs appear on the scene, with the vision and courage to recognize the economic facts, the day of two cars in a workingman's garage may no longer be an idle dream—though perhaps it will be a nightmare to those who must cope with future traffic congestion.

While bending our efforts toward building a successful enterprise, and at intervals pondering the problems posed by labor unions, we realize that other groups, far better organized than the unions, are seeking to take over these labor organizations, as well as many other associations, with the objective of destroying, if possible, our country's economic strength. It is not surprising that one so enthusiastic over the merits of free enterprise as I should be apprehensive of inroads made in this country and elsewhere by the Russian Communist conspiracy.

However, preoccupation with subversive intrigues, or, for that matter, with many other problems facing those who run businesses, is not my only concern. There have been other interesting and absorbing facets in my life.

XXI.

Home and Family

I

Our family life has always been a major interest for Molly and me. The homes we have lived in have followed somewhat the pattern of our expanding hotel system. As Sheraton grew, so also, not too surprisingly, did the size of our residences. An economic consideration, however, also entered our calculations, for when houses exceed a certain size their worth often diminishes in proportion, providing interesting opportunities for those not averse to the larger homes of an almost forgotten era.

We built our first house back in 1929 in a quiet section of Cambridge. It had one bath. Many years later, when Sheraton had reached more impressive proportions, we acquired one of the more pretentious summer homes in southern New Hampshire, with thirty rooms and some ten baths. Both houses, curiously enough, cost us the same amount—ten thousand dollars. However, there was a notable difference. The first we built ourselves; the other, almost unsalable because of its size, had been abandoned seventeen years before we purchased it.

Our offer for this long-deserted Dublin, New Hampshire, estate, representing perhaps the value of the eighty acres surrounding it, was partly influenced by its location high on a shoulder of Monadnock Mountain, an ideal place for an amateur radio installation. The modest offer was eagerly accepted, the former owners having grown allergic to the ever-recurring real-estate taxes. An interesting commentary on the shrinking value of large New England estates emerged when we discovered in an attic room an invoice for shrubbery, mostly rhododendrons which after more than fifty years still line the half-mile-long driveway. Early in the century these plants had cost just what we paid for them fifty-two years later, but in the latter instance, eighty acres of land and a once magnificent mansion were included for good measure.

Trees ranging in size up to four inches in diameter flourished in the middle of the driveway, and acres of waist-high grass were a reminder of some once luxurious lawns. When the question of tearing down the structure was considered, we found it cheaper to reshingle the house, replace the broken windows, all of heavy plate glass, and apply here and there some needed paint. Soon we had restored the once impressive splendor.

Today, some four years later, our Dublin "cottage" is again an interesting New Hampshire landmark with an exciting view of Monadnock to the west, a panorama of hills and valleys covering some sixty square miles visible to the south and east, and a great seventy-foot steel tower to the rear, supporting impressive radio antennae that permit two-way communications with most of the outside world. The house itself, of exceptionally good construction typical of the early days of the twentieth century, despite years of exposure to the elements, required only trivial interior repairs.

One exception was the great hallway into which the main stairway descended. The Zuber scenic wallpaper displayed on four sides had mostly fallen away. We carefully reassembled it, as if it were pieces of a jigsaw puzzle, thus revealing a sixteenth-century horse race in Siena, Italy. Two missing panels were a problem until fortunately we noted the address of the Alsatian supplier. We wrote him, describing the missing sections. Although fifty-two years had passed since the house was built, by return mail we received two panels that fitted with faultless precision—even to the horses' tails which matched to perfection the equestrian posteriors on the adjoining panels. A note included with the shipment told us that earlier patterns, dating back another century and a quarter were also available; but for these, if possible, an extra week's notice would be appreciated.

Furnishing the new home, once it was repaired, was an exciting and not too costly undertaking. The living room, larger perhaps than some hotel ballrooms, could accommodate immense rugs and massive pieces of furniture—ones which at auctions attract little interest from bidders. There are few people today with space for a fifty-foot Aubusson rug, and since the intricate patterns scarcely permit of subdivision, we were able to secure one of these at a purely nominal price. If it had been a quarter of its actual size, the cost might have exceeded that of the house and all its surrounding acres.

Auctions in Newport, Rhode Island, were a fruitful source of supply for us, since large estates in that region were often broken up, casualties, no doubt, of an ever-rising income tax. Bidding on items such as Flemish tapestries, Chippendale settees, French Empire bedroom sets, or perhaps an occasional concert grand piano, could produce an exciting assortment of beautiful things for well below the cost of furnishing a much smaller home.

This buying of objects of beauty at auction sales led to a Sheraton activity which is now an important adjunct to our hotel decorating department. We organized a subsidiary to acquire objects useful to hotels. With Bill Clough, a former Harvard classmate, at its helm, this company's sole activity is to expose its representatives to auctions in search of luxury items destined to give glamour to some of the more resplendent hotel suites. The annual dollar volume of these purchases of period furniture, bric-a-brac, statues, Oriental rugs, pictures, and other decorative pieces, reaches several hundreds of thousands of dollars. How many of those attending brilliant banquets in various Sheraton ballrooms admire the spectacular eighteenth-century candelabra that often embellish head tables may not be accurately known, but these striking contributions to a hotel's decor usually reflect the daring of Willis B. Clough, of the illustrious Harvard class of 1918, in topping the next highest bid as some important estate was being dissected under an auctioneer's hammer. Massive crystal chandeliers now suspended from many Sheraton banquet-hall ceilings may previously have sojourned for a generation or two over dinner tables of great Long Island estates, having come originally, perhaps, from historic German or Austrian castles. If these sparkling relics of a former scintillating era are appreciated by the many who see them each year, credit is due to Bill Clough.

The Franklin MacVeaghs of Chicago originally built the house which we restored in Dublin. MacVeagh had married the only daughter of the president of one of Chicago's great banks, a circumstance accounting, no doubt, for countless shares of the bank's stock, once worth close to a thousand dollars each, registered in the family name. Dividends alone, in days that ante-dated the income tax, could perhaps have built many houses a year like the one we acquired, and carpenters in days when the century was young were fortunate to receive for a long day's work a fraction of the hourly income their better-paid counter-parts receive today. Judging by the size of the servants' quarters, there must have been dozens of retainers on hand in an era when the going rate was four dollars a week.

As I have said, William Howard Taft, in whose cabinet MacVeagh served as Secretary of the Treasury, was an occasional visitor in Dublin. Summer cabinet meetings were sometimes held there, and foreign ambassadors, according to legends still extant, presented their credentials to the President in the MacVeagh house.

Recently I saw a large portrait of Franklin MacVeagh in the

private office of Robert Anderson, today's Secretary of the Treasury. It is the first thing one sees on entering the secretarial inner sanctum. I had been invited to Washington to discuss my theory —or obsession, as some might insist—that fluctuating common-stock levels play a major role in creating and intensifying recurring business cycles.

Lord Bryce, British Ambassador to Washington, and Mark Twain were summer residents of Dublin when President Taft visited New Hampshire. Three large maples facing our summer home today, nearly fifty years later, were planted by these famous individuals—that is, two of the maples, those attributed to Taft and Lord Bryce, are considered authentic. A claim that the third was planted by Mark Twain is occasionally questioned by skeptics, but the Hendersons resolutely ignore such heresy.

2

Because of the large number of rooms in our Dublin house, we can easily care for, during summer months, all our children and an ever expanding collection of grandchildren. This affords us a means of becoming better acquainted with our immediate progeny.

Our son Barclay, now in college on the Pacific Coast, and daughter Mitzi are the only members of the original five who remain unmarried. Barclay, during summer vacations, rarely hesitates to call his mother on the phone to mention casually that some students may be coming for the weekend, and a dozen or more, lady friends included, frequently appear. Molly seems accustomed to these sudden invasions and raises no objections. Fortunately there are ample facilities. Barclay's proficiency in keeping our Dublin rooms occupied, at least during weekends, makes me wonder that the hotel business never attracted him.

He hopes eventually to become a doctor, if able to survive the scholastic rigors of twelve years of training.

With hobbies, with a business which makes occasional demands on the time of its president, and with an occasional interest in golf, though still, after forty years, a beginner, I understandably have not always been a perfect father to our many children. Excepting on Sundays, it is usually their mother to whom falls the task of parental supervision. Sundays are an exception, for, particularly with the younger ones, we often hold what we think of as our special brand of Sunday children's hour. On these occasions I seek to convey to our sons and daughters a sense of the responsibilities I feel all parents should impress on their eventual successors.

These Sunday affairs have also afforded us an opportunity to learn from our children what the teachers in their schools were telling them. This at times was mildly startling. I gather our American economic system is not popular with most of those who instruct our sons and daughters. It required many of those Sunday-afternoon family hours to convince our contingent of the next generation that there might be two sides to many questions of the day. Fortunately we have been able to ignite at least a modest backfire.

Emphasis to our children has always been on the importance of accepting only with caution their father's or any other point of view, weighing impartially and, above all, unemotionally, both sides of an argument—a procedure apparently rare at least among some of their teachers. Unless more parents discuss with their children the merits of our free-enterprise system, I think the rising generation will largely support some form of socialism or collectivism, and, if so, the greatness of what was once America may be undermined by those who, however well-meaning and sincere, have little knowledge of, and often no first-hand experience with, the mechanisms they are likely to destroy. Few teachers seem to understand the role business has played in making America great. They seem often to prefer to respond to their own strong emotions, which deflect them from an appreciation of our existing economic pattern.

Other matters thrashed out in these so-called children's hours cover such diverse subjects as politics, corruption in government and other fields, astronomy, history, science, and particularly current events. It was in connection with discussions of our solar system that we sent for a powerful astronomical telescope to observe the moon, the planets, and the heavens in general. Counting the satellites orbiting around Jupiter and the rings surrounding Venus, discovering that the second star in the handle of the Big Dipper is actually two stars when seen through powerful lenses—these were some of the compensations for engaging in these interstellar explorations. Magnifying the moon one hundred and sixty fold, so that only a portion was visible in the telescope's field of view, and noting the rapid movement of our impressive satellite was among the more interesting experiences we shared with our younger children.

Discussions with our sons and daughters, however, are not exclusively a one-way street. Discovering the subjects they are learning about always interests us.

When possible, during these hours, we tried to struggle with questions involving controversy. Playing the "devil's advocate" is a role that usually falls to me—one that most people will concede should not be wholly unfamiliar.

For example, Great Britain's difficulties with the Suez Canal were among the topics we often discussed. When the seizure of the canal by Colonel Nasser was prominent in the news, the possibility of intervention by the affected nations received much newspaper comment. The threat to world peace seemed quite real, yet inaction could also be hazardous, for it could permit Nasser to resort to a technique Hitler often used in his earlier depredations, that of "divide and conquer." By making individual deals with various nations wishing to use the canal, Nasser could eventually compel the interested nations to capitulate. As were all others, I was naturally troubled. If the recent difficulties with Cairo stemmed from decisions made when Colonel Nasser first seized the canal, and if I should now claim a degree of implication—as I did facetiously on a previous occasion with respect to the beginning of the First World War following my ill-fated ten-mark-gold-piece experience—it might be harder this time to laugh off.

Fearful of the "divide and conquer" approach, I suggested, through long-distance phone channels having contact with the White House, that nations interested in the freedom of the canal should form a "users' union" based on the domestic labor-union strategy of applying joint pressure. A few days later, the Users' Association was announced. A week or so later, a *Life* magazine article describing this concept, with symptoms of being Washington-inspired, appeared on the newsstands. It not only outlined the proposed plan, but even presented the labor-union analogy to illustrate the point. Of course chance, requiring far less than the one-in-a-million odds to which by now I was accustomed, may have accounted for this apparent coincidence. And, in view of the abortive issue of the early attempts to deal with Nasser, I should perhaps be cautious in claiming even remote authorship of a policy that so completely backfired on the occasion of the ill-fated British-Israel "putsch."

One of the fortuitous circumstances for which Molly and I have long been grateful is that our five children virtually comprised two quite separate families. Ten years separated the youngest of the first contingent from the oldest of the succeeding three. This ten-year gap, coinciding closely with the duration of the great depression, made it possible to grow up twice, so to speak, with our children. Now, with grandchildren arriving, the process is again being repeated.

Up to now, only our eldest son, Ernest III, has shown an

interest in the hotel business. He has recently become treasurer of the company. Besides fulfilling the duties of his office, and teaching his father the hotel business, one of his principal duties has been supervising Sheraton's growing family of motor hotels.

Penny, our middle-sized daughter, did on one occasion exhibit an unprecedented and seemingly inexplicable interest in her father's business affairs. As a junior at Smith College, she was spending a few days' vacation with us in Boston. Suddenly she developed an astonishing urge to see her father's hotels, particularly the Sheraton-Park in Washington, once known as the Wardman Park Hotel.

We had made some major improvements at the Sheraton-Park. The property had been modernized and wholly air-conditioned, and a two-million-dollar banquet hall and spacious exhibition facilities had been added. Eager to see the changes, I took Penny with me to Washington.

We arrived late, but this did not discourage my "shameless" daughter. Reaching for the phone, she dialed a number she apparently knew.

"Sorry," a landlady told her, "he isn't home."

"Shall I call at eleven?" Penny asked.

"Sorry," came the voice, "it's an important engagement. He won't return until late."

"How about midnight?" Penny tried hopefully.

"Sorry," came the reply, "it's a very late business appointment. You will have to call in the morning."

With all enthusiasm gone from her voice, Penny consented to join her father in exploring the new banquet hall, one of the largest and most dramatic in the country. A debutante ball was in progress, and we could look down on it unseen from a balcony not in use that night.

Eighty of the capital's most luscious debutantes, all in lovely white gowns, were being presented to Washington society, and the climax of the evening arrived as we looked down from our point of vantage. Two great orchestras joined together, the dimmers were set at a level to create the desired effect, and two searchlights cast their beams on the red-carpeted stairway as the first of the eighty debs majestically descended. Her father, an admiral, ablaze with his decorations, was on one arm. On the other was her escort for the evening, a handsome U. S. Army major, a White House aide, bearing the necessary complement of shining gold braid. While a thousand guests below stood breathless, Penny took one look at the tall, handsome major and announced, "I hate him, I hate him." As she went on, I thought I could detect incoherent references to "an important business engagement."

The next morning, it seems, an acceptable alibi was forthcoming. Perhaps, after all, the daughter of an out-of-town admiral, lacking a wide acquaintance in the capital, might have been assigned an obliging White House aide, drafted for this special occasion. At all events, all was forgiven, and a year later Penny became the bride of Major J. Carleton Petrone, Jr., a former White House aide.

The wedding reception, held on the mall in front of our Louisburg Square home, revived a famous Boston tradition, dormant for over a century. Jenny Lind was married in that same enclosed plot of grass on the side of Beacon Hill, the property of the twenty-two families whose houses abut on Louisburg Square, a garden which visitors to Boston sometimes think of as a small piece of London transplanted to the New World.

With Penny married and only the two youngest left under parental jurisdiction, and one of these, Barclay, a freshman at Reed College in Portland, Oregon, our immediate family seems to be facing attrition. However, if while under the parental roof, they have absorbed a sense of responsibility and integrity, and a desire to get ahead, then we will have discharged the greatest of all obligations confronting American parents. And if these lessons were impressed with sufficient firmness that our children will in turn pass on similar admonitions to their own children, Molly and I will feel our primary duty as citizens has been performed.

In the meantime, as our own family shrinks, our many grandchildren, just as do the hotels in Sheraton's corporate family, continue to multiply. Barclay, while at college, has at times been able to watch the progress of the glamorous Portland Sheraton with its luxurious swimming pool and exquisitely landscaped grounds, a Sheraton contribution to Pacific Coast architecture. The recent acquisition of the leading hotel in Cleveland and the principal one in Mobile, Alabama, is bringing Sheraton into two areas not previously invaded. Little by little, Sheraton is approaching the time when, throughout the nation, few if any great cities will remain untouched by our ambition to provide topflight hotel facilities designed to bring acclaim from a critical traveling public.

XXII.

Sheraton Throughout the Nation

SHERATON's activities, spreading into more and more American cities, have provided us with a splendid opportunity to become acquainted with much of our country. The fabulous growth of oil-rich Dallas, the incomparable charm of New Orleans or San Francisco, the Southern atmosphere we once liked so well in Augusta, Georgia, the excitement of New York, or the newness of Los Angeles all tended to heighten our pride in these United States. Our growing interest in our thrilling fiftieth state, represented by four leading Waikiki Beach hotels, has given us an opportunity to become familiar with what we are sure must be the world's finest climate.

In the bustling city of Detroit we have the Sheraton-Cadillac, the largest hotel in Michigan. It gladly acknowledges its indebtedness to the automotive industry by displaying in its great lobbies large, colorful replicas of the emblems of the leading manufacturers that put this country on wheels—General Motors, Ford, and Chrysler. Tens of thousands of Detroit visitors, as they register at the new and modern registration desk of the great Sheraton-Cadillac, can readily admire these. But our interest in Detroit is not limited to this impressive hotel. There is also a Sheraton subsidiary which participates in the activities of that city.

Shirley Murphy, who heads Thompson Industries, the subsidiary which makes parts for the automobile companies, concluded that his enterprise should expand. The Martin Electric Company of Detroit, manufacturer of welding equipment that could produce hundreds of metallic welds at the touch of an electric button, offered an opportunity. The principal customers of Martin, large auto-makers, would set up on appropriate dies a few sheets of steel, and when the all-important button was pressed, hundreds of movable electrodes, bearing currents of thousands of amperes each, would descend upon the metallic surfaces, emitting crackling sparks, acrid odors, and the incandescent glow of sputtering electrical contacts. In a matter of seconds an almost complete auto body would emerge for transfer to the lacquer-ovens.

Bill Martin, president of the company, had been advised to sell rather than face the uncertainty of tax-collectors' valuations should a question of inheritance taxes inconveniently arise. Tax laws can be harsh where a single owner of a business is concerned.

The purchase of the Martin Company was therefore arranged by Thompson Industries. As it is a Sheraton subsidiary, Sheraton's principal officers participated in the legal maneuvers, involving a multiplicity of signatures, deeds, certified checks, contracts, and other documents associated with these long-drawn-out "closings." When checks and notes, aggregating several millions, finally changed hands, we sighed with some relief. The Martin Electric Plant and its corps of skilled craftsmen were now a part of Sheraton. We forthwith hailed some taxicabs and headed for Detroit's Outer Drive to inspect the newly acquired property. Heretofore we had seen only the voluminous financial audits.

Arriving at the Outer Drive address, the taxis came to a halt. We must have seemed unusually pleased. We had evidently made a very shrewd purchase, for the plant was enormous. With a pride of ownership reminiscent of that secondhand motorcycle of my boyhood days in New Hampshire, we started up the great stone stairs so that, theoretically at least, we could take over this magnificent enterprise. The next moment our taxi driver was shouting to us. "A mistake," he apologized. "The wrong address. That," he said, "is the Chrysler Factory."

Perhaps we should not have been expected to recognize a several-hundred-million-dollar automobile plant. After all, we were only hotel men.

In Cincinnati, another Sheraton city, the one my great-grandfather Judge Thomas Henderson originally helped to lay out, we were again exposed to momentary embarrassment. I was not quite sure whether to be pleased or amazed on arriving at our Sheraton-Gibson Hotel, the largest and surely the most profitable of the Queen City hotels, though I could not necessarily vouch under oath that scholarly doubt might not prevail as to our claim it was the best. At all events, allowing for a trace of prejudice, we still believe the Sheraton-Gibson is entitled to a most distinguished rating.

Extensive redecorating and air-conditioning had just been completed when I arrived to visit the newly transformed property. Despite efforts on my part to discourage such unnecessary attention, Joseph Curry, the genial manager, had met me at the airport. On arriving at the hotel's main entrance I was astonished to find a brass band, forty pieces strong, deployed throughout the lobby. Its tumultuous greeting, expressed in strains of "Hail to the Chief," was overwhelming. Joe Curry, quick to capitalize on such situations, started to apologize. "I hope you don't mind this little gesture of welcome," he said. "We are all so glad you are here." He failed somehow to mention that John L. Lewis had preceded us by only a few seconds. The coal miners' chief was to address a convention at the Sheraton-Gibson Hotel.

It is an interesting commentary on ever changing times that John L. Lewis was receiving the kind of ovation that might have been accorded only a generation ago to Andrew Carnegie or perhaps Charles M. Schwab.

Augusta, Georgia, was once an important Sheraton city, but this is no longer so. The sale of the Bon Air Hotel a number of years ago marked one of the rare instances when Sheraton sold a hotel at a loss. Furthermore, the sale was a major error, for a few days after the deed was signed announcement was made of a proposed multi-billion-dollar hydrogen nuclear plant across the river from Augusta, which would bring undreamed-of business to the region. Almost overnight, following the sale, the value of the Bon Air trebled. Hereafter perhaps we should inaugurate a private version of a secret intelligence administration.

Another city to which Sheraton destinies were once closely bound, though the properties have since been sold, was Daytona Beach, Florida, a prosperous resort where we once owned the two leading hotels. One of these was directly on "the world's finest beach," or perhaps I should say the second finest, now that we have taken over four Waikiki Beach hotels. The two Florida hostelries later became casualties to the principle that chain-hotel operators lack the needed touch to make such very seasonal operations successful.

Our recollections of Daytona Beach include pleasant memories of the owner of a popcorn concession on the beach near one of the hotels. Being fond of popcorn, we soon came to know him.

The arbiter of this popular beach franchise had once attended an Eastern college. His former roommate was in Chicago, the head of a branch of some prominent brokerage firm, and therefore obviously quite prosperous. Despite a considerable disparity in their incomes, the two classmates had retained their early friendship, and each spring they met on a fishing trip in Maine.

On these annual occasions, the former roommates spent many

hours each grieving over the misfortunes of the other. The opulent Chicago broker would implore his old-time friend to abandon the impractical popcorn enterprise, pointing out that he could start in Chicago as a security salesman and would surely soon be promoted. A branch-office managership could eventually be within reach and his salary and commissions could reach fifty thousand a year.

The purveyor of popcorn was not impressed. Why didn't the misguided broker renounce the turmoil of a great bustling city, give up those early hours battling strap-hanging throngs vying for a nine-o'clock office deadline? Why not end this self-inflicted misery for the joys of a popcorn-vender's life? The beach was large; there was room for two.

Neither could convince the other. Perhaps the old adage that one man's meat is another man's poison still retains validity.

One of our loyal customers at Daytona Beach was Charles McCormick, head of McCormick & Company, Inc., of Baltimore. Charlie brought us much patronage. More important, as author of what he called "multiple management," he brought us ideas we could use.

Charlie's uncle had ruled the great Maryland spice concern with a firm hand, clearly dedicated to the cherished thesis that a subordinate's sole duty was to follow instructions given him. The Baltimore company had faltered as harder times approached, and at this point young Charlie stepped into his uncle's shoes. Surely the sheriff would not be far behind, for Charlie, according to his uncle, had quite impractical ideas. He actually believed employees could contribute to management, and even help restore faltering profits.

The depression of the thirties faced the nation as Charlie's "impossible" schemes went into effect. Strangely, despite harder times, customers were beginning to return, and better products appeared on the market. The business, once more expanding, gave signs of approaching new levels of prosperity.

Charlie's "visionary" techniques, which revitalized his company's earnings, consisted of establishing so-called junior boards of directors with decision-making power in policy-making fields. Decisions were subject only to approval of the senior board of directors. Use of the board's veto power, however, was as rare as a Russian veto is commonplace in the U. N. Security Council. For practical purposes, the McCormick junior boards were helping run the business.

Members of the McCormick operating committees were recruited, in periodic rotation, from among the younger executives of the company. This gave the members valuable experience and the company a profitable source of ideas.

It was because of learning from Charlie McCormick of his multiple-management program that we set up our "board of operations." This entity is one of our chief policy-making bodies. Its membership, likewise subject to rotation, comes half from our Boston staff executives and half from among our hotel managers. A dozen or more serve on this board until the rigors of rotation bring on replacements. Many of the constructive policy decisions responsible for Sheraton's growth originated in the deliberations of our operating board, a process for which we are indebted to the "visionary" head of the McCormick Company.

Besides Daytona Beach, there were other cities with which Sheraton's growth was closely identified. One of these, Providence, Rhode Island, we sometimes view with mixed emotions.

The Biltmore Hotel in Providence, an impressive community-built project, was the result of millions raised by local residents to provide the Rhode Island capital with a modern attraction. It had fallen upon troublesome times during the days of the depression, and additional funds were needed to meet pressing obligations. A new stock issue designed to raise two hundred thousand dollars had been offered existing shareholders, and, as an added inducement, each new share would command ten votes. Half the issue, if corralled, would virtually control a multi-million-dollar hotel. We set out to acquire as many shares as we could buy.

We canvassed the shareholders, seeking to buy the new shares to which they would be entitled. During depression days few were interested in additional investments, and so we acquired a large portion of the issue; but, according to our best estimates, we fell slightly short of the needed majority. When a member of the "opposition" commented on the close race, wishing us better luck the next time, we accepted defeat graciously and eventually sold our shares. Several years later, with business somewhat improved, we finally bought the hotel, but the price was up by some two million dollars. When finally in possession, we examined the records dating back to the time of our ill-starred proxy battle. The stock ledgers gave us a shock. It seemed we might once have actually held a majority of the voting shares. We still wonder if we played a gigantic poker game and perhaps held a winning hand without realizing our strength. If so, we were playing for rather high stakes. Had we called the hand, we might have won the Biltmore at a saving of two million dollars.

In another of the cities where we were once established, our stay was of short duration. Soon after we purchased the local hotel, we were informed that the customary "little white envelope," useful in making our stay more "welcome," was not in its proper place. The amount expected was small, but the principle involved had little appeal. We refused to rectify this "oversight." Shortly afterwards things began to happen. Insuperable obstacles arose from the most unexpected sources, and we could see clearly that business under the circumstances would not be very "profitable." A few months later we resold the hotel.

Whether the little white envelopes finally reappeared we never discovered.

Despite our disappointment some years ago on reaching Dallas, Texas, just as a new Statler hotel was announced, we were presently to have a chance to dry our tears. The great Southland Life Insurance Company, with headquarters in Dallas, had decided to rival the glamour of Radio City by building a mammoth Southland Life Center designed to eclipse anything previously seen west of the Mississippi. Sheraton might participate in the venture if we could project a hotel that could surpass any previously erected. This seemed quite interesting, and soon the Sheraton-Dallas, a twenty-eight-story structure was underway. The grand opening in April 1959 was a spectacular event even for Texas. Now that we are a part of Texas, we are convinced Sheraton has really "arrived."

Baltimore, where we have the Sheraton-Belvedere, is a city we have always admired, perhaps because it resembles Boston. Despite a reputation for unexcelled perfection, our hotel did once face a delicate crisis. A top vice president of Boston's largest bank, an institution responsible for much of Sheraton's progress, had asked for a reservation in Baltimore. We eagerly awaited his comments, for a bank loan in the millions, an advance he would personally have to approve, was under discussion, and we wished to make sure he would be impressed. He was, but somewhat unfavorably; his reservation, withdrawn from the files to assure special attention, had been misplaced, and when he arrived all the rooms were gone. A decidedly second-rate hotel was the only recourse. Later, with trepidation, we awaited word on the prospective loan, which, amazingly, was granted.

Here in New England, in one of our earlier hotels, we made an interesting discovery, though we never put to use the information gained on that occasion. The hotel was of unusual interest, for we already had several hotels in the system, and a reputation for good food had become essential. The hotel we took over had enjoyed wide recognition for its culinary excellence; customers crowded its restaurants. Soon we hoped to learn the secret of this great reputation.

On taking over this eminent hotel, Elmer Boswell, following his usual inspection, reported his findings with amazement. The praise for the excellence of the food apparently had rested on the somewhat doubtful foundations of a continuous stream of radio and newspaper announcements proclaiming with monotonous repetition the pre-eminence of the hotel cuisine. True, some clever chefs could concoct some excellent sauces, but what was underneath was a decided shock. The hotel offered the lowliest items known to the purveying fraternity. Steaks were neither "prime" nor "choice" nor even "good," according to government grading standards. The chickens, to our credit, were of a variety unknown to us; we had not even heard of "Texas Cheaters." Subsequently, under Sheraton jurisdiction, prime cuts of beef and pure White Rock AA chickens appeared on the revised dining-room menus, less firmly buttressed, perhaps, by the magic of clever publicity. Even today we occasionally wonder whether guests of that distinguished hotel ever really knew the difference when the more costly delicacies were placed before them.

We cannot altogether suppress a degree of curiosity as to whether "subtle" advertising and war propaganda may not have something in common when it comes to molding our strong convictions.

In Pittsburgh, where we presently fly the Sheraton banner from the stately Penn-Sheraton Hotel which overlooks magnificent Mellon Square, I was once invited to address an important group of leading business tycoons. The occasion was the unveiling of an impressive mural sculptured in steel, aluminum, and glass, erected through the generosity of the three industrial giants which, by producing these important products, had made Pittsburgh famous. Because of the honor accorded our hotel, I prepared the speech with especial care, and before leaving for the once smoky but now immaculate city, I decided to listen to it on our home tape recorder, to hear how it would sound to a distinguished Pittsburgh audience. The results were inconclusive. I heard only the first few words before I fell fast asleep.

Alerted by this timely warning, I scrapped my manuscript and spoke the next day extemporaneously. It was probably better that way, for Sheraton shares rose thereafter on the New York Stock Exchange. Had I retained the prepared address, all present might have felt a compulsion to sell Sheraton stock short.

Louisville, Kentucky, is another city where we are proudly represented. A new specialty dining room in our Louisville Sheraton is currently enjoying great success. We named it after a famous eight-foot giant of a hundred years ago, Jim Porter, and our new Jim Porter Room has almost become the "tail that wags the dog." Both the hotel and its new and lusty offspring are doing very well; but my most vivid recollection of Louisville antedates the acquisition of the former Seelbach, now the Sheraton Hotel. I was there during the Kentucky Derby when this hostelry was still an important link in Gene Eppley's hotel chain. As guests of Gene Eppley, we met a fabulous oil tycoon also in Louisville for the races and were seated in a box adjoining his. I, a novice at the sport of kings, had come from faraway Boston to attend this spectacular event.

Although still remembering the months I once spent in raising three incubated chickens in order to earn two dollars and eighty cents, nevertheless I made up my mind that this time, come what may, I would splurge. The main event, I felt, called for ten dollars right on the favorite's nose. In the adjoining box, our new Texas oil friend had bet twenty thousand dollars on the same horse and seemed only mildly interested in the outcome. He was telling me a Texas story, the point of which I, intent on my ten-dollar bet, apparently missed.

The race started off well. Number seven obligingly took the lead, but gradually lost steam. Finally, with some difficulty, he managed to come in fourth. I was shocked to see ten dollars evaporate with such ease. My Texas friend, the story completed, suddenly remembered the race. Had our horse come in? He evidently was not unduly interested.

Later, when the celebrating—or drowning of sorrows, as the case might be—was in progress, I passed one of the sumptuous Seelbach suites, the one my Texas friend occupied. The door was open, and he beckoned me in. He did not even recognize me, but, seeing my official-looking Speed Graphic camera complete with requisite flash appurtenances, had mistaken me for a professional photographer. Would I kindly take some pictures of his guests? Apparently the misfortunes of the afternoon had not crippled his resources, for he still could flourish a fairly robust bankroll. On the outside were hundred-dollar bills. Inside, I suspect, may have been thousands. Peeling off three of the hundred-dollar size, he handed these to me. Momentarily annoyed at this munificent gratuity, I returned the bills to his shirt pocket, where some Chinese laundryman would doubtless discover them. Ever since I have cursed my uncooperative New England conscience.

Chicago for us is important, for there are two Sheraton hotels in that city. An angry complaint once reached the startled general manager of the illustrious Sheraton-Blackstone. A phone call from a decidedly irate woman expressed displeasure at the carelessness of a guest in a large corner suite. "I demand," the complainant insisted, "that when he retires he be asked to pull down the shades." The circumstances were unusual, so the manager asked where the lady lived.

"Two blocks away," she replied.

"How, at that distance," the manager inquired, "could you have been so seriously annoyed?"

"Oh," she explained, "I have a telescope."

It was at the same Chicago hotel during the Republican National Convention of 1921 that momentous decisions were reached in Room 507. This was the occasion when the famous "smoke-filled room" became part of the language of our American way of life, when Warren Harding was given the official nod that broke an apparent deadlock in Republican convention deliberations.

Our second Chicago hotel, now called the Sheraton Towers Hotel, rises forty-two stories above Michigan Avenue, looking down, we suspect, on its neighbor, the stately Tribune Tower. Its four hundred and fifty rooms are soon to be augmented to more than a thousand through the medium of a large and luxurious addition.

In Washington we are proud owners of two quite famous hotels, the Sheraton-Carlton, and, as I have said, the former Wardman Park, now the Sheraton-Park Hotel.

The Sheraton-Carlton's principal claim to fame, aside from being Washington's most expensive hotel, is that John L. Lewis is usually seen there for luncheon, seated at his own sacrosanct table in his own private corner of the main dining room. I suspect people more often think of the Carlton as a John L. Lewis caravansary than as a link in the Sheraton hotel system.

The former Wardman Park, once looked upon as a great white elephant, now as the Sheraton-Park is one of the nation's truly great hotels, bursting with distinguished guests. With its newly built banquet hall, capable of serving two thousand at Washington's great state dinners, it is home to many of those high in Washington government, social, and business circles. It is also probably one of the few hotels in the world displaying in its lobbies and in several of its elevator foyers authentic eighteenth-century furniture, pieces which in some instances have appeared in prominent American exhibitions. As our capital's largest hotel, now air-conditioned and beautifully modernized, it is today one of the nation's very distinguished addresses.

Charles E. Wilson, former General Motors president who left his company's leadership to accept a cabinet post under Eisenhower at a minute fraction of his former salary, when selecting a suite at the Sheraton-Park was asked by his wife if he really could afford it. "Do you know, Charlie," she reportedly remarked, "it will cost nearly all your new salary?"

In Washington today our two hotels are apparently doing their share toward maintaining Sheraton's prestige.

In all Sheraton cities throughout the United States and Canada we have tried to render at least some services for which no dividends are expected, and for which few, if any, thanks are likely. These extra services are Sheraton's contribution to the American traveling public. One of these self-imposed responsibilities is to expose hotel employees periodically to physical examinations. This applies especially to those working in hotel kitchens and dining rooms. A traveler may never know the origin of some troublesome germ bent on plaguing him, but this creature is not likely to have been reared in a Sheraton hotel, thanks to these medical precautions. A second contribution, one we hope will be rarely appreciated, is the presence of emergency oxygen equipment in our larger hotels. Still another mechanism for providing safety for Sheraton guests is under consideration, and imminent adoption is a probability. It is an electronic device to sound an alarm at the telephone switchboard should smoke develop in some corner of the building. These precautions are designed to protect the public, and even though visible dividends are unlikely, they are a matter of pride to all connected with the company.

In looking back over the years, although we realize errors have at times been made, we also know these were often the foundation for much of the company's progress, for mistakes are usually the most effective teacher. We expect our managers to be tolerant of errors of subordinates, for it is from such lapses that we gain the wisdom on which we can build in the future. Should the same mistakes somehow recur, however, our complacency diminishes perceptibly.

Looking cautiously into the vista of the years ahead, we are fairly sure that at least some errors will not recur. Should, for instance, the Empire State Building again be offered at a fraction of its potential value, we would be less likely to turn it down. However, if our progress continues at the rate we are forecasting, we may, according to company projections, double in size in another five or six years, and perhaps attain our immodest goal of becoming a billion-dollar company in ten or a dozen years. And if we reach this objective, we are quite sure we shall have done so without sacrifice of an early ambition—to prove false the concept widespread in the "muckraking" days of the nineteen-twenties that a company could not prosper without recourse to corporate chicanery.

Appendix

Controlling Business Cycles

K HRUSHCHEV'S recent boast that the Communists would ultimately bury capitalist countries was perhaps predicated in part on the hope that another serious American depression would bring this country to its knees. Russia has succeeded in eliminating to a large extent the type of cyclical swings that have at times caused such havoc to our economic system. Are we unable to control these phenomena? Must we consider them a continuing necessary evil, or can we, as we have done with cholera and other plagues, find a cure.

There seems to be a definite cure available—one that in the long run is not too costly, although like other medicines the taste may be somewhat unpleasant for a moment. The cost of a serious depression, on the other hand, could represent a loss of millions of dollars for every dollar the "medicine" might cost.

The plan for regulating the major swings of the business cycles is based on reducing the impact of changes in the supply of the nation's "liquid wealth" caused largely by fluctuating values of so-called security dollars—the widely fluctuating value of common stocks.

This theory of the relationship of security dollars to the business economy is based on the simple fact that since security dollars are readily convertible or exchangeable for ordinary dollars at short notice, they are in many respects equivalent to

[263]

monetary dollars. Accordingly, changes in the general level of security prices have an impact on our monetary system as do changes in the amount of available money. Security dollars represent potential purchasing power, just as do currency dollars, savings bank dollars, credit dollars, or any other kind of readily usable dollars that make up our reservoir of liquid purchasing power.

A holder of a $10,000 government bond can buy a $10,000 house just as readily as one possessing this amount in currency, in the savings bank, or in his checking account. The existence of interest-bearing coupons does not prevent a government bond from representing potential purchasing power. Similarly, if the liquid wealth is represented by $10,000 at market value of General Motors stock, the potential purchasing power makes equally possible the purchase of the same house, but with one difference; if the market value of the security dollars has fallen by 50 per cent the owner may then perhaps bid only half as much for the $10,000 house. His liquid wealth has been sharply reduced.

In relating security dollars to our monetary system, it must be taken into account that many security dollars never enter the stream of commercial activities, being perhaps permanently locked up in the strong box. For this reason, the total amount of security dollars outstanding, when considered in terms of potential purchasing power, must be "weighted" to compensate for a slow turn-over. A rough calculation suggests that, when comparing security dollars with currency and bank dollars as an influence on prices, a weighted value of only 20 per cent of outstanding common stock dollars should be considered. However, even 20 per cent of all such security dollars, because of the large amounts involved, may be equal to all currency and bank dollars outstanding at a given time. This was almost so in 1929. Three years later, when stocks were nearly valueless, currency and bank dollars had shrunk relatively little (currency in circulation actually increased); yet the price index was down nearly 50 per cent. The quantity theory of money simply didn't work until a weighted value of approximately 20 per cent of all common stock dollars was taken into account as an integral part of our total liquid purchasing power. Thus fortified, the quantity theory of money, or perhaps more accurately, the quantity theory of "liquid purchasing power" becomes a workable concept.

When in 1929 the heavy liquidation in the security markets took place, managements of business enterprises ran to cover as fast as they could. No wonder the business indexes turned sharply down, thereby inducing further security liquidation. Can anyone really believe business would have come so near to a standstill within three years if the security markets had not been decimated, or if the liquid wealth of the country had remained at its 1929 level? Psychological factors, of course, were also present. Inability to borrow with securities of little value as collateral also played a part. However, the inability to sustain purchases because of the lack of potential liquid purchasing power was perhaps the greatest factor that led to a self-intensifying depression. Neither the psychological factors, the lack of collateral, or the vanishing liquid wealth would have caused any serious problems had the Dow Jones averages remained at their 1929 levels. This is another way of saying that the fall in security dollars *caused*, rather than simply foretold the approaching depression.

More recently, subsequent to July, 1957, the great breaks in the market averages foreshadowed an inevitable downturn in business indexes. Following several days when crashing stock prices trimmed billions from the nation's reservoir of liquid wealth, Sheraton's executives, concerned over future business, canceled nearly six million dollars' worth of projects in order to assure adequate liquidity, should the down-trend become pronounced. It is quite likely that in thousands of other business conference rooms similar actions were taken. Again in this instance, the change in security markets was a cause, not a forecast, of changing economic conditions.

It is true that there have been instances when a rise or fall in security markets has not been followed by a comparable rise or fall in business activity. I think, on the other hand, that movements in the security markets have consistently influenced the *trend* of business indexes. As an illustration, in September, 1955, on the occasion of the sharp drop in security markets following President Eisenhower's heart attack, business did not actually turn down. However, the sharply rising industrial trend evident for nearly two years came to an end, and two years of a "sideways" movement took place. Following this "sideways" movement, the market breaks of late 1957 did produce a downward trend to business indicators, and as a result a severe recession followed. In each instance, a change in the industrial trend *followed* the actions of the security markets—interrupting the upward momentum in 1955, and causing a downturn in 1958.

An added reason why changes in the level of security prices affect the trend of industrial activity is the failure of our conventional accounting system to allow for fluctuations in the value of our American dollar.

If, during a given year, the price level falls, as it did during 1930 following the great stock-market decline of that period, then at the end of the year each dollar retained was worth more than at the beginning of the year. If the decline in the price level amounted to 10 per cent, this would mean, at least on average, that the dollar had appreciated by 10 cents. Accordingly, if during the year a $100,000 company appeared to have suffered a $5,000 loss, the value of its securities, based largely on reported earnings, would presumably have declined. Business activity for this company would be curtailed, and retrenchment would presumably become necessary. Dividends would doubtless be omitted. However, the cause of the trouble would be largely in an accounting system that forced the company to report a $5,000 loss. Actually, of course, if dollars at the end of the year were worth 10 per cent more, the company, despite the "apparent" loss, with $95,000 of net worth remaining, would in fact have enjoyed a substantial "profit" for the year—the $95,000 in more valuable dollars at the end of the year being worth substantially more than the 100,000 cheaper dollars with which the company started the year.

Unfortunately, this defect in our accepted accounting system, this failure to reflect the changing value of a dollar, aggravates the ravages of our business cycle and tends to accentuate upward and downward spirals. Each time earnings appeared to decline during the great depression, as dollars became scarcer and more valuable, security prices suffered further declines, shrinking anew the supply of security dollars, or so-called liquid purchasing power. According to this revised quantity theory of money, each further drop in the security markets made dollars even scarcer, and therefore still more valuable. No wonder a vicious spiral resulted.

The breaking of this downward spiral occurred in 1932 following the inauguration of President Roosevelt. Shortly after taking office, he announced the abandoning of the gold standard. This decision, coupled with other inflationary acts, set off a great speculative spree that was followed by sharp advances in the stock market. The downward spiral of three years' duration was broken. The rise in the market was premature, and stock prices fell again; but the downward trend of industrial activity was changed to a sidewise movement upon which recovery could start. Just as the great depression gained its impetus from the stock-market crash of 1929, so too was its final reversal sparked by the great security-market rally during the summer of 1932.

With the interrelation of security markets and business indexes better understood, the trigger action of earnings on security prices becomes worthy of study. This trigger action arises from the fact that common stocks usually sell at from ten to twenty times earnings applicable to these shares. A small change in a company's earnings accordingly becomes converted into a very much larger change in the market value of its securities. The significance of earnings on our cyclical trends is in this way exaggerated by this trigger action.

There are several observations that tend to reinforce this theory of the impact of fluctuating security dollars on our economy. For instance, in England, France, and Germany, the depression of the 1930's, though severe, was of less intensity than that experienced in the United States. With investments in common stocks less prevalent in European countries, shrinkage in liquid wealth was less pronounced. This could account for the reduced severity of the great depression in those countries. Russia, having no Moscow Stock Exchange, is able to boast virtual immunity to the great depressions that hit capitalist countries. Russia has no common stocks to fluctuate.

Again the fact that the greatest of all American depressions followed directly the tremendous orgy of common-stock speculation of the 1920's suggests once more the interrelation between common-stock values and industrial activity.

Another aspect of this theory seems to explain in part the relative freedom from severe depressions during the past two decades. In 1929 currency, bank deposits, and government bonds, all relatively stable forms of purchasing power, represented a relatively small segment of the country's liquid wealth. In those days common stocks represented a very large proportion of the potential purchasing power. Accordingly the impact of changes in security prices on our economy was quite significant. In later years, following the great depression, as a result of large increases in the amounts of government bonds outstanding (a relatively stable form of liquid wealth), the ratio of sharply fluctuating security dollars (common stocks) to our total liquid wealth was small. Because of this more favorable ratio, less severe depressions could have been anticipated—a circumstance that, though in part due to other favorable factors, has nonetheless been observed.

It is of course true that the effect the stock market and business activity have upon each other is not just a one-way street. Emphasis has been primarily on the effect of security prices on business trends, since the reverse is not disputed. There is, however, an important difference in the interplay of these forces that accounts in part for the fact that business and security prices occasionally move in opposite directions. One reason for this seeming discrepancy may be that the level of security markets is determined more by the investors' estimate of future trends in business, perhaps six months or a year later. The effect of changes in the level of security prices on our economy is perhaps more immediate.

It should be re-emphasized that the effect of expansion or attrition in the number of security dollars outstanding is less pronounced than is the impact of a similar increase or decrease in currency, credit, or bank dollars, since the latter are more frequently drawn upon to satisfy wants. However, if careful research confirms that the suggested 20 per cent is the correct "weighting," when taking account of security dollars, then the decline of some sixty billion dollars on the New York Stock Exchange during the last half of 1957 should have had the same effect on the American economy as would a twelve-billion-dollar shrinkage in monetary dollars (20 per cent of sixty billion dollars). It would seem that either eventuality might have produced similar results.

During the 1957–58 recession, prices of certain sensitive raw materials declined, whereas prices of many services and of certain manufactured goods increased—presumably in response to wage increases granted despite the recession. An unbalanced national budget of some twelve billions had to some degree offset the shrinkage in the value of common stocks. Substituting the liquid wealth represented by added issues of government bonds growing out of unbalanced budgets, together with a temporary easing of a tight money policy apparently brought us rapidly out of the recent recession, laying the foundations for a new wave of expansion in business activity, once more stimulated by a rising stock market.

It appears that the interrelation of business and the level of security markets can best be visualized as resembling two moving marbles connected by a rubber band. The two for a time could travel in opposite directions. In the long run, as the elastic stretches, there comes a tendency for both to travel in the same direction. As security markets rise or fall, they seem to exert pressure upward or downward as the case may be, on the trend of business indexes.

This interaction seems to explain why, when both business and the stock market are rising or declining, these trends reinforce each other. The upward or downward spirals of bull or bear markets feed upon themselves until such time as investors reach the conclusion that the economy has stretched too far in one direction, or perhaps until some significant national event has affected the security markets. Any sharp and sustained trend in our economy seems in the majority of instances to have been preceded by a substantial rise or fall in the value of securities.

Bull markets like the ocean tides may be advancing relentlessly, but this does not preclude waters from receding in the course of a rising tide, when individual waves have spent their power on the beach. Likewise, as a change in the level of security prices exerts a strong pressure on business activity, other influences may for a time pull in an opposite direction. In the long run, the influence of security price levels appears to be a dominant factor.

The so-called "Dow Theorists," who claim to predict sustained bull or bear movements with a high degree of accuracy by observing when security prices break out of a given range, are usually right simply because security price changes ordinarily *cause* corresponding changes in economic trends.

It has at times been pointed out by economists that only twelve to fifteen millions of the 173 million men, women, and children of this country own shares of stock, and therefore fluctuations in the market affect relatively few people. On a percentage basis, this is true, but it should be recalled that these twelve to fifteen million people control a large proportion of the liquid wealth that comprises much of the nation's potential purchasing power. It should be remembered that nearly all of the billions in security dollars can be exchanged, just as can dollars in the bank, for currency dollars, provided, of course, all are not offered for exchange simultaneously. The principal differences between dollars in the bank and security dollars are:

1. The extra day or two required to convert security dollars into currency dollars.
2. Bank dollars may change in value due to inflation or deflation. They may even earn a small return if banks pay interest on deposits. Dollars invested in securities, though often less vulnerable to inflation, will increase or decrease as stocks go up or down.

Both banks and the stock exchanges provide at times the facilities for setting aside temporarily unneeded funds. In these days of inflation who can say which is the safer custodian for surplus cash? When the time comes to buy a house or an automobile, some will take the money out of the stock market, others will borrow using common stocks as collateral. More perhaps will take the money out of banks. The majority perhaps will buy the house or automobile out of income. If, however, security prices fall, not only does this raise a psychological barrier to certain purchases, but perhaps more significant, the security dollars held may no longer provide the necessary purchasing power. They may have shrunk too much or provide insufficient collateral for the needed loan. Unfortunately, it requires only a small reduction in the number of cars sold, in the number of houses built, or the number of business transactions effected to start a downward trend. Speculators observing such a trend are likely to start selling securities, and as security prices fall, a recession becomes a reality.

But a drop in common stocks can have further repercussions on our economy. As equity values drop, big corporations may become more conservative. The size of contemplated bond issues, supported by diminishing equity values, may be trimmed down in order to be marketable. Although in the case of certain large companies this problem may not arise, it could be of real significance to many companies for which expansion depends on the ability to raise additional capital.

In the same way, lower security markets, particularly if the trend appears to be downward, often have an adverse effect on the marketability of new stock issues. The number of jobs a corporation can provide is often directly related to its ability to market additional common shares. This relationship between jobs and the level of security markets furnishes added evidence of the relationship between the level of security markets and the level of business activity.

Again, bank borrowings, when common stocks are used as collateral, sometimes make necessary curtailment of commercial activity if common stocks lose their value. Funds originally earmarked for projects that might involve many jobs must occasionally be used for reducing bank loans when collateral begins to shrink. Margin calls, although rare nowadays compared with their prevalence during the great depression of the thirties, nonetheless can still have an impact on our economy. The sale of a new car, for instance, and the jobs that the building of that car could have involved, might not materialize *because* security prices had declined.

Again there is the matter of billions distributed annually in the form of legacies. Such distributions often represent wealth that is quickly spent. Much of this wealth often comprises security dollars, and accordingly the level of security markets will presumably affect the demand for automobiles, homes, or other items often purchased by legatees.

To ignore the significance of common stocks as a factor in the purchasing power of the nation is simply unrealistic. The only room for argument is the extent of the impact—whether a proposed "weighting" of perhaps 20 per cent, when comparing security dollars with other monetary dollars, is the correct amount to offset the fact that bank dollars will spark business transactions more readily than ownership of security dollars.

If we accept the theory that some proportion, possibly 20 per cent of all common stocks, represents funds that, like cash or bank deposits, will sooner or later be used to satisfy tangible wants, then a revised quantity theory of money should be considered. This revised theory could be called the quantity theory of liquid purchasing power. It could be stated as follows:

The value of a dollar is inversely proportional to the sum of all currency, credit dollars, and bank deposits outstanding— *plus* 20 per cent of the market value of all security dollars represented by common stocks.

The old-fashioned and now discredited quantity theory of money broke down in 1932, when the price level fell by nearly 50 per cent without a corresponding drop in the number of monetary dollars in use. This revised quantity theory seems to offer a satisfactory solution to this dilemma.

I do not wish to convey the impression that changes in security values are the only force that governs fluctuations in business activity. Even if ownership of securities of fluctuating value were completely eliminated, an expedient that would seriously impair our prosperity, even then changes in the tempo of business would not entirely disappear. Periods of tight money, inventory adjustments, dislocations due to weather, new inventions, labor policies, military threats, etc., would continue to exert pressures on our economy. The reason why fluctuating values of security prices play a major role in our economic picture is that they accentuate a trend once developed. This is in contrast with many of the other hazards to our economy, which often tend to be self-correcting.

High money rates, for instance, attract larger savings, which in turn can ease the shortage of available funds. Likewise, excess inventory accumulations tend to correct themselves because of the cost and risk involved in carrying large stocks of raw materials or finished goods.

In contrast, a prospective decline in business activity is likely to induce selling of securities, which causes a shrinkage in security values—a diminution of an important reservoir of liquid wealth, one that constitutes a segment of our potential purchasing power. As a result some purchases are postponed, causing production indexes to turn down. Some jobs may be lost, and corporate earnings tend to fall. This is a signal for further liquidation of common stocks, and thus a downward spiral develops.

Many constructive steps and certain fortuitous circumstances since the great depression of the thirties have reduced the severity of business cycles. These changes include:

1. The tightening of margin requirements in times of speculative exuberance.
2. The reduced ratio today of the value of all common stocks

compared with the value of outstanding government bonds, a more stable form of security dollars.

3. Restrictions on speculative abuses, and on conditions under which "short selling" is permissible.

4. The tendency to recognize the dangers of speculative orgies coupled with treasury department and Federal Reserve Bank efforts toward controlling booms and busts.

The tight money policy of the Reserve Banks has often been constructive and necessary to discourage speculation at times when an excessive rise in common stocks threatened to spark a dangerous boom. Tight money also helped retard inflationary increases in consumer prices, virtually the equivalent of a general sales tax.

Although a tight money policy was effective early in 1957, it seems that subsequent liquidation in the security markets in the summer of 1957 could have been recognized sooner as a signal for earlier reversal of the tight money policy. Too much medicine can also harm a patient.

A very real danger of excessive bull markets lies in the altered ratio of the value of common stocks to other more stable sources of liquid potential purchasing power, such as bank deposits, government bonds, etc. As more of our national liquid wealth is represented by common stocks, the greater becomes the impact of fluctuations in the value of these common stocks on our economy.

Although some steps have been taken that diminish the effect of changing levels of common-stock prices on business activity, the task of relegating cyclical storms to a point of relative insignificance depends on actually isolating the "germ" responsible for these phenomena, so that a satisfactory cure may be prescribed. There is strong evidence that the offending germ is the impact of changing security values in our economy.

If depressions as we know them are primarily (though of

course not exclusively) the result of fluctuating security dollars, the question arises: Can we eliminate severe depressions and substantially reduce the extent of recessions by limiting the fluctuations in so-called market averages? This, of course, does not contemplate regulating individual securities, but would apply only to general market averages. Acutally, a step in this direction has already been taken through occasional changes in margin requirements. This concept could perhaps be enlarged to cover actual incentives to purchase shares at times when markets were shrinking, or by imposing margin requirements of up to 100 per cent or *even more*, should market averages climb too high. Although by no means impossible, margins exceeding 100 per cent could be imposed by requiring additional cash deposits in addition to the full purchase price of common stocks.

A more practical method might be to take advantage of the trigger action of earnings on security prices. It would be based on a variable rate of corporate income tax, one which in the long run would equal the present rate for corporations, but which would rise or fall by perhaps five or ten percentage points, according to whether the economy was progressing or receding too rapidly in relation to normal economic growth. The difference in tax revenue to the government in any year would be made up by the Federal Reserve Banks, which would provide advances to the government when the economy was depressed, and take funds out of circulation from tax-paying corporations as reimbursement during periods of excessive expansion. In this way average earnings of all corporations would remain relatively stable, for the tax load would be lightened in hard times and increased during periods of excessive business exuberance.

Such action by the Federal Reserve Banks would resemble the function of a storage battery, which stores up energy when an excess of electricity is in the lines, and discharges into the lines when there is a temporary need. With more nearly level corporate earnings, employment would remain more stable and a very real antidote to cyclical swings would be built into our economy.

If the above program is adopted, it might end the greatest single weakness in our free enterprise economy.